WHAT YOU THINK IS WHAT YOU GET

An introductory textbook
to the study of

The Alexander Technique

Donald L. Weed, D. C.

A GIL BOOKS Publication
Published by Groups In Learning

A Gil Books first edition

Previously published by:
1445 Publications,
Thalwil, Switzerland.

Published by Gil Books in association with ITMA.
Gil Books is part of Groups In Learning.

Groups in Learning,
10 Charlotte Street,
Bristol BS1 5PX.
Tel: +44 (0)117 925 3413

Interactive Teaching Method Association
PO Box 181
Bristol BS99 7BH
Est. 1991 for Graduate and Post-Graduate Training in the F. M.
Alexander Technique.

A catalogue record of this book is available from the British Library.

ISBN 0 9526320 5 5

Cover design and layout by David Scott.

Printed and bound in the UK by
Redwood Books, Trowbridge, Wiltshire.

"For everyone who will do the work."

This work is an exercise in finding out what thinking is.

F. M. Alexander

The most remarkable aspect of F. M.'s experiments proved
that the only true guidance needed
was his sequence of directional thinking
which must carry through
no matter what movement is to be accomplished.

Marjorie Barstow

The whole of it is a mental achievement,
not a physical thing at all.
It is a form of thinking.

Sir George Trevelyan

As time went on, I began to understand the Technique.
Strangely, the learning process seems to go on forever.

Marjorie Barstow

ACKNOWLEDGEMENTS

The writing of a book is always a group project, no matter how lonely the process may seem to be.

There have been many people who have made major contributions to this book.

Marjorie Barstow and Frank Pierce Jones are mainly responsible for the training I have had. While the information I received in class time was priceless, I learned as much or more just by being able to be around such wonderful people. Without their help and friendship, I may never have gotten well, let alone become a teacher.

Sidney Friedman was the person most responsible for the development of the Basic Principles course.* If he had not given me the opportunity to work in classes as a student teacher at Washington University, I would never have gained enough confidence early in my career to keep challenging myself to become a better teacher. More importantly, without his providing me with students who had to do homework to pass my courses, I might never have found out how valuable nineteenth-century-seeming educational techniques would be in learning this revolutionary, new work. Most importantly, he had the confidence in me to go along with all of my "improvements" in teaching, even when I am sure they didn't make sense to him. Thank you, Sid.

I am also very grateful to my colleagues at The Performance School. They let me bring the Basic Principles program into the school's curriculum, even though there were some strong reservations. Without the opportunity to teach the class in a longer format, with little or no experiential work, the course could never have evolved into its present form. Without the stimuli provided by our common vision, projects, and efforts, I might never have had the chance to find out what I really believe is the basis for standards of knowledge in this work.

My proofreaders, Heather Kroll, Kevin Ruddell, and Peter Lewis, are to be congratulated for having struggled their way through bits and pieces of early manuscript, and thanked for having provided me with the clues and keys I needed to learn how to make my writing a little more comprehensible on a first reading.

Karen is to be thanked, by all of us, for keeping the office and apartment running through Hell and High Water Music.

Lesley is to be thanked for teaching me more about possibilities, and reminding me that "not being allowed" was just a nightmare from my past.

And all of my students, old and new, are to be thanked for teaching me most of what I know, now, and in the future.

D.W.

---

* Editor's Note: See Appendix C, *Basic Principles*.

TABLE OF CONTENTS

AN OPEN LETTER TO THE SECOND EDITION

Dear Don,

What a great, great book you have created! It is just what the Alexander Technique world needs - yes, yes, yes!

I am sitting here at the dining room table, thinking of you, and hoping that many people are reading your book, *What You Think Is What You Get*. How true that is!

As I think back over the twenty years plus since you first came to me for lessons, and I remember how you were when you began and how you are now, I laugh a lot. I am very proud of all of the changes you have made, and very proud to have had a part in your making them. And now, you have handed me your very own book, ready for me and everyone else to read.

I consider it a great privilege to be asked by you to add a few words to your second edition. However, now as I start, I can see what a great task it will be. The things you have written in your book are so good, they are disturbing.

You call your book a textbook, and so it is. But, it is a different kind of textbook, because it is on a different subject: the Alexander Technique. By writing a textbook, you have opened up another direction for the investigation of movement and the technique.

Every time I start to read your book, my thoughts slip back to those early days when there were only three books written. What you have done in your book is what F. M. did in his, but in a different way.

I know that there will be people who will not like what you have done or who will think that the way you have approached the work is too different. There are many people like this who aren't willing to change, or who can't read or talk about something new and different without turning up their noses. These people can't see what I know, and I know that your book is a valuable tool that should be used by every student and teacher in this work.

When I see people react in this way, I want to shout to them, "Hey! Aren't you being just a little bit stubborn?" I want to say to them, "You can turn up your noses if you want to, but your noses are going to get scratched if you don't open your eyes!" Too often they just won't open their eyes and try something new. They'd rather stumble blindly along doing what they've always done, and believing that they are right.

After spending many hours working with your book, one of the things that pleases me the most is that it gives a fresh approach to F. M.'s "work." It is almost like fresh breezes flowing through the air. Your ideas and suggestions, like those breezes, are moving, and we need to keep up with them. How cleverly you have taken F. M. Alexander's discoveries and organized a moving structure around them, so that these discoveries can be better understood and used. Every thought you have written is so well explained, and then put to practical use. Your ideas are open and flowing - ready for action, and more action.

Now, as I read page after page, I begin to realize how much more I have yet to learn about that which I thought I already knew. The way you have opened my seeing! As I read your book, and think about the things you have written, and try them out for myself, I notice more and more that my own eyes are getting brighter and better. This is truly exciting for me.

Another thing which pleases me about your book is how timely it is. Just as there seems to be a growing demand for teachers, here comes your book, not only to help all of the new students, but to guide the new, young teachers as well.

A few weeks ago, I gave a workshop. I was surprised and delighted at the number of students who had copies of your book. Because they were reading your book, they were thinking differently, and asking better questions. I do not think the workshop would have gone as well if there had not been so many students who had read your book. I do think that all of my workshops would go better if all of my students would read it

Thank you for writing What You Think Is What You Get. As students of the F. M. Alexander Technique, I believe that we should all read your book again and again. If we did, we would all be better students and teachers, and, in time, we would come to appreciate the time and care and energy you have given in the creation of this book.

While writing this letter, I read a little poem on my desktop calendar which I thought was pretty good. I think it says what you and I are both trying to tell our students. With one little change, I'd like to share it with you:

> [Nature] has given us two ends
> > With a common link,
> With the one we sit
> > With the other we think.
> Success in life depends on
> > Which we choose,
> Heads you win,
> > Tails you lose.

Thank you once again for writing your book.

Cheerfully,
Marjorie L. Barstow
Lincoln, Nebraska

INTRODUCTORY REMARKS

There are a number of introductory books available on the Alexander Technique. All of them are designed in some way or other to intrigue the general reader enough to pursue further information or lessons. As marketing material, they serve a valuable purpose, but I believe that they fall far short of being of value to the serious student.

The best books now available on the work are those written by Alexander, either in their entirety, or in Edward Maisel's collection, *The Alexander Technique* (formerly *The Resurrection of the Body*), and *Body Awareness in Action* by Frank Pierce Jones.* In fact, Jones' and Maisel's books are the primary texts that I use in my introductory course entitled Basic Principles. None of these books serve as a good introduction to the work, however, because they are so packed full of information that they make better reference books than primers.

What I believe is presently missing from the resources available to a student is a good basic textbook which a student can read repeatedly to help understand the basic issues and ideas involved in the Alexander Technique. What the serious beginning student deserves is a textbook which presents Alexander's work in an informative way, which identifies the major issues, which gives the student a good starting point for his study of this work, and yet, is sufficiently complex that one or two readings will not exhaust the value of the book.

What You Think Is What You Get is directed to fill the gap between the eye-catching introductory books presently available and the denser resources of Jones and Alexander. It is meant as a beginning point of study.

The material in *What You Think Is What You Get* is all based on the writings of F. M. Alexander. The format and the selection of material comes from my fifteen years of experience learning how to help students own the ideas of this work.

While a clear point of view has emerged over the years, no dogma, credo, or perspective was imposed on these ideas when they were introduced. Only those concepts and ways of presenting the material which have worked remain. In fact, many of the ideas presented here were in great conflict with my own ideas when I first tried them out in class. Many of the ideas presented here are the survivors of long, and often

---

* Editor's Note: The publishing information for some of the books referred to in this edition has changed.

Body Awareness in Action by F.P. Jones is currently available as *Freedom to Change*, (Mouritz, London).

The Resurrection of The Body, edited by E. Maisel is now published as *The Alexander Technique, The Essential Writings of F.M. Alexander* (Lyle Stuart, New York).

Man's Supreme Inheritance is now published in the UK by Mouritz.

Constructive Conscious Control of The Individual is published by STAT Books of London by arrangement with Gollancz.

The Use of The Self, is published in the UK by Gollancz (London).

The Universal Constant in Living is currently out of print in the UK.

heated, arguments with students and colleagues. The ideas in this book are not presented in this way because they have been derived from a prior doctrine. They are presented in this way because they work in this way. I ask the indulgence of every reader to suspend judgement about any section until he or she has completed the section.

This is not meant to imply that by completing a section the reader will always have been brought back into harmony with the material. Much of the material is controversial, and almost all of it is provocative.

If, as Alexander claims, the major portion of a student's difficulty is the student's incorrect conceptions, then one of my tasks as a teacher is to find a way to aid students in identifying and eliminating their mistaken concepts. As a result of constantly addressing these most vulnerable issues when dealing with students, my teaching style has been characterized as confrontational. What is always confronted in class, however, are the ideas that people have, not the people who have them.

In the Basic Principles class, material is presented in a seeming lecture format until some idea, issue, or comment sets off a reaction in one of the students. Then, whatever the point of contention may be, all of the energies of the teacher and the class are directed to the pursuit of this point until the problem is resolved or until no further questions can be easily asked or easily answered. As such, this teaching style is very dependent upon the reaction of each individual student to the material, to him or herself, to me, and to the other students.

For this reason and many others, I prefer to call this process the Interactive Teaching Method. One of the key tenets of the Interactive Teaching Method is to engage the student actively in the discussion. Experience has shown that there is no better way to engage a student fully than to threaten some precious, previously-held concept or belief.

In the classroom, this lends a kind of provocative edge to much of the interaction. This inner (and often outer) turmoil creates an atmosphere which is occasionally uncomfortable, but one in which positions and beliefs are more clearly stated and examined. The purpose of these transactions is not to foist any particular position or concept on anyone, but to create an arena in which everyone, including the teacher, can actively re-examine their own points of view.

It has been a tremendous challenge trying to translate these procedures into text. In the classroom, armed with the knowledge of the material and years of experience working with thousands of students, it is possible for me to tailor the proceedings to match the present needs of either the majority of students, or the neediest student, at any given time. Because all of these issues, problems, and difficulties are universal, focusing on the needs of an individual still serves the needs of everyone. In addition, the neediest student is liable to present the strongest and most eloquent articulation of a particular point of view.

There is often a direct relationship between how clearly a position is stated, and the ease with which the difficulties created by that position can be relieved. By dealing with each issue and idea as it is evoked by classroom experience and discussion, there can be a more effective and lively identification of problems and solutions.

Over the years, the use of the Interactive Teaching Method has been proven to accelerate the processes by which students gain command of this work and a capacity to do it easily on their own.

The major obstacle in bringing this interactive form of teaching onto the page was in trying to find a way to present the information without the feedback guidance provided by the students in a class. I became quite concerned about how I was to direct the presentation to students who weren't there, or, worse, how I was to present the material to every possible student at once. The concern grew to the point where it began to threaten the project, until I remembered one of the principles I teach in class.

One of the tools which I encourage everyone to try is to make mistakes often. Many teachers in success education state that if you are not making a lot of mistakes, then you are probably doing something wrong. One of the first tools to acquire in learning to experiment, a necessary aspect of learning the Alexander Technique, is a willingness to make mistakes and a willingness to be wrong. For me, the person who most embodies this essence of willingness and courage with respect to experimentation is Marjorie Barstow.

Recently, I have begun trading work sessions with Marjorie. In exchange for extended private lessons, I do Restructuring* with her. Both of us have experienced a great deal of change and improvement through this exchange.

One time, after I had done a particularly involved and long session with her, Marjorie was packing for a trip when she noticed how poorly she was moving. She then decided that she wasn't going to do any more packing until she had improved her own manner of movement.

She later told me:

"Every time I started to move, I caught myself doing the same old things I didn't want to do and I started over. I kept catching myself, going back, and starting over so much that I just started laughing at myself. Finally I was laughing so hard that I decided that I wasn't getting anywhere, so I decided to take a nap."

A very important starting point in the study of the Alexander Technique is a willingness to experiment and a willingness to be wrong. Therefore, I decided to go ahead and write the book in the way that made the most sense to me, and accept it if I was wrong.

Another important technique that I teach with regard to mistakes is to learn to make mistakes loudly. This is a concept which I learned

---

* Editor's Note: Restructuring is a neuromuscular re-education technique developed by Donald Weed.

singing in choruses. The choir directors always said to make your mistakes loudly. That way it would be so much easier for the directors to find where the mistakes were in order to correct them.

The same thing applies to making mistakes in learning this work. I teach that if you are going to make a mistake, make it big! Make it loud! There are no style points awarded in Alexander lessons.

What is important is that everyone become more alert and clear about what they are thinking and how they are training their thinking to become a more valuable source of direction and guidance. By stating your ideas as clearly as possible, they are more available for examination and improvement.

Therefore, I decided to make the statements in this book as loudly and as clearly as I can. Once I have put these ideas out there, we will all have a chance to discuss them to see where we can prove I am wrong.

Another advantage of teaching live classes over writing things down in a book is that, in class, I am able to pick and choose which of the stories I will tell and which of the issues I will bring up, and in what order. In bringing this classroom information into book form, I realized I would be limited to just a few stories, in just one order, which talk about just a few certain issues, without the benefit of immediate feedback as a guide. I became concerned that there would be no one way to present the material to everyone because I believed that I had never found a consistent way to teach any of my classes. It was not until I realized that I did have a consistent way to teach my classes, and that I did have an "audience" present, that I was able to overcome this last difficulty.

You see, in class, I consistently observe the meanings and implications of all that is said and done and relate these experiences meaningfully to past experiences and the ideas found in the work. While it was true that I was mostly alone while I wrote this, I could still "interact" with an idealized composite of all of my previous students. In that way, I could present issues and discuss ideas which reflected the most common needs my students have had, and answer the questions they have most commonly asked.

In a sense, what I have done in writing this book is that I have told the story of how some mythical series of classes might have been taught to a mythical and ideal group of students.

Because I have decided to include in this book many, if not all, of the personalities and possibilities which might occur in class, it is unlikely that anyone will be able to read this book straight-through and not find at least some of it redundant, or simplistic, or bewildering or just plain wrong. My recommendation is that you keep reading and re-reading it. As you change, so will the information in this book.

One of the experiences which most frequently happens in teaching these classes is that, inevitably, at least one thing I say will make someone in the class very angry. When this happens, the person involved will fight this idea loud and long. Many students are often brought to the edge of dropping the class out of anger because, in their opinions, I had demonstrated my unfitness to teach by saying some stupid thing.

Just as inevitably, sometime in the near future, these same students find themselves in an argument with someone else. As they reach the climax of their argument, the only words which state the ideas they are trying to communicate are the very words I had used previously, and which the student had fought so long and hard against in class. It is to their credit that they go ahead and say those previously offensive words. It is also to their credit that they tell me about these experiences later, albeit somewhat sheepishly.

All of these different features of a live class presentation being carried out at once in print means that it is unlikely that any single presentation style can accommodate all of the needs of the text. The writing style of the text, therefore, is a mixture of formal and informal styles. Where possible, every effort has been made to make the material conform to common standards of good writing.

Occasionally, a sentence structure or word choice which works in lecture will resist translation. Similarly, the needs of conveying large amounts of precise information accurately and with the sense of simultaneity involved have sometimes created sentences of such length and awkward structure that they exceed most of Alexander's sentences and begin to approach Faulkner.

According to my proofreaders, diligence and reading repetition will yield the full scope of the content of these gargantuan sentences, but these particular sentences will never be confused with "good writing."

While I am forever and deeply indebted to my primary teachers, Marjorie Barstow and Frank Pierce Jones, I have learned much from the others who have taught me or who have worked with me as colleagues or who have let me teach them.

Whatever success these efforts enjoy, the credit belongs to them.

Whatever faults are here to be found are mine alone.

OPENING THOUGHTS

CHAPTER 1

FIRST QUIZ

First of all, are there any questions?

If you have picked up this book, you should have a lot of them. Like, what is the Alexander Technique? How does it work? How did it begin? How can it help me?

Frank Jones begins his book, *Body Awareness in Action*, with a similar question: "What can I do to be saved?" Although the question carries with it a plaintive tone reminiscent of the early seventies, the question it asks, and the questions it implies, still have validity for anyone who is seeking self-improvement.

I will assume that because you have read this far, you are interested in improving yourself and you are primarily interested in finding out if the Alexander Technique can help you. That last question may be the only question for which you will receive a quick and easy answer from me in this text.

Yes, the Alexander Technique can help you.

The Alexander Technique can help you in your everyday activities. It can help you in your specialized activities. It can help you walk. It can help you talk. It can help you do more, with greater success, in less time, using less energy.

But, there is a price.

You must think. You must discipline yourself. You must be willing to change.

Perhaps the willingness to change is the greatest price you will have to pay, because it is the First Law of the Alexander Technique that people are willing to do anything to get better as long as they don't have to change.

Years ago, a student dragged her boyfriend into one of my classes. She thought that since the work had done so much good for her, she wanted her boyfriend to enjoy the same special benefits. He didn't want to be there, and I never want to have any student in any of my classes who doesn't want to be there. So we made a kind of mutual agreement that I would leave him alone, and he would try not to look too bored.

When it became apparent that his girlfriend wasn't going to give up in her insistence that he have a lesson, I asked him if he wanted to get it over with, or whether he wanted to walk out. He decided that it would cost him less in the long run to have the lesson than to put up with his girlfriend's harping about his not having a lesson, so he sat down in the teaching chair.

First, I explained the basics of the transaction that was about to transpire when I put my hands on him. As soon as I put my hands on him, however, he was transformed.

His slouched and hunched-over appearance disappeared. His face became more symmetrical and attractive. His voice lowered an octave. His eyes, previously dull and listless, were now vibrant, alive, and seeking.

Even before I could ask him what he had noticed about himself, he had leaped to his feet, towered over me, shook my hand more forcefully than before, thanked me in a full and commanding voice which filled the room, and left.

He never came back to class.

This was in October.

Throughout the year, I kept seeing this fellow in the student newspaper. He was usually being singled out for some kind of honor or award. The one constant in all of the interviews was about how he had been such a late bloomer, and had only recently begun to achieve the potential he had always demonstrated.

That May, right before graduation, I saw him walking across the quadrangle. His appearance and gait, if anything, had improved since last I saw him. He looked up, saw me, and having recognized me, ran across the quadrangle. I immodestly imagined that he was going to thank me for acting as the catalyst in the fabulous year he had been enjoying.

When he reached me, though, he shook his fist in my face and shouted, "I've been trying to forget everything you taught me since I met you!"

Once I got over the shock created by my expectations about what he would say to me, I asked him to explain why he was so angry.

He told me that ever since I had worked with him, he had continued to think about what I had said. As he thought about it, he continued to change. I asked him if he hadn't gotten better, and improved, and enjoyed great success. He said, "Yes," but then, he added mournfully, in a way I will never forget, "But, don't you see? I didn't want to change! I was happy the way I was!"

He taught me a very important lesson that day.

Sometimes people don't want to change.

Sometimes they are so content with themselves, that they happily accept how things are. The only reason why they show up in classes like mine is that they were either coerced, as this fellow was, or they have become secure in the belief that most classes that look like mine are unable to cause genuine change.

Since this incident, in almost every introductory class I teach, I have felt the obligation to warn people: "If you don't want to change, stay away from this work." As my friend Bradley Ehrlich says, "The Alexander Technique is a catalyst for change," and a very powerful one at that.

If you want to get better in yourself, and in everything you do, read on. If you don't want to change, stop now before its too late.

If you've decided to go on (and I am glad that you have), I have a little task for you.

Take out a piece of paper and a pencil. Put your name and the date at the top of the page, because you are going to take a little quiz. It's very short. There is only one question. But, even though the quiz is short, it is very important.

In my classes, this quiz is the first thing that we do. It accomplishes two things. First, it helps to acquaint me with the students in the class, their background, their training, and many of their most basic ideas. Second, and much more importantly, it provides a baseline against which each student's progress can be measured.

That's the major reason why I want you to write out your answer to this quiz now. Later, after you've read this book and had some lessons in this work, I want you to go back, take the quiz again, and see how much you have learned.[1]

The question I would like you to answer is, "What is the Alexander Technique?"

Be brief. Be concise. Be complete.

Answer the question as though someone that you care about has just asked you, and you want to answer as completely as possible, and in a way which will give them something of value while making them want to learn more.

Some of you will be new to the work and believe that you don't know anything about it. If that's the case, then say so. Write it down.

If you think you don't know much about the work, but you might know something, write it down.

If you are a long-time student or teacher and you know so much about the work that it would take a long time to answer, take this opportunity to write down the best short definition you can. Make it something that is lively and informative and that sings of the reasons for your own excitement about Alexander's discoveries.

If you are a teacher, you answer this question often. See if you can find a new way to answer it which pleases you.

Go ahead. Write out your answer now. I'll wait.I have asked hundreds of people to take this first quiz. I never cease to be amazed by the wealth of information that it generates. Quite often, an answer will begin with an apology for how little the person knows about the work, and then it will end with an eloquent response.

---

1. I would appreciate it if you would send me a copy of both the quiz you take now and the one you take after you have finished the book. I would also appreciate it if you would send me any ideas, or papers or whatever else you may write as you continue your study of this work.

While I may not be able to respond personally to all of them, I learn so much from reading what others write that it makes me both a better student and a better teacher of this work.

It really doesn't matter how you answer the question, though, because whatever answer you give is the correct answer. I asked you for your answer to the question. Whatever you wrote is your answer, so it must be right. About the only way you could get this quiz question wrong is if you copied somebody else's answer, and even then the only problem that would arise would be if you didn't give credit to that other person.

You see, I don't think there is any one right answer to this question because I don't think anyone knows what the Alexander Technique is.

CHAPTER 2

THE DECISION GAME

The quick thinking reader will have already figured out that I include myself in the group of people who don't know the answer to the question, "What is the Alexander Technique?" This is why I keep asking people. This is why my classes often sound more like a heated debate in the House of Commons than a poetry reading at high tea.

The best answer I have received so far to this question on a first try was by Dr. Connie Amundson of Seattle, Washington.

Dr. Amundson wrote, "The Alexander Technique is the study of thinking in relation to movement."

This definition is, in itself, controversial but, from the instant I heard it, I realized that someone had finally put into words what I believe will be the next great understanding in this work.

For years, those of us involved in the work struggled to come up with a definition which encompassed all of Alexander's work. Alexander never gave us such a definition. In fact, he didn't even give us the name "Alexander Technique." He always referred to what he did as "the work." Once, in a defense of this practice of not naming his work, he wrote in a letter, "How can you name a thing that is so comprehensive?"[1]

One benefit which has come from asking students to write down answers to this quiz question is that there has been a synergistic relationship between the task of phrasing these definitions and an increase in making new discoveries in the classroom. Often a change in phrase will lead to an enlightening new experiment, and vice versa.

Ten years ago, Marjorie Barstow asked me, 'What can we do to get these people thinking?' By sharing her phrasing of the task in that manner and at that time, Marjorie confirmed in me the validity of the direction I had taken in my teaching and encouraged me to continue it.

I was further inspired as she went on to say, "I'm convinced that the next great breakthrough in teaching will occur when we can finally get students to realize that it is their thinking that's important, not their movements or their feelings."

I had been actively working on this idea in my teaching, even before Marjorie had said this, but it took Dr. Amundson's answer on her first quiz before it ever occurred to me that this idea should be part of the definition of the work.

Before Dr. Amundson's answer, my definitions had abounded with heads, bodies, relationships, movement, following, ease, delicacy, improved performance, conscious control, etc. By defining the work in this new and different way, she has given us a way to focus in on what is important by placing emphasis on the relationship of thought to movement.

---

1. Maisel, Edward, ed., The Resurrection of the Body, Shambala Publications, Boston, Ma., p. viii

In spite of the clarity of the phrase "the Alexander Technique is the study of thinking in relation to movement" or perhaps because of it, there will be many people who disagree with this idea. Many of the people who disagree will seem equally or better credentialed than Dr. Amundson or myself. What is someone to do when two or more experts disagree, particularly in a field where you have little knowledge or expertise yourself?[1]

This issue comes up most often for me with regard to health care. Very often, a patient who is seeing me for a second opinion with regard to surgery is faced with making a choice between opposite recommendations. Similarly, all new parents who do any research into the field are faced with a difficult decision about whether or not to have their babies vaccinated.

In fact, once one starts to think about "experts" and opinions, one quickly realizes that all of our decisions have to be made with the support of some experts and the condemnation of others. And the fact that large numbers of experts of great prestige hold a given position does not make that position any more right than if their numbers or honors were smaller. For instance, I'm reasonably certain that most of the world's most prominent experts agreed that Columbus would sail off the edge of the world.

In his excellent book, *No Hidden Meanings*, Sheldon Kopp tells us, among other things, that, "all important decisions must be made on the basis of insufficient data." Often they must be made in the face of stiff opposition. All you can do as you approach any given decision is find out all that you can about the subject, or, if there is too much material, you can shop around in various sources until you begin mostly repeating what you already know, and then make a decision. All you can do is endeavor to make your best guess at any given time. If you are right, terrific! If you are wrong, you can change.

I find as I work with people that many of them have a difficult time making decisions. They have been so used to compromise and trying to make everything work at once, right away, that the idea of systematically analyzing what they know to make a choice seems foreign to them, especially when the decisions involve issues which are complex and involved. For these people, I recommend that they use the Elephant Eater Technique.

James E. Tolleson, one of the foremost teachers of success education, asks anyone faced with a difficult and complex task, "How do you eat an elephant?" For many of us, this conjures up images too grotesque and bizarre to include in a family book, but the question remains, "How do you eat an elephant?"

---

1. Some people try to limit the phrase "Alexander Technique" to just the way that Alexander taught the work. To which I usually reply, "Since we have evidence that Alexander taught in a number of different ways, which way did you have in mind when you limited your definition to the 'one way' in which he taught?" If the person then says the way he taught the people closest to him, then I point out there is such variety and disagreement among those people about what and how Alexander taught that it seems unlikely that any of them could really tell us how it was done. Therefore, the contention that the work or the name assigned to the work should be limited to "the way Alexander taught" is, at best, merely meaningless, and at worse, the articulation of indefensible prejudice. A further development of this entire discussion can be found in Appendix A.

The answer to this is really very simple.

You eat an elephant the same way you eat a chicken: one bite at a time.

For people faced with the problem of elephant-eating a difficult decision, like how do I reconcile all of these diverse opinions about the Alexander Technique and what is it and how should it be taught, I recommend a tremendous tool for taking one bite at a time which I call The Decision Game.

The Decision Game is a very simple game to play. What causes people difficulty in playing the Decision Game is their habit of trying to "mush"[1] everything together and reaching thoughtless compromises prematurely. The Decision Game requires very different behavior indeed.

To play The Decision Game, one first picks an issue or some aspect of that issue. Instead of trying to understand it better immediately, one then tries to state the issue in the two most opposite and illuminating ways possible. Then, using your left hand for one statement and your right hand for the opposite statement, point up and to the left side with your left hand as you say, "Between (position statement A)" then, point up and to the right side with your right hand and say, "And its opposite (position statement B), which is more likely to be true, more likely to be what I want, more likely to help my career, etc.?"

This procedure will force you to take a stand on the essence of the decision you want to reach.

For example, "Between cleaning my room, and going to a movie, which do I really want to do? " "Between asparagus and green beans, which do I want for dinner?" "Between Mozart and Salieri, who is the more enduring composer?"

After a little practice, many people become so good at playing The Decision Game, they can do it without using their hands.

I recommend that even once you have built up your confidence playing the game, you use the gestures anyway when the decisions are more difficult. For those of you who teach, I recommend that you play 'The Decision Game out loud with the gestures when you are explaining something in class.[2]

The real value of the Decision Game to the Alexander Technique is that we can use it to identify some very basic issues, and find out where

---

1. In the Basic Principles classes, we call this tendency to mush (pronounced moo-sh) all of your points and ideas together The Dog Sled Theory. Often by merely teasing apart the various ideas which have been mushed together and then using consistency in logic and definitions of terms, the student will find his own solution to self-imposed problems.

2. The real art involved in playing The Decision Game has to do with the way in which you phrase your choices.

As you start to use this technique, there are three things to keep in mind. Firstly, you must search for the key issue involved. Secondly, you must make sure that your choices represent genuine choices or opposites. Additionally, my recommendation is always to make your choices as colorful and humorous as possible. The more actively you involve your intellect in phrasing your choices in interesting ways, the more likely you are to break through into a new insight or decision.

we stand on them. For instance, between (left hand) "We know what the Alexander Technique is," and (right hand) "We don't know what the Alexander Technique is," I have already declared for the second choice. The reason why I think "We don't know what the Alexander Technique is" is that there are so many different answers given by so many different people. Before Dr. Amundson, nobody could even give me a simple definition which was both complete and satisfying.

When we know what something is, we can usually communicate what it is, or, at any rate, agree about what it is. For instance, most of us can agree on what a tomato is. Or what music is, though we may argue forever about what good music is or even if there is such a thing as "good" music. (For instance, is "good music" music which is well behaved? And if it is, then weren't the stodgy musicologists right every time they said that a new pioneer like Mozart or Wagner wrote bad music because it broke all of the rules?)

If one were to listen to all of the definitions available for the "Alexander Technique," these mutually-exclusive diversities would quickly eliminate any possible hope of agreement More to the point, for every teacher or lesson one could point to and say, "That's the Alexander Technique," I can produce at least one other "expert" who would say, "No, it is not!"

This kind of turmoil doesn't disappoint me. Rather, it excites me. Actually, as a chiropractor, I'm quite used to this kind of doctrinal infighting among peers.

Even after one has successfully played The Decision Game, it may be apparent that the investigation has not gone far enough to reach a conclusion. At this point, it is often helpful to use another technique we have developed in the Basic Principles classes called "Asking the Next Question".

When a question in The Decision Game remains largely unresolved, it is often helpful to see if it is possible to formulate another question which might explain the first question more clearly. This second question is, of course, the Next Question.

One of the best strategies for asking these Next Questions is to work your way backwards as far as you can to the underlying premises and assumptions. Then, you can look at the question you first wished to answer once more to see if any further Next Questions need to be asked.

Often it requires asking very many Next Questions before the logjam of indecision with regard to the initial question can be answered. Sometimes even when you have searched as far back as is seemingly possible, the initial question will remain unresolved. Almost always though, any stubborn question will yield to the answers gleaned from the appropriate Next Questions.

In the case of the question we have at hand - whether or not anyone knows what the Alexander Technique is - a valuable Next Question to ask might be whether or not Alexander's work is finished.

If, for instance, you decide that the work is finished, then it would be possible for you to hold the position that the Alexander Technique is definable and, therefore, one can know what it is.

If, on the other hand, you think as I do, that Alexander's work and the technique for teaching that work is not finished but is rather constantly evolving in significant ways, then it would be difficult to define the work in any complete or conclusive way and you would probably have to concede that you don't know what the Alexander Technique is.

For me, I don't think it is possible to know finally, once and for all, what anything is if it has the possibility of changing dramatically with just a thought. Further, if you believe as I do, you would have to believe that not only is the work unfinished, but that we all have the duty, in fact, the obligation, to contribute to the work as we learn it.

This is where the genuine excitement in this work lies for me.

Not only do I get the advantage of learning information and procedures which have demonstrated to me clear and growing benefits, but everything which I can contribute to the work will be a significant contribution which will benefit others as well.

This is what I tell all of my students, too.

Anything which they contribute - anything which you contribute - to this new, evolving, and unfinished work, will be a significant contribution which will help others as much as it helps yourself.

Sometimes even Asking the Next Question will not bring clearly into focus the solution to the initial question. At that point, the practiced decisionist engages in a discipline called Scoring.

Scoring in The Decision Game is accomplished by making the same distinctions as before ("Between A and B"), and then, thinking of the two choices as a continuum. You decide where you would "score" your opinion with respect to the midline between the two extremes. Then, because the rules of the game state that the point between the two decisions, the midline, behaves as though it is an infinitely high, infinitely steep mountain with perfectly smooth friction-less sides, whichever side you favored when you scored your opinion becomes the position that you hold.

Even if you do not or cannot believe that this newly held position is the true position, you carry on "AS IF" it were. By acting on this "AS IF" principle, one of two eventual outcomes will result. Either the action and decisions engendered by the "AS IF" decisions you have made will be proven false subsequently, or they won't. In those cases where your adopted position has proven false, you can re-play The Decision Game with improved information and benefit. In those cases where your "AS IF" decision has proven true (or failed to prove false), you have taken a course of action which so far has proven to be of benefit.

In other words, Scoring prevents Fence Sitters Folly,[1] the process of keeping yourself mired in inaction while you can't make up your mind. By scoring your decision, and accepting the strong statement of the position you favor, you can now act based on one of the positions or the other.

The best thing that could happen if you act as though one of the choices was right is that the choice was right, you did act, and you accomplished your goal. The worst that can happen if you act as though one of the choices was right is that you could be wrong. If you are wrong, you can then learn from your mistakes. You can learn how you were wrong, how to institute new and better procedures and thereby improve your chances of reaching your goal once more.

In fact, usually, the only procedure you could follow which could genuinely be called a bad procedure would be if you would sit around doing nothing because you couldn't make up your mind which choice was right. Once you begin sitting around in this way, it is more likely than not that you will continue to sit around and never reach your goal.

Except when it does, almost nothing good ever comes from sitting around.

So far, we have used The Decision Game to identify two important issues with regard to how one sees the Alexander Technique. The answers to these questions are basic and in large part will determine almost every other answer which you make about the work. Right now, maybe you should take some time to write out your own answers to these two questions as a way to see where you stand.

First, between "We do know what the Alexander Technique is," and "We don't know what the Alexander Technique is," which statement do you think is more likely true? Where would you score yourself on this issue?

Second, between "Is Alexander's work finished and whole?" or "Is it unfinished and evolving?" which do you believe is more likely true?

In case you weren't sure, when I wrote out my answers just now, I decided to behave "AS IF' this work was unfinished and evolving.

---

1. Fence Sitter's Folly is the name I give to the policy of remaining compromised in the middle of a decision. After having made a decision about which way you really believe the issue at hand should be decided. it would be sheer folly to remain "sitting on the fence" with regard to that issue. Even when you haven't made a decision about what you want to do, "sitting on a fence" rarely advances you because it limits your capacity to generate more information. With more information, your troubling choice may become easier.

It constantly amazes me how a person can remain paralyzed by indecision. By using The Decision Game, a person forces himself to take a position on a given issue. This, in turn, may make it easier to take positions on subsequent or related issues. In this kind of case, taking a position is just another way of making up your mind about what to do.

By focusing on small manageable steps with clear, definite decisions, you can begin to form a course of action which will bring you what you want. Bite by bite, decision by decision, issue by issue, what you are really thinking about something and what you want to do about it will become increasingly clear.

As your goals and needs become clearer, it will become easier to create strategies for reaching them.

As your strategies improve, your rate of success in reaching your goals will improve as well.

Consequently, even if I knew everything there was to know about what the work is now (and I don't), I still couldn't say I know what the work is because I do not know what it will become.

These are my decisions today on these two issues. Everything which I decide and write about from here on will reflect these decisions.

It doesn't matter whether you agree with me or not on any issue. The important thing is that we are both willing to take a stand, share it with one another, and be willing to change to the point of view which makes the most sense, no matter whose point of view it originally was.

Many times during this book, and in all of my other books, we will be playing The Decision Game. I recommend that you try it out in everything that you do. I think you will find it of great value.

Since you had to answer the first quiz in the last chapter, and now that we know each other better, it seems like a good idea that I should share with you my answer to the first quiz.

I don't know how many times my answer has changed to that question, nor can I guess how many times it will change in the future. That doesn't matter. Every time I change my answer, it means that I've learned something in between.

Now that you have some more background, I think you'll see the sources of some of my definition. Some of it may still be unfamiliar or difficult to agree with, but we will talk about all of this definition before we are done.

Don Weed
August 20, 1989

First Quiz

The Alexander Technique is an as yet unfinished and constantly evolving investigation of the relationship between thought and movement behavior, and how the retraining of the conscious mind can be used by individuals to bring about continuous and constructive changes in the quality and efficiency of their general standard level of performance in all of their activities.

CHAPTER 3

YOU CAN DO WHAT I DO

One of the most important things which F. M. Alexander ever said is something which he is reported to have been quite fond of saying:

"You can do what I do, if you will do what I did."

Sadly, this phrase has been both dreaded and ignored since he said it.

To some in search of the secret of the Alexander Technique, this is the ultimate bad news. This means that, just as there is no secret to success, there is no secret to the Alexander Technique. There is only work.

The people looking for a secret to the Alexander Technique are looking for a short cut. They are looking for a way to get the benefit of the work without having to earn it. These are the people most likely to ask, "How can I do the Alexander Technique?' They are also the people that, when you tell them how to do it, will be sure that you are withholding something.

To others, this phrase of Alexander's represents the clearest, most concise game plan for learning the work. One only needs to do what Alexander did. Too often, though, these people choose to limit their concept of what Alexander did to a certain manner of posture and movement or to a certain way of teaching or even a certain way of moving their heads in relation to their bodies.

But, Alexander did more than that!

He observed himself in his manner of performing activities. He reflected upon these observations. He challenged his ideas with experiments.

Elsewhere (see Appendix A), I have written at greater length about the five part process of investigation which Alexander constantly employed and which is central to the work. If we are going to say that we are going to do what Alexander did, we can't just mean that we are going to project his directions and let our necks be free, etc. We, too, have to follow this process of observation, postulation, experimentation, evaluation, and adaptation.

We have to be willing to look at anything and everything including Alexander's ideas as he was willing to look at them, in a constructive, but critical, way. We have to reason these ideas out and then work to prove or disprove them in a practical manner.

There is a tendency in many of us to see Alexander's work - or at least our understanding of it - as some unassailable writ. We often approach his ideas and writings as though the parts we understand and agree with are, *prima facie*, accurate and true. They are worthy of learning as is, and hence, beyond investigation or proving.

Those parts of his ideas and writings which we don't understand or with which we disagree we tend to ignore, discount, apologize for, or "improve" as we read about them or encounter them in practice. Once again, the result is to avoid or minimize the amount of time and effort spent in understanding the principles and concepts which comprise the work based on those principles and concepts.

It's as though people still believe that, with enough lessons from a sufficiently skilled or venerated teacher, they won't have to bother with a careful and close examination of who they are and how they work. They won't have to come to understand that, in this work, what they do is not nearly so important as how they do it. They won't have to learn to forego their concepts of correction for a concept of conscious control. They still believe that with a sufficient number of high quality lessons they will not have to examine, evaluate, dismantle, and reconstruct their entire means of taking in information and formulating responses, but will still be able to acquire the benefits of Alexander's work.

And, unfortunately, to some degree, they can.

In my classes, I make a distinction between the three kinds of improvement in efficiency that are possible.

Because efficiency is a measure of the relative amounts of effort required to achieve a particular end, any change in the performance of a given activity which requires less effort for similar or better results would represent an improvement in efficiency.

The three ways to improve efficiency in the performance of an activity are 1) to change the protocol, 2) to decrease the effort used in the performance of a previous protocol, and 3) to change the direction of the manner of use of the self in the performance of the protocol.

Both of the first two kinds of improvements are ways which are familiar and available to anyone who has tried to improve the efficiency of their performance. As we shall see, only the third way is uniquely the province of Alexander's discoveries.

A protocol can be thought of as the steps taken to perform an act.

By evaluating the steps in a given protocol, sometimes a change in the order or nature of the steps taken will create a more efficient performance of a task. Sometimes the change in protocol can be external to the performer, like getting a different or better tool. These kinds of changes are of value, but they don't require any knowledge of Alexander's work to do. Therefore, they are not limited to Alexander's work.

What is less clearly not a unique part of Alexander's work is improvement of efficiency by a decrease in effort. This is the kind of increase in improvement which I call doing the same thing less.

If someone performed an act with a distorted psycho-physical equilibrium and a great deal of strenuous effort, then a simple way to perform the same act more efficiently and with greater comfort would be to perform the same act with the same psycho-physical disequilibrium but with less effort. This, without question, would be a more efficient movement, and the degree of change might be significant, but would it really represent a change with regard to Alexander's discoveries?

It is true now and will probably be true for some time that students come to the work to learn to reduce discomfort or distress in movement of some kind. While some come to the work to improve the quality of their performance, most come to the work to solve a problem just as Alexander did in dealing with his hoarseness.

It is important to remember that Alexander satisfactorily resolved his vocal problems very early on in his process of discovery (lines 148-154 out of 778 lines in the Maisel edition). He achieved this improvement primarily by a change in protocol, and possibly a decrease in effort. But, it isn't until much later in his narrative that he tells us that, with regard to changing the use of himself in activity, his efforts were misdirected (lines 362-364). It isn't until line 386 that he tells us he even began to consider the manner of direction of the use of himself.

This is after he solved his vocal problem to a large degree. This is after he discovered the three harmful tendencies in speech. This is after he discovered the connection of the three tendencies to his general stature. This is after he discovered that in order to maintain a lengthening he must move his head forward and up. This is after he had learned that the misuse of himself in "taking hold of the floor with [his] feet" was the same wrong use which interfered with his vocal mechanism as well as the whole of his psycho-physical mechanism in activity. This is before he discovered the nature of the direction of the use of himself in activity and before he discovered any of the procedures which trained him how to think while directing himself in movement

And yet, there are a number of practitioners who teach that in order to do what Alexander did all we have to do is move as he moved. They teach "forward and up" and "back back" as a kind of politically-correct, ritualized gymnastic while minimizing the training of their students' processes of thought.

It is as though thinking becomes a way of facilitating the all important postural and movement behaviors rather than the key to acquiring the condition of conscious control which can generate any movement at will. There are even groups of teachers who are now into peripheral reflex facilitation or the proper way to sneeze.

It is as though by creating the physical, postural, movement efficiency characteristic of the Technique, they believe their students can work backwards through their "psycho-physical unities" to improve their processes of thought. But this cannot possibly work because, as we shall talk about later, it is not movement which creates thoughts, but rather thoughts that create movement.

It is the training of a person's ability to think in a certain manner which lies at the heart of this work, not the ability to move or stand or sit in any particular way. Improving the relationship of one's head and body in activity without a corresponding retraining of one's thinking to alter the means of directing the use of one's self in activity is a hollow victory unworthy of being called the Alexander Technique. It is like a marriage without intercourse: it fulfills the formal requirements but the probability of bearing fruit is exceedingly low.

After discovering the misdirection of his efforts, Alexander looked into the manner with which he directed his efforts. And so must we. Alexander challenged his thoughts with reflective examination and then challenged them again. And so must we. He used practical experimentation to discover which of his ideas worked and which did not And so must we.

We all have an obligation to pursue this work each day as if from the beginning because Alexander did just that, and this process of pursuit of knowledge about himself and the workings of his mechanism became part of how he learned. It was part of "what he did."

I understand that there are some people who, out of respect, I suppose, think of and/or teach Alexander's work as being whole and finished. As I have said elsewhere, it is inconceivable to me that this would be true. Each person will have to decide for him or herself which they are going to believe: does F. M.'s work represent some finished, whole, or "revealed" truth or does it just represent his best shot to understand himself and the way he directed himself in activity? Are we going to "deify" Alexander and thereby make off-limits for investigation his words, and whatever of his procedures we understand, or are we going to accept him as a brilliant self-credentialed colleague who is going to assist us in the common goal of exploring his work?

To me the choice is clear.

It is often said that, by giving someone a fish, you make them dependent upon you. If you teach them how to fish, however, you will free them forever. Alexander didn't give us some sort of overly precious and delicate fish to eat unexamined. He taught us HOW to fish! He didn't leave us at his mercy through a dependence upon him. He gave us the tools with which to do this work for ourselves.

But, in order to do this work, we have to do what he did. Not only in terms of the manner of our movement work, but by the retraining of our thinking as well.

Alexander also learned to teach the work, and he learned to write about the work. He took upon himself the added tasks and responsibilities involved in knowing the work so well that he could communicate it to others.

The determining factor in learning this work can't be the number of lessons: Alexander didn't have any, and A.R.[1] only had six. It can't be receiving proper kinesthetic information from a properly trained teacher because neither Alexander brother ever had anyone "put hands on" them

---

1. Albert Redden Alexander (1874 to 1947) was F.M Alexander's brother and the first person other than Alexander himself to become a teacher of his work.

when they were learning. It can't be simply the number of hours spent in class because even well- respected teachers admit to "the occasional dud" making it through their entire programs. It is not even the degree of aptitude or ability we bring to learning the process which is significant.

A man whom I consider to be one of the best teachers in the world had a tremendous difficulty in relating to students when he first began teaching because his coordination was so good to begin with that he couldn't understand why others didn't change as quickly as he.

At the other end of the spectrum, my nickname in my first training class was "Old Stone Hands" and, on the basis of my natural aptitude, understanding, and condition, I was no one's favorite teaching partner and avoided at all costs.[1]

All one needs to do to become accomplished in this work is to follow the procedures outlined here and in Alexander's books and in the rest of the Commentaries and in the other books and in your teacher's classes.

There are sufficient maps available to find your way if you will do the work.

Like my first T'ai Ch'i instructor used to say, "Everybody can do it. Some a little slow. Some a little fast. But, everybody can do it"

You just have to do for yourself what Alexander did for himself.

In my opinion, the entire scope of the activities which describe Alexander's life and exploration of this work (the "how" with which Alexander "did it") is the minimum amount of tools and effort which must be used to learn this work.

"You can do what I do if you will do what I did." It seems like such a simple phrase, but if we were to practice it to its greatest depth of meaning, we couldn't help but accomplish for ourselves at least the same degree of constructive conscious control which Alexander enjoyed.

---

1. I've often wondered if my difficulties as a beginner in this work weren't somehow an advantage. Nothing came easily. I couldn't see anything. I couldn't feel anything in a lesson. I couldn't understand what most people in my classes were excited about.

From the beginning I have had to work for everything I have achieved in this work and the tools which I acquired and refined along the way have served me and others well.

If there are one or more aspects about the practice or understanding of this work which concern you, the reader, because you don't get it or see it or feel it, put your concerns aside and just get busy.

If I can go from where I was to where I am, and where I am going, you can do anything. All that is required is that you do the work - you do what {F.M.} did.

AN INTRODUCTORY LESSON

CHAPTER 4

ONE THOUGHT

When I teach an introductory Alexander class, I always start by telling my students that Mr. Alexander's work begins with One Thought. It's a simple thought and easily remembered. In fact, I tell them that if they remember nothing else from my presentation except this One Thought with which the work begins, then I will consider my efforts successful.

The One Thought that I want them to remember is this:

> **the poise of a person's head**
> **in its dynamic relationship with his or her body**
> **in movement**
> **is the key to freedom**
> **and ease of motion.**

When it is written down and said out loud, it seems quite easy to understand and somewhat obvious. But, it wasn't obvious to Alexander. This statement represents a series of principles and discoveries which took him many years of experimentation to find.

When Alexander began his study, he was trying to solve a specific problem -throat troubles which threatened the loss of his voice during his dramatic recitals.

First, he tried the experts' solutions to his problems. When those solutions didn't work, he had to accept personal responsibility for being the cause of his difficulties. To find his own solution, he had to train himself to observe his manner of using himself in the activities of ordinary speaking and reciting.

While doing this, he noticed that he had a tendency to do three things each time he began to speak: 1) pull his head back, 2) depress his larynx, and 3) gasp or suck air in through his mouth right before he began speaking.

Once he had identified these three tendencies, he had to work out which of the three was controllable. In turn, he found out that he could not directly control the depressing of his larynx or the sucking in of air prior to speaking. He did find, however, that the pulling back of his head was not only directly controllabie, but he was capable of controlling the other two faults indirectly by the prevention of pulling back his head.

After that, he had to see that these three tendencies were not only a misuse of the parts involved in vocal production, but that they constituted a misuse of his entire mechanism. This misuse could be caused by movements generated by ideas as simple as a distortion of the relationship of his head to his body in movement, or as subtle as his attempts to carry out faithfully a correction given to him by a respected teacher.

This statement of the One Thought with which we begin our study of this work - though simple and easy to remember - distills years of brilliant investigation and reasoning by Alexander into an excellent starting point, and, as such, deserves further investigation itself.

ONE THOUGHT

the poise of a person's head

People often wonder why I begin this statement with the word "poise".

There are many reasons.

First of all, I use poise because people are unfamiliar with it. It gets their attention. It lets people know that something new is being presented. The word "poise" demands their attention in a way that a familiar word would not.

Secondly, it prevents people from deciding immediately that they already know what I am saying because the word choice introduces a sense of uncertainty.

Most importantly, the major characteristic of the word "poise", which distinguishes it from "position" and "posture" is a sense of motion.

Obviously, "position" refers to placement. For something to be in its position, it has to be in its place and stay there. In the case of movement behavior, position would refer to the placement of body parts with respect to other body parts.

The word "posture" suggests a static state as well. Most people have a sense that there is a right "posture," a right way to be. Many can even recite a litany of appropriate directions for acquiring "good posture": "Chin in! Chest out! Shoulders back!" and so forth. These people believe that if they could only maintain these optimum placements of their parts, they would have good posture. That is a static concept.

One of the strengths of Mr. Alexander's work is that it recognizes that we are made to be in constant motion. More importantly, we ARE in constant motion, no matter what our usual concepts about motion imply.

Even when we are "still," there is movement within us.

There is breathing, of course, and heartbeats, but I mean more than this. There are constant shifts and adjustments of our parts in relation to one another even when we don't think of ourselves as "moving."

Because "poise" is different, new, and best implies motion, I use it when I state the One Thought with which to begin the study of Alexander's work

The Alexander Technique is about many things and one of the most important is movement

ONE THOUGHT

the poise of a person's head
in its dynamic relationship with his or her body

In the course of his lifework, Alexander made or articulated many discoveries about who we are and how we work. One of the most basic of these discoveries has to do with the importance of the relationship of one's head with one's body as the controlling factor in movement and coordination. This head/body relationship is basic, powerful, and occurs first in the sequencing of all movements. Alexander talks about this relationship as being the primary control of use in all activities.[1]

As we study the Alexander Technique, we will have much to say about the nature and importance of this relationship. For now we will just remember that the first part of the first thought involved in the study of the Alexander Technique has to do with the poise of one's head in relation to his or her body.

ONE THOUGHT

the poise of a person's head
in its dynamic relationship with his or her body
in movement

It is important to remember that one of the major sources of confusion in this work (and in many other kinds of work, I suppose) is that we often use a simple term in more than one way within the same context, often within the same sentence. Often we are not clear about having made these changes or about the reasons why we made them. Even more often, we don't realize we have made them in the first place.

This usually innocent carelessness lends itself to criticisms of the limitations of language which in itself provides further absolution from the effort to communicate clearly.

---

1. Some individuals restrict the use of the term "primary control" to mean only the positive formula suggested by Alexander in a phrase from the first chapter of The Use of the Self, "To lengthen, I must put my head forward and up." As I will endeavor to prove elsewhere (see Volume One of the Alexander Commentaries). It not only makes more sense to think of "primary control" as referring to all movements and directions involved with the relationship of the head with the body (as Alexander himself talks about it in the preceding sections in his discussion of lengthening and shortening the stature), but it also gives us the ability to avoid the unpleasant experience of having the primary controlling factor in movement popping into and out of existence depending on the relative direction in which one's head is moving with respect to one's body at any given moment.

It is not my place or intent to suggest that language is not limited. Language is limited.

My point is to suggest, as I often will throughout these books, that the limits that are real in such cases are greatly augmented by the limits that are perceived.

I have been told that in order to keep a circus elephant from wandering off, all that is required is to tie a rope around its leg which is similar to the ropes used to tie it up when it was younger. As a baby, the elephant learned that the other end of a rope tied to its foot is ALWAYS tied to a stake that the elephant can't move. As an adult, it "remembers" that all ropes are tied to stakes it can't move. Consequently, even if the rope isn't tied down on the other end, the elephant won't try to walk away.

The elephant is limited because it assumes it is limited. It accepts limitations based on the authority of its own assumptions.

Many of us are limited like this. We decide beforehand what our limits are without trying to reach further. In fact, some of us are so much smarter than elephants that we don't have to have someone tie a rope around our legs before we limit ourselves.

Just because we believe our language to be limited is no reason for us not to do our best to use language well. Language is a tool, not an answer. If we become impressed by our perceived limits about language to the point of becoming lazy, we may end up not experimenting or challenging our limits as Alexander challenged himself and his limits.

Without challenging our limits, we may never know the joys, the wealth, the riches we may share by overcoming personal limitations if only for just one sentence, one phrase, or one idea.

I do not believe that the teaching of this work can always be done through language alone, but I will guarantee that the amount of learning which can be done by "words alone" is much larger than we perceive it.

A. R. Alexander, F. M.'s brother, was the only other teacher for which Mr. Alexander seemed to have consistent and high regard. Not only did A. R. claim that he needed just six lessons to learn the work, but he BOASTED that he never had to have hands placed on him.[1] In other words, the entire training of the only teacher in whom F. M. had enduring and consistent faith was through words alone!

This is all a long preface to explain why I have included the phrase "in movement" in the One Thought.

Yes, I realize that I said that we are always in movement and some of you may think that this is just me being redundant, over and over, again and again. But, by including the phrase "in movement" I wish to emphasize this point once more.

We are always in movement.

More importantly, "in movement" is a kind of concession to our more common ideas about what movement means. Movement in this sense is meant to convey being in activity where activity is construed to be purposeful movement, such as walking, talking, or scratching your nose.

---

1.   Both the story and the verb came from Marjory Barlow during a lecture at the 2nd International Congress of Alexander Teachers at Brighton, England.

At the same time, there are also the internal movements of parts interacting with parts even when we are standing, sitting, or lying "still."

So, "in movement" in this context can mean both of these kinds of actions, both internalized and purposeful movements, and this is why I use the phrase because I intend both meanings at once

ONE THOUGHT

the poise of a person's head
in its dynamic relationship with his or her body
in movement
is the key to freedom

I rarely have to explain to anyone what a key is. It's anything which can be used to allow access to something which has been withheld.

In this case, the key is an idea, the first of many which we will be discussing.

It is also a movement about which we will have more to say later.

Right now, however, I want to discuss the second half of this phrase in greater detail.

For years, I used to say the phrase "freedom and ease of motion" as though it was a single noun: "freedomandeaseofmotion." Some of my colleagues still do. By saying these words in this way, what I gained in time was greatly outweighed by what I lost in meaning. By making this phrase into a single noun, I was cheating myself and my students of a profound truth, i.e., that Mr. Alexander's work is the key to freedom. Period.

Boundless freedom.

Unqualified freedom.

Freedom that means every bit of whatever "freedom" means to you.

By the time a person has learned to monitor and control this relationship to his advantage, he will have developed skills and understandings which will enable him to realize his dreams and to acquire all of the tools he will need to exceed all of his self-imposed limitations.

Sometimes I think we lose sight of the great scope of the value of this work's potential.

For these reasons, I choose not to make the phrase "freedom and ease of motion" into a single noun, but rather I choose to talk about freedom in as large a sense as I can, because personal freedom in its largest sense is one of the great by-products of this work

ONE THOUGHT

the poise of a person's head
in its dynamic relationship with his or her body
in movement

is the key to freedom
and ease of motion.

The other by-product of this work that this beginning thought tells us about is ease of motion.

This is a phrase which has become a specialized, technical term among many of the students who have worked and trained with Marjorie Barstow.

By "ease of motion," we mean the accomplishment of tasks and activities with a particular quality in the performance of these tasks. The nature of this particular quality includes, among others, the elements of strength, efficiency, clarity of intent, and freedom from distortion.

I have found that, for most people, the concept of ease of motion can best be conveyed in a simple three-word phrase: Fred Astaire dancing.

We all seem to be able to recognize in Mr. Astaire's dancing exactly the kinds of qualities that are meant by the phrase "ease of motion." His dancing also demonstrates another important point about coordination and control of movement

Control of movement has at least as much to do with the turning off of muscles as it has to do with the turning on of muscles. Mr. Astaire always used just as much strength and effort as his actions required, and no more.

Now, I suspect that once I started talking about Fred Astaire some of you started to think to yourselves, "Now he's gone too far! I can understand that this Alexander Technique stuff can help me. I might even move better, look better, feel better, and have more energy. But, I couldn't possibly learn to move as easily as Fred Astaire danced!"

HOW DO YOU KNOW?

Beware of your own elephant ropes!

At this point in my introductory classes, I will often do some demonstration teaching of Alexander's work. Mr. Alexander tells us in his second book that experiential lessons with a teacher are of great value in showing the new student his needs in regards to re-education: "There is only one way in which a teacher can really convince a pupil [of the need to learn this work] and that is by demonstration upon the pupil's own organism."[1]

By teaching these lessons in a group, it is possible to demonstrate the truth of this One Thought to the class's satisfaction. It also gives the teacher a chance to emphasize several aspects of the One Thought with which this work begins.

One of these aspects is the concept of "in relation to."

When I first begin working with each student (usually with the student sitting or standing), I ask everyone in the class if the student has the necessary prerequisites for a lesson: first, does the student have a head,

---

1. Alexander F.M., *Constructive Conscious Control of the Individual* Centerline Press, Long Beach, Ca., p.126. It is intersting to note that at this point F.M.'s interest is in proving things to his pupil, not in teaching him.

and, second, does the student have a body? I simply refuse to work with any student who does not have both.

As the students are trying to figure out how to react to my silliness, I ask them more seriously if there is a relationship between the person's head and body. After they consider this for a while, they begin to understand that, because we are talking about two aspects of the same person, by necessity, there is a relationship between each person's head and body.

I then ask them if this relationship is static or in motion.

By now, whatever laughter there once was has stopped, because this question requires more involved thought than the students suspected was coming.

During the course of my writings, as during the course of my classes, students will be presented with hard choices and tough decisions.

I do not expect or want anyone to accept any decision I have made. I do want everyone to go through the same kind of processes of evaluating and deciding things for themselves as I have. I don't care if you decide to agree with me or not. I only care that the quality of the process by which you reach your own decisions and the amount of effort that you put into reaching your decisions is at least as good as my own.

I bring all of this up only because we have just reached one of these points of decision.

When faced with the question as to whether this relationship is static or dynamic, most students opt for some kind of mixture. They report that their heads were in a fixed relationship to their bodies until they "changed positions." While they were moving their heads from "position" to "position," then, the relationship was dynamic. Once they got to the new "position," the relationship became fixed again.

Some people are very comfortable with this explanation.

I am not.

What if the reason why the movement of the head seems fixed at some times and not at others is because the smallest unit of movement which we perceive is too big? What if we could become more and more sensitive, more refined in our ability to perceive smaller and smaller units of movement? If we did, then wouldn't the times this relationship between our heads and bodies was dynamic seem to increase, and the times this relationship was fixed seem to decrease?

This is what we observe in students who take lessons.

As their sensitivity to themselves in movement increases, the times they report their heads to be "not moving" dramatically decreases and the times they notice movement in this relationship increases. In fact, this trend is so universal as students become increasingly sensitive, that it has led me to postulate, as I have stated above, that we are constantly in motion, and that the relationships of all parts of us with respect to all other parts are constantly in motion. As we shall see, some of these relationships are more important than others, but they are all dynamic.

<u>ONE THOUGHT</u>

**the poise of a person's head
in its dynamic relationship with his or her body
in movement
is the key to freedom
and ease of motion.**

CHAPTER 5

TWO DISCOVERIES

Depending on how specific and detailed one chooses to be, the list of Alexander's discoveries about who we are and how we work could be very long indeed. If one decides to limit oneself to those discoveries which are basic to the work and which make the work unique, the list becomes much shorter. In fact, all that Alexander discovered can be distilled into two discoveries.

The first discovery which Alexander made was that in every movement you make there is a change in the relationship of your head with your body which precedes and accompanies the movement, and which will either be helpful to you or get in your way. In other words, every time you move, there is a change in the relationship of your head with your body which initiates movement throughout your mechanism.

This movement will take on one of two major characteristics.

Either your head will move in such a way as to increase the amount of muscular tension in your neck, to distort all succeeding relationships within you (which will pull you out of shape), and to lower the general standard level of performance of your coordination of motor activities, or, your head will move in such a way that there will be a reduction in the amount of muscular overtension, your system will subtly shift to conform to more natural and attractive internal relationships and your motor coordination in the performance of activities will be enhanced. The enhancement of your coordination in the performance of activities will improve the quality of the performance itself.

Because the Alexander Technique can train you to monitor and ultimately control this relationship of your head with your body (albeit indirectly), the nature of your coordination and the level of quality of your performance in activity becomes a matter of choice. Through the Alexander Technique, constant improvement in both coordination and performance quality is readily attainable.

You see, every movement is actually made up of two movements.

The first of these movements is the kind of movement we were talking about before when we talked about the movements between parts. We call this movement the relationing movement and to understand it better, let's first take a look at a basic concept from anatomy.

Anatomists distinguish between the two different kinds of "skeletons" that make up the rigid framework of our bodies. They divide the skeleton (and the attendant soft tissues) into two different parts: the axial skeleton and the appendicular skeleton.

The axial skeleton is made up of the skull, the spine, the ribs, the sternum, and, according to some authors, the hyoid.[1] The axial skeleton constitutes the central rigid framework for the head and body. The remaining bones - shoulder blade, collar bone, humerus, etc. of the upper limb and the innominate, femur, etc. in the lower limb - make up the appendicular skeleton.

The relationing movement, the first movement to occur in every movement, takes place primarily in the axial structures. This relationing movement either improves the capacity to perform by creating a flexible lengthening of the axial structures relative to the movement at hand or decreases the capacity of the individual to perform by changing the relationship of the axial structures in such a way as to compress or overstretch them for the task at hand. The resulting condition of these structures, in turn, will influence the relative efficiency of the relationing movements in the appendicular structures as well.

The second aspect of movement in every movement is that combination of changes in joint angles which are peculiar to, and characteristic of, the action being performed. In this regard, we might call these combinations of motions the gestural movement.

Gestural movements may be restricted to one joint, or may be expanded to include all of them. Gestural movements may involve either the axial or appendicular skeletons, or both. Gestural movements may involve brief, momentary protocols, or may take place over a very long period of time. Whatever the nature of the gestural movement, it is always preceded and accompanied by changing relationing movements which either help the quality of performance of the gestural movement or get in the way.

As you will see, the choice - help or hurt - is up to you.

TWO DISCOVERIES:

1) In every movement you make, there is a change in the relationship of your head with your body that precedes and accompanies the movement, and which either helps you or gets in your way.

In other words, every movement is made up of two parts:

i) A relationing movement performed primarily by axial structures which determines the quality of the gestural movement.

ii) A gestural movement which is the combination of movements which make up any specific action and which can involve any part of the body.

---

1 This is a curious inclusion because the hyoid is not actually a bone and is made up entirely of cartilage. The reason for its inclusion is most likely the fact that, even though it is not a bone, the hyoid acts like a bone as a very important attachment point for many muscles in the front of the neck.

The second thing that Alexander discovered is, if anything, more important than the first discovery.

As a result of his reasoning and experimentation, Alexander discovered that the conscious mind has the capacity to override every system, including the natural ones.

When he began his studies, he believed, as many still do, that there were certain aspects of our system and our functioning which were beyond our capacity for interference. He believed that there were some things that we just can't mess up with our meddlesome minds and ideas.

As it turns out, he later decided that this concept was wrong. In fact, it was our ability to impose our concepts and ideas upon our movement behavior, and even our structures, which was responsible for the bizarre and bewildering variation in performance and appearance that is evident in any large group of people.

For instance, many of my students have the idea that it is necessary to tighten the buttock muscles to maintain standing. It is not. The "natural systems" of the body work in such a way that once a person is standing no muscular effort is required in the legs to maintain this posture, and, if, as some authors claim, muscular effort is required, the muscles involved are located in the calves. In the standing posture the gluteal muscles should be uninvolved.

My students who think they have to tighten the muscles in their buttocks to keep standing all have tight buttock muscles. Many of them have heavily overdeveloped muscles and they mistakenly blame their unwanted "size" on fat. In most cases, this extra size is the result of a kind of continuous isometric contraction of these muscles, and the only reason for this enforced contraction is the student's mistaken concept about the need to keep these muscles tight.

Similarly, many people do not realize that there are two functional joints in the elbow region. Everyone is familiar with the hinge-like joint in the middle of the arm which allows us to bend our forearms toward our upper arms or to straighten our arms out. Not everyone knows that there is another joint in the elbow region about an inch closer to the hand.

This joint is called the radio-ulnar joint, and its purpose is to allow us to roll the moveable radius bone over the top of the relatively fixed ulna bone. This allows us to turn our palm up relative to our arms, as when we are receiving change at a cash register, or to turn our palm downward, as when we type or play the piano, without having to move the upper arm.

I wish I had a nickle for every pianist who claimed to be an expert about the arm and about its requirements for efficient movement who didn't even know that this joint existed!!! I think I could comfortably retire on the interest from the principal that such a piano tax would generate.

The fancy name for this movement is pronation and supination of the forearm. It is normal for this joint to move 180 degrees or one complete half turn from palm up to palm down without moving the upper arm. I cannot remember meeting any adult who still had this full range of motion without having some form of previous help. The major reason why I think this is true is that most people don't know that this movement is possible. Over time, this conceptual fault has resulted in an artificial restriction.

Even when we are told what is possible, we are so certain that our belief is correct that we will often deny our own experience. My favorite example of this happened one time when I was working with a pianist on a piano technique called a tremolo.

A tremolo is accomplished by a rapid alternation of pushing down on one key with the thumb and then a second key (usually an octave away) with the little finger. I was struck by the ingenuity of this particular pianist because she was performing this movement without using the radio-ulnar joint at all. By a combination of finger, wrist, shoulder, and body movements she was able to alternate the notes quickly, but she complained about fatigue.

When I showed her how to accomplish the same thing using this "new" joint and movement she argued with me that what I was showing her wasn't possible, even as she did it. Then, after she had been doing this movement of rapid alternation using her arm in the way it was made to be used for some time, she stopped and turned to me and said, " I can't do this!"

"You can't do what?" I asked innocently.

She then brought her arm up, turned it back and forth perfectly, just as I had shown her, and said, "I can't do this."

"You can't do what?" I repeated inoffensively.

"This!" she shouted wildly, as she continued the movement.

"What?" I asked again, somewhat fiendishly.

This time as she continued to perform the movement and was about to say, "This," once more, it gradually dawned upon her that in order to show me the movement she claimed she couldn't do, she had to perform the movement itself. In fact, she performed it very well. Still, her conviction that she couldn't do that movement completely overrode her own understanding that she was doing the very thing she claimed that she couldn't, even as she did it

Once she understood the contradiction, we both laughed.

Her conviction about her inability to perform this movement was so strong, however, that the very next thing that she said was, "Well, I still can't do it."

Furthermore, these kinds of "misconceptions" do not require ignorance to be intact.

Once I had a registered nurse in one of my classes when I was talking about the elbow region. When I claimed that there was a special joint in the forearm that accomplished pronation and supination, she loudly exclaimed, "No!" Intrigued by her response, I asked her to show me how to pronate and supinate without using that joint She then twisted and turned her humerus (her upper arm bone) in her shoulder joint while holding her elbow region in place.

Now this was a person who had studied anatomy, passed exams, and taken a cadaver dissection class. She "knew" all of the information about the region, but, her own personal idea of the way the region worked was different from what she had studied. In fact, she believed her personal idea more than the information she had learned. Therefore, the way she turned her forearm conformed to her personal idea rather than to what she had learned about her body structures or to the structures themselves.

When I told her that the arm was constructed differently than she demonstrated and that it moved more efficiently in a way that was unlike how she moved it, she didn't believe me. In fact, in spite of her command of the information in that region, she completely denied that her arm moved in the way which I described. When I offered to show her how her arm really worked, she almost dared me to try. When I actually moved her arm as it was made to be moved, the experience was in such conflict with her ideas that her eyes flew open in surprise and she cried out, "You broke it!"

Our conscious minds have the capacity to override every system - our sensory system, our manner of movement, even our reflexes.[1]

Alexander discovered that what we think and how we think it can have a tremendous effect on the functioning of our mechanism. Like the relationing movement of our head with our body, the effect of our manner of thinking can be for our benefit or our detriment. And it doesn't matter whether you decide to believe either of these discoveries. They are in operation whether you believe them or not.

No matter what you believe, you are going to precede and accompany every gestural movement (activity) you perform with relationing movements of your axial and appendicular structures in such a way that you are either helped or hindered. You are going to "create and operate" yourself based upon your ideas of what is right and wrong, and your system will adapt itself to fit your ideas in a kind of self-fulfilling prophesy, even to the point of distortion and structural damage in activity.

Or, as Flip Wilson's character Geraldine might say, "What you think is what you get!"

You can believe this or not. You can ignore this information or not. It doesn't matter. What I am sharing with you is true, and there are many other places where you can find this same information.

---

[1] In orthopedic testing, Jandrassik's Maneuver is used to eliminate the conscious interference by the patient in testing for deep tendon reflexes of the legs.

The patient is asked to lock his fingers together and pull outward on his hands as if to pull them apart.

Often, a patient will be so busy pulling on his hands, he will forget to interfere with the patellar reflex and a normal response can be elicited. This response is possible because the patient is no longer preventing it by conscious interference.

What makes it uniquely Alexander's is that he says that the manifestation of this truth occurs even at the level of planning, the level of structure, and the level of motion behavior. What you think and how you think it determines, to a great extent, what you will be and become.

This being so, then doesn't it make sense to learn about the operative and formative principles which Alexander articulated? Doesn't it make sense to learn these principles which Alexander articulated and which you can use to acquire a universally constant improvement in your general standard level of performance? Doesn't it make sense to learn and use these principles so that you can free yourself from your own self-imposed limitations in even the most basic movements?

Of course it does. And that's why I'm here to help you.

ALEXANDER'S TWO DISCOVERIES

I.

In every movement you make, there is a change in the relationship of your head with your body that precedes and accompanies the movement and which either helps you or gets in your way.

In other words, in every movement there are two movements:

i) a relationing movement performed primarily by the axial structures which either creates a flexible lengthening that improves the coordination of the movement or which creates a general collapse that lowers the coordination of the movement, and

ii) a gestural movement which is made up of changes in angles of the joints of any part of the body and which defines the actual movement itself.

2.

The conscious mind has the capacity to override every system, including the natural ones.

WHAT YOU THINK IS WHAT YOU GET.

CHAPTER 6

THE MONKEY TRAP

In his book, *Body Awareness in Action*, Frank Pierce Jones tells us that "a simple way to trap a monkey is to present him with a nut in a bottle. The monkey puts his paw through the bottle's narrow mouth, grasps the nut, then cannot withdraw his paw because he will not (and hence cannot) let go of the nut." [1]

Whenever I am teaching an introductory series to a group of students, I like to include this story because people understand it easily and quickly. They can understand how a monkey might see a nut in a bottle, grab it, and not let go. Because the monkey could just barely squeeze his empty paw into the bottle, and because holding the nut in his paw makes his paw larger, the monkey is trapped.

In terms of Alexander and his work, the nature of this transaction is very simple.

When the monkey sees the nut, it acts as a stimulus and the monkey wants the nut. In this way, the nut becomes the "end" the monkey wishes to "gain." By acting immediately upon the desire to get the nut directly, the monkey falls into the trap which, in the Alexander Technique, we call "end-gaining." His attention is on the end he wishes to gain (the nut), so he pays little or no attention to the circumstances present or the manner in which he will gain his end. In fact, he just reaches for the nut and grabs it.

In and of itself, the act of reaching directly for the nut is not a problem. If the nut had been out in the open, it would have been a suitable strategy. In fact, it may have been the most efficient strategy possible. But, this particular nut is not on the ground. It is in a particular kind of bottle.

Now, the movement strategy, which had once served the monkey extremely well and which had helped him to survive before, endangers him. If the monkey persists in his old strategy, it will prove deadly.

There is nothing wrong with the strategy. The strategy and its effectiveness haven't changed. What has changed are the circumstances which surround the use of the strategy.

What was once of great value is now a danger because the conditions in which this strategy would be employed are different. If the monkey persists in his usual manner of response, if he continues to put his attention on the end he wishes to gain, if he seeks to gain his end directly, and if he doesn't put his attention on learning how to change the manner of his response to this new, nutty stimulus, he will be caught.

1 Jones, Frank Pierce, *Body Awareness in Action*, Schocken Press, New York, 1976, p. 4

At this point, I always ask my students to take a few minutes and tell me some other solutions to the monkey's dilemma. I'd like you to do this, too.

Take a few minutes and write down as many different solutions as you can think of to this problem of getting the nut without getting caught. I'll wait for you.

When you are finished, read on.

I am always surprised by how enthusiastic and creative people can be at this point. The responses almost always turn into one of the most fun times in the whole class. I have been doing this demonstration for fifteen years now and I am still getting new solutions.

How many solutions did you have? I'd like to share with you now the three most common categories of solutions.[1]

The first category is the largest and it often contains the most creative solutions. The first solutions that students think of are for getting the nut out of the bottle.

Some of the ways that have been suggested are: 1) shake the nut out, 2) break the bottle,[2] 3) for Looney Tune fans, there is the world-famous chewing gum on the end of a stick, 4) a hydraulic engineer once suggested washing the nut out on a wave of water, and 5) recently, the last three classes I have taught have suggested sucking the nut out.[3]

The second category of answer involves performing some sort of operation on the nut while it is in the bottle so that the nut opens. Then, the smaller, edible pieces of the nut can be safely extracted.

The last solution is the one that people rarely think of. I am always very proud of the people who do think of it. It involves a form of solution which requires a "trick of mind" that many people find hard to accomplish.

In order to understand this mind trick better, let's see if we can find the solution to a simple problem which was once posed to me in a math class.

Picture if you will nine dots set out in this fashion:

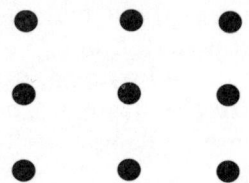

---

1. If you've thought of a solution that doesn't seem to fit any of these categories, please send me a postcard tell me about it. I love to find new solutions.

2. For afficionados, this category runs the range of getting a hippo to break the bottle for you, which has dual attraction of not cutting yourself on the broken glass and opening the nut as well (although no good solution has been found yet to the problem of ingesting broken glass), all the way to the monkey using the diamond on her engagement ring to cut out the back of the bottle and reach for the nut through that larger opening.

3. I have no idea what this means.

Your task is to connect all nine dots by using only four straight lines and without raising your pencil from the paper once you have started drawing lines.

Go ahead and try to work this out. The answer can be found in Appendix B.

As we have seen in Appendix B, the solution is found in being able to go outside the self-imposed limits of the problem as you perceive it. No one told you to stay inside the "box". In fact, there is no "box" to stay inside of.If you had trouble solving this puzzle, it was probably because you perceived these dots as a "box" and made another rule of your own about having to stay within these perceived, but unreal, boundaries.

In a similar way, people make up their own "perceived rules" about turning over on my portable adjusting table when I am giving them a chiropractic adjustment.

Because the portable table is so much smaller and so much less stable than the tables I use in my office, many people complain as they go from lying on their back to lying on their stomach and vice versa. Almost everyone is uncomfortable as they do it.

There is one special group of people who are not uncomfortable when they "change sides." These are the people who, when I ask them to turn over, stand up first, and then turn appropriately as they get back on the table. They have no trouble turning at all.

Rather than staying on the table and twisting precariously because they perceive that there are rules which say that they have to stay on the table, these people just step outside of the "box" and take care of their needs.

The more I teach and the more I work as a physician, the more strongly I am struck by the number of problems that people cause for themselves because of self-imposed limitations from perceived but unreal rules.

Some of my patients believe that they have to perform certain exercises or move in a certain way because of their injuries. In most cases, these peculiar ways of moving only serve to aggravate their condition. Further, very few of these patients are easily able to see their own participation in the exacerbation of their conditions.

This kind of behavior is really no different than the elephants who tie themselves up to perceived stakes in the ground. Except, perhaps, that it is more insidious. At least with the elephants, their handlers are using a real rope to trick them intentionally. In the cases of my students and patients, all too often these restrictive "boxes" or "ropes" are being created by the captives themselves.

How does this relate to our friend the monkey?

Well, the third solution to satisfying his desire to get a nut is for him to get another nut.

Just because he sees the nut in the bottle and it makes him want to have a nut, it doesn't mean that he has to have that nut. There are a lot of nuts around, and, if the monkey doesn't believe that, he should come to some of my classes.

Once we believe that we have found all or most of the solutions to the monkey's problem, I ask my students what they have done differently than the monkey who was caught.

Eventually, they tell me that there were two differences.

First, they point out that all of their solutions are more indirect then the one the monkey used.

Rather than going immediately for their end in a direct manner, they stopped; looked at the situation; made decisions about what was involved in the problem; and then addressed themselves to find a solution appropriate to the specific problem at hand.

The use of this kind of procedure constitutes the second major difference between the approaches of the monkey and my students.

In Alexander terms, instead of keeping their attention on the end they wished to gain, my students put their attention on the means, the process, whereby they could gain their end. At the heart of Alexander's work is this invitation to forego trying to gain your end directly and to keep your attention on the means whereby you will gain your end instead.

Whenever my students are anxious about whether or not they will ever gain their ends, I remind them that if they simply perform the process they have reasoned out to gain their end, and if the process they have reasoned out is appropriate, they cannot help but reach their end.

In fact, they can't avoid it.

In the same paragraph in which Frank tells the story about the monkey trap, he goes on to say, "Most people are caught in monkey traps of unconscious habits" [1] These people cannot escape because they do not perceive what they are doing to trap themselves while they are doing it.

If we are ever to get out of the "boxes" of the monkey traps of our unconscious habits that Frank describes, we will need a powerful tool. We will need a new way to look at ourselves, our movements, our feeling sense, our thoughts, and our concepts. We will need to learn how to look at these things in such a way that we will no longer be bound by them. We need to learn to look at them so that they will come to serve us rather than bind us to the tyranny of habit.

In order to put this new tool into use, we will need courage, discipline, and a willingness to work and experiment.

Alexander has supplied the tool.

The rest is up to us.

---

1 Jones, Frank Pierce, Body Awareness in Action, Schocken Press, New York, 1976, p. 4

PHYSIOLOGIC CONSIDERATIONS

CHAPTER 7

HOW MUSCLES WORK

The best way to understand what is going on inside of us as we do this work, is to look at some basic concepts about the way in which our systems are put together and how they function. In this way, we can get a clearer picture of what is going on in an Alexander lesson. Once we have a sense of our mechanism and how it works, this will give us a foundation upon which to retrain our thinking processes so that we can make Alexander's work our own.

First of all, let's take a look at the way in which muscles work.

Before you become concerned that you are going to have to learn a lot of anatomy and physiology, we are only going to look at the basic principles of movement physiology and see what they tell us about the work.

Each muscle is made up of many fibers which are grouped together and attached into bundles. These bundles are grouped together into larger bundles, and then still larger bundles, until the largest grouping of these bundles of fibers is given a single name to designate a muscle. In fact, there is a way in which giving a single muscle name to these groups of fibers is a kind of false distinction, in that it is possible for various small parts of a muscle to fire at any given time while the rest of the muscle is at rest.

Muscles come in many shapes and sizes, and perform many different kinds of activities. It is the nature of the activity performed which will often determine the size and shape of the muscle. The muscles which we are most interested in for this discussion are the ones which provide movement at the joints.

The most typical model for the kind of muscle we are interested in is one which is attached by a tendon to the bones on both sides of a joint.[1] The working part of the muscle, called the belly, lies between the two attachments. When the muscle is working - when it is turned "on" - the belly of the muscle contracts. As this happens, it pulls on the attachments on the ends of the muscle, bringing the ends closer together. This contraction of the muscle is what provides the power to move the bones. In

1. When we think about our skeletons, we usually think of the bones that make it up. In order to understand movement, however, we have to think of our skeleton as being made up of bones and joints.

A joint is the space between two bones in the skeleton. If there were no joints, our skeleton would be in a single piece like the shell of a crab, and we would be unable to move. So, the combination of bones and joints which make up our skeleton is what allows for the balance between the strength of the rigid framework which the bones provide, and the ability to move provided by the joints. As we shall see, it is the function of our muscles to provide the power to move us at our joints.

other words, it is the muscles of our body which provide the major source of power for movement, alignment, and distortion.

Many people are quite enamored of the concept that gravity is the great villain in the melodrama of our poor posture. "Gravity is king!" one of my instructors from chiropractic school used to love to say, "All must bow down before gravity!"

I am no longer swayed by such statements. It seems to me that gravity does some wonderful things for us. As Marjorie Barstow used to say, it does keep us from floating off into space. But, within the closed system of our bodies, the effect of gravity is very small, while the effect of our muscles, directed by our thoughts, is very large. If this were not the case, how else could we stand?

Perhaps the most important point regarding gravity is not so much its relative influence upon us, as the probability that, over time, we have developed sufficiently as a species to function in harmony with our environment in spite of gravity. In his Noble Prize speech, Nicholas Tinbergen said:

> It is highly unlikely that in their very long evolutionary history of walking upright, the hominids have not had time to evolve the correct mechanisms for bipedal locomotion. This conclusion receives support from the surprising, but indubitable fact that even after 40 to 50 years of obvious misuse one's body can (one might say) snap back into proper, and in many respects more healthy, use as a result of a short series of half-hourly sessions. Proper stance and movement are obviously genetically old, environment-resistant behaviors.

Our bodies are normally very strong and can resist gravity in widely varying ways. It is only in cases of severe disability or disorder that people do not have the ability to function effectively within the constant gravitational field we all experience. While it would require a tremendous force to cause the distortions we experience and observe, it is clear that a single, relatively weak, unidirectional force such as gravity cannot account for the diversity of variation in these distortions. It does take a powerful force to cause the differences we see, but gravity is not the culprit. The force which fuels these distortions in each of us is the power and force of the conscious mind.

To summarize, the kind of movement which is produced depends upon which muscles are contracted, the order in which they are contracted, and the force with which they are contracted.

Simply put, in any movement, some muscles are used primarily for movement, some for creating a stable support against which the movement muscles can pull, and some are used for fine correction of the movement once it has been initiated.

As you have probably already guessed, this process can become quite involved. While it is essential for your teacher to know and understand these processes, you need only concern yourself with just a few basic ideas.

The most important thing to remember about muscles is that, when they work, muscles get shorter. There are a number of elegant explanations about how this is done, and not a little bit of controversy, but the one thing that all of these movement models agree upon is that when muscles work, they get shorter.

The second most important thing to know about muscles is that, when they are not working, they do not get longer. They get less short.

This may seem like a picky distinction or a word game, but it is actually much more important than that. Although there is a mechanism for muscles to make themselves shorter, there is no mechanism for them to make themselves longer.[1]

As teachers and proponents of Alexander's ideas, we often talk about "lengthening." Too often, in a practical sense, this encourages students to "do" something to lengthen. Students should not be encouraged to try to "lengthen" their muscles, because, philosophic discussions aside, it is not possible.

The act of "lengthening" which generates the feeling sense impression of lengthening comes primarily from the cessation of muscular working. This allows the muscles to become less short, not to lengthen.

Muscles do not get longer. When they are not working, muscles get less short.

For example, it is not unusual for a student in an Alexander lesson to appear taller during a lesson. My own personal record for such an event in a standing lesson was a measured six and a half inches, where the standing height of the individual was six and a half inches higher at the end of his lesson than it was listed on his drivers license (which probably means the increase in height was even greater since most men get taller and lose weight on their driver's licenses).

Now, in understanding what happened, it is important to see that the student did not really get taller. He got less short.

As I am sure some of you have already guessed (or seen elsewhere in class), the student's previous lower height was the result of the distortions caused by excessive muscular pull throughout his system, creating in him

---

1 For those of you who wish to propose eccentric contraction as an internal mechanism for muscles making themselves longer, I will refer you to Brunnstrom's discussion of eccentric contraction in the book Brunnstrom's Clinical Kinesiology (Lehmkhul and Smith).

Briefly, according to Brunnstrom, eccentric contraction occurs when small numbers of fibers contract in association with the elongation of the gross muscle to provide fine movement control and a braking action. Although the disposition of the muscle as a whole is to get longer under external force the mechanism of the intramuscular force itself remains contraction.

There is an intriguing possibility that the contrary contraction of some fibers during the general "lengthening' of the muscle as a whole for purposes of control may provide a kinesthetic and conceptual basis for some of the unnecessary tension in cultivated movements, but this discussion lies beyond the scope of this present project.

a very exaggerated slump. In other words, his decreased stature was caused by the shortening of a number of muscles.

As I worked with him, the distorting pulls of the various muscles generally became less. In other words, the muscles involved in the distortion worked less; as a result, the muscles involved in the distortion got less short; the distortion diminished; and the student's height increased.

No one gets taller in this work. What happens is that, as the distortions, which are actively making the person shorter, are diminished or prevented. The person becomes less short, just like the muscles themselves get less short when not working.

The third most important thing to remember about how muscles work is that they can be thought of as being grouped in opposing pairs.

For just about every muscle in the body, there is another muscle or group of muscles which pull the bone in a direction opposite to the direction of the first muscle's pull.

For example, the best known muscle in the upper arm is the Biceps muscle. I call it the "Popeye" muscle because this is the muscle little kids show to you to prove that they are as strong as Popeye the Sailor Man. The action of this muscle, located anatomically on the front of the arm, is to bend the forearm towards the upper arm at the hinge joint in the elbow.[1] Located on the back of the arm is another muscle called the Triceps whose job is to straighten the bend caused at the elbow joint by the Biceps muscle.

While the structure of the opposing pairs of muscles throughout the body is not always this clear, the principle remains much the same. For just about every muscle which moves a bone one way, there is another muscle which moves it back.

The fourth most important thing to remember about how muscles work is that muscles only have a direct effect on the joint the muscle crosses. The direct effect of a muscle ends at the muscle's attachments.

On the face of it, the idea that the direct effect of a muscle occurs only in the joint or joints which the muscle spans, and goes no further than the attachments of the muscles, may seem obvious. My experience with students shows me, however, that in terms of practical application, the majority of people do not understand this principle at all.

Let's take as an example someone with a tremendous slump who is having a lesson.

The major cause of this person's slump (and just about everyone else's) is that, as part of the general pattern of his misuse, the muscles at the front of his body have gotten excessively short and have pulled his body unduly forward. As we have seen above, if his front body-muscles would

---

1. It is worth mentioning that the contractions of the muscle fibers in the biceps in the process of moving the forearm is what causes the muscle to bulge and become hard. It is not moving the arm by some mysterious means which causes the muscle to bulge while this may be obvious to some, it may not be to others.

It is the shortening of muscles which causes movement; "movement does not cause "muscles."

stop overly contracting, the interference would diminish, the distortion would lessen, and the slump would decrease. On this, we could all agree.

There is a strategy for getting rid of this kind of slump which many people follow, however, on which we might not agree.

Have you ever heard of (or been) someone who during this kind of lesson tightened his or her legs? It's really quite a common response even when it is not noticed. And really quite ineffectual. Actually detrimental. When it is noticed, most people can agree that it isn't a good way to change a slump and, in fact, because of the increase in muscular tension in the legs, it probably causes more problems than it solves.

But why doesn't it work?

Two reasons.

Firstly, the muscles most commonly tightened are attached to, or end at, the base of the pelvis or lower. Consequently, their actions cannot directly affect the area of distortion which lies primarily beyond these attachments.

More to the point, the student's problem is being caused by too much contraction of certain muscles of the chest and torso. Further contraction of other muscles in the leg will not prevent the interference and distortion created by the overly-contracted torso muscles. Only diminishing the amount of undue contraction in the muscles which are creating the slump will provide a real solution.

Even if one were to contract the muscles whose action opposes the "slumping" muscles - an idea we will talk about later - all one would succeed in doing would be to have two sets of muscles overly contracted. You might be "straighter," but you will still be carrying out the act and motion of slumping.

And this is the fifth most important thing to remember about muscles in relation to this work.

Movement is carried out by the sum effect of all of the muscular forces being brought to bear on the body at any given time. Since the greatest efficiency of movement would involve the greatest amount of work done for the least amount of effort, we can easily state the minimum amount of effort needed to perform any activity.

I call this formula the Motion Needs Equation:

1) For every movement, some muscles will have to be fired (contracted) to power the movement; some muscles will have to be fired to create the stability required to perform the movement; and some muscles will have to be fired to provide mid-course corrections for fine tuning the movement.

2) For each of these actions, there is a minimum amount of effort required to meet the needs of the motion involved.

3) Any effort greater than this is unnecessary and wasteful.

4) All other muscles not involved in these three functions serve purposes which are not required for the performance of the given motion and hence should be turned off throughout the movement.

If we return to our friend who is tightening his legs to prevent his slump, we see a number of ways in which this activity is contrary to the motion needs equation.

First, because of the location of the leg muscles, because their end attachments are lower on the body than the areas involved in the slump, these muscles cannot be considered to be used for the purpose of making the motion involved or for fine-tuning the motion once begun.

More importantly, the addition of even greater amounts of effort to remedy a problem caused by too much effort to begin with is a strategy that makes no sense.

I suppose that someone might argue or believe that the leg muscles could be used to stabilize the body in order to perform the action of "straightening up" to eliminate the slump. Certainly if one were to try to eliminate the slump by activating the muscles which straighten the body and thereby increase the forces involved, there might be a need to stiffen the legs to stabilize these additional unnecessary muscular forces.

But, this slump (and most other body distortions) is being caused by too much muscular effort in the first place. A more reasonable approach would be to eliminate the original fault.

By putting these last three rules together, we can begin to see the body and its condition in a new and exciting way.

Motion is caused by a contraction of muscles which is greater in one directon at a given joint and which causes one bone to turn around another bone at that joint in a manner which makes the ends of the contracting muscle come closer together.

If the contracting force of an opposing muscle, pulling in the direction opposite to the pull of the first muscle, was of the same amount of force as the first, then the bone would not turn around the joint and there would be no motion.

But, there would be movement.

In fact, there would be two movements: one pulling in one direction and the other pulling in the opposite direction.

This kind of kinetic stalemate is what we mean when we say that someone is "holding a position." It is not that these people are being "still" so much as they are involved in a kind of escalating tug of war in which they are using the muscular force of contraction necessary to move in at least two directions at once. The resulting muscular overcontraction serves no useful purpose but rather layers on successive amounts of purposeless force. This purposeless force of muscular overcontraction is what we mean by tension.

As an Alexander teacher and a doctor, I often hear clients complain that they "carry their tension" in their shoulders or neck or legs or wherever. They believe, incorrectly, that tension is some kind of entity, some kind of condition with a life of its own that can be carried around like coins in a pocket.

When I work with these people and relieve an area of tension, quite often they tell me that their "tension" has moved to another area. I will tell you what I tell them.

There is no such thing as tension!

No such THING.

"It" isn't carried around. "It" can't be transferred. Tension is nothing more nor less than a persistent movement of muscular overcontraction which a person habitually carries out, often as part of a more complex pattern of habitual movements.

Tension is simply a movement which you carry out continuously against yourself. And that's good. Because if you caused it, you can stop it.

These are the major elements of muscle physiology which have a bearing on the Alexander Technique. By putting all of this information together, we see that the power of our muscles is the most important element in the creation of our distortions.

When our muscles are working in a balanced way which satisfies the motion needs equation for a given movement, this use of our muscles provides harmony and an increased quality of performance in activities. When the use of our muscles is out of balance and in violation of the motion needs equation, the muscles produce distortions and a decrease in the quality of performance.

How our muscles come to be in maladaptive conditions and, more importantly, how we can learn to retrain ourselves to perform in more constructive ways lies at the heart of the Alexander Technique.

In order to move ahead in learning about these procedures, we must first look more closely at the relationship between movement and thought.

CHAPTER 8

THE IMMACULATE CONTRACTION

While muscles provide the power for movement, it is our nervous system which provides the direction of our movements.

Muscles are only machines which contract on command.

The message to contract comes from the nerves.

Some of these messages which reach the muscles, such as reflexes, are built into the system and cannot be changed directly. Other messages are elaborate, on-going strategies for turning certain muscle groups on and off in specific sequences. These sequences constitute the design of a given movement.

It is impossible to change the design of a movement once the message has been sent out of the motor area of the brain.

It is only before that point, as the movement is being designed, that a change in strategy can occur.

The design of a movement is a thought. The only effective tools which can be used to change a thought are thoughts themselves. Consequently, it is the redirecting and retraining of our thinking which will provide the means of escape from our monkey traps.

When most of us consider the nature of thinking, our opinions are usually based on some model or other which minimizes the role of conscious thought.

The simplest and most common representation of this is to draw a circle as if it were a pie with a small wedge-shaped piece cut out of it. In most people's concepts, the small wedge would be labeled "conscious" and the rest of the pie labeled "unconscious."

In practice, people seem to believe that this model can be applied equally well to locomotion as to the vegetative processes. The implication is that there is only a small part of the locomotive processes of thought which is conscious and reasoning.

Because Alexander's discoveries and techniques deal with the conscious and reasoning parts of us, if this restricted model of the realm of conscious guidance was true, then there would only be a small part of our processes with which this work would be effective. This limited role of conscious mental activity isn't consistent with the way F. M. presents his work, nor is it consistent with the kind of changes one observes in people as they continuously employ the work. As I worked with more and more people, the discrepancy between this pie-wedge model and the events which happened in classes became more and more evident, and I sought an answer to account for my observations.

One day, as I was teaching an Alexander workshop to a drama class at a junior high school in Portland, Oregon, one of the students brought up this very problem by asking what was the difference between conscious and unconscious thought, and which of the two was larger and more important

To answer him, I drew a pie chart on the board with conscious thought in the small wedge shaped piece, and with the rest of the pie labeled "unconscious." He told me that my drawing was the way he had been taught the mind was organized in science class, but, by the way I was talking about consciousness, it seemed to him that I had made the conscious part of the pie seem much bigger.

I explained to him that the value of a model, like the pie chart, was to be able to express some larger, less comprehensible phenomenon in a simpler and more comprehensible way. Sometimes the process of reduction or evaluation could contain an error and, therefore, the model might be wrong. Still, the advantage of having a model is that when the observations no longer fit the model, you can change the model to fit the observations. More importantly, you can test a model by running different experiments and comparing the results against the predicted results which would have happened if your tested model had been true. In other words, if the model which you are presently using either no longer fits the observations or is proving to be a handicap in your advancement, then you can change the model to a more advantageous one as long as your past and future observations are consistent with the new model. Therefore, with regard to conscious and unconscious thought, perhaps the pie chart diagram is an appropriate diagram, but perhaps the values should be reversed. Perhaps it is true that there are two categories of thought - conscious and unconscious. Perhaps the difference in size is so large that one of the two is much larger than the other. But, what if the actual case is that the larger of the two kinds of thought is conscious thought?

It was at this point that my sponsor to the class cleared his throat and got my attention. Apparently I had gone into a twenty minute discussion with myself which he felt was no longer appropriate to an introductory Alexander class at the junior high level. So I took off my mad professor persona and returned to the class and the fun we had been having earlier while learning about Alexander.

But I never forgot the implications of those comments.

What if the largest part of our thinking processes is actually conscious? Or if conscious thought isn't the largest part, what if the size of the piece of the pie which represents consciousness is larger than we take it to be?

After my monologue in the drama class, I began an experiment which I continue to this day.

I have acted in my practice and taught in my classes "AS IF" the model of the relationship of conscious to unconscious thought could be represented by a pie chart with a single wedge, but that the largest part of the pie was conscious thought.

If this model was true, then one would predict that most, if not all of the decisions which underlie specific movement behaviors are conscious and, hence, able to be expressed. If the decisions for these behaviors are knowable and able to be expressed, then these decisions and the behaviors that they cause would certainly be capable of being altered by Alexander's procedures.

If the client could be trained to redirect his thinking in a more constructive manner, then the mental power the client could bring to bear on his own problem would become an ally instead of an obstacle.

Consequently, to prove or disprove this model, I set out to see how many times I could find a specific decision or thought which underlay a client's unusual movement behaviors.

In the last twenty-five years, I have not found one unusual habit or movement behavior which could not be traced back to some specific conscious decision.

The most common way to trace one of these underlying conscious thoughts is to talk with a student in class about where a particular behavior may have originated. The answers are often absolutely intriguing.

The most dramatic of these examples occurred with a student from Washington, D. C.

When watching him walk, two distortions became clear very quickly. First, the movement of his legs was very exaggerated. Second, instead of moving his legs straight forward, he moved both legs to the side as they came forward. In fact, his walk was one of the most bizarre, nonpathologic gaits I have ever observed. When I questioned him about why he walked in this way, he told me why, immediately and emphatically.

When he was at military school as a teenager, he kept hitting the heels of the student marching in front of him in close order drill. No matter how often he tried to stop hitting the other student's heels, he found that he couldn't. Moving his legs in this exaggerated and peculiar manner was the only way he had ever found to avoid the heels of the person marching in front of him.

We will have more to say about our marching soldier and his decisions, but for now, it is sufficient to note that, on initial observation, his pattern of leg movements was bizarre and inexplicable. With further investigation, based on the analysis and decisions the marching student had made, the way he moved his legs was not only reasonable, but it made sense.

I have also found in my investigations that the precipitating cause of a bizarre or exaggerated behavior does not have to be a specific solution for a specific event.

I once had a patient who had a horrendous problem with "tension." As we talked about in the last chapter, she really didn't have "tension." What she had was the habit of using tremendous amounts of muscular force in opposing directions constantly so that, even when she was lying still, it was very difficult for someone else to move her arms, legs, and neck because of the force of her residual "tension." This continuous pulling of her own muscles against herself was so strong and so constant she was suffering from fatigue and the pain of overuse syndrome even though her life was not very active.

I worked with her as a Restructuring client for almost three months.

Although she would get relief in sessions, she did not show the kind of on-going improvement between sessions which is characteristic of Restructuring. During her re-examination, I was explaining to her that when a client goes this long without significant improvement, I usually make a referral to someone else because I am not helping them. I told her that I knew that there was some reason why my treatment techniques were not preventing the return of her pattern of using extreme amounts of muscular effort to "hold onto" her muscles, but I couldn't figure out what it was. Until the cause of her holding onto her muscles could be found and eliminated, I didn't think she would get any better while under my care.

After I had told her once more that I couldn't figure out the unknown cause of her problem, I turned away to do another examination procedure. As my back was turned, I heard this tiny little voice, like a four-year-old's, say, "But if I let go, the world will fall apart."

Here was a movement behavior strategy based on decisions made by a very small girl when faced with the dynamics of a very dysfunctional family. At one point in her life (and, in further discussions, my patient was very eloquent when talking about this particular time), events and circumstances were so threatening that the only thing she could think of to do to help was to tighten all of her muscles to help "hold things together."

When things worked out in an acceptable way during the time she was doing this excessive "holding", the little girl had become convinced that things worked out so well because of how she had tightened her muscles. Therefore, she decided she had a responsibility to herself (and to everyone else) to keep her muscles tightened, no matter what.

Forty years later, these decisions had created overuse syndrome and premature degeneration in her arms and spine, as well as movement distortions and general muscular inefficiency.

But, she kept doing them.

Like our marching cadet, we will talk more about our world-saving body-contractor, and why they both persisted with their maladaptive behavior, but, for now, it is only important to see that their behaviors came from their ideas. Their behaviors came from conscious thoughts which remained active, in place, and acted upon, despite the passage of time and the changing of circumstances.

After having traced hundreds of such examples back to the decisions which initially created the movement behavior, I have yet to find a movement behavior which I could not trace back to such a decision.

Consequently, I feel quite confident that a more appropriate and useful model to represent the role of conscious thought to unconscious thought is a pie-shaped model in which the small wedge represents unconscious thought and the larger region represents thought which is conscious.[1]

So, movements are caused by the contraction of muscles, and muscular contraction is caused by the sending of messages along the nerves to the muscles involved.

These messages are called impulses in the peripheral nerves, but they are the sort of thing which we call thoughts in our brains. Once we have established that commands which are sent to the muscles originate as thoughts in the brain, then we have a way of finding out something about the thoughts which an individual has.

First of all, we must begin with a basic decision about the relationship of thought and movement.

I believe that most, if not all, movement behaviors begin with a thought.

If I am going to move in some way, I must first make a decision to move in that way. This decision then becomes organized into a strategy for movement, and the movement becomes issued as commands to the muscles involved.

In this way it can be said that muscles are activated by thoughts. I believe (and I am quite confident that Alexander would agree) that if there was a movement, then there was a thought which preceded and directed it.

In other words, there is no such thing as an Immaculate Contraction.

If you were to ask me to touch my ear, in order for me to do that, I must carry out all of the mental operations involved.

For example, I must give consent to do the action or withhold it. I must decide which hand to use, which ear to touch. I must calculate the probable pathway of movement to follow. I must decide how much force to use, and so forth.

In other words, once I have decided that I will touch my ear, I must devise a strategy for carrying out that action.

How these strategies are devised and carried out is a topic well beyond the scope of our present efforts and a target for a great deal of excellent

---

1. In class we make a distinction between three initial levels of consciousness: conscious, aware, and acknowledged.

There is an extremely large number of our actions which are conscious. The percentage of these conscious actions of which we are aware is much smaller. The percentage of the conscious actions of which we are aware, that we are willing or able to acknowledge at any given time, is smaller still.

The fact that we may not be aware of an action, or the fact that we may still not acknowledge some action or other of which we are aware, does not make these actions any less conscious.

Unless there is the presence of a severe organic or behavioral condition, for an action to be classified as less than conscious, I would have to find an act or movement behavior for which no underlying conscious decision or decisions could be found.

To date, I have never found any unusual habit or movement behavior that could not be traced back to some specific, fully conscious decision.

research. There is one aspect of this subject, however, which would serve us well to pursue.

Frank Jones talked about the distinction between behavior which is public and behavior which is private. While all of a person's behavior involves both thought and movement, only the movement occurs in a public arena. Thus, it is only a person's movement which can be detected by our senses. Because a movement can be detected by someone's senses, it can be said to be public. Only those behaviors which are public can truly be known by others.

While it is true that we can learn to make reasonable inferences about a person's thinking by analyzing their public behavior, the thinking itself remains private and unknowable. If this were not the case, then deception (self and otherwise) would not be possible. However, because of how our nervous system interfaces with our muscles, there is a way that we can work backwards from our public movement behavior to find out something about our private thinking processes.

While we cannot "know" what was going on in a person's private thinking behavior, we can "know" how they moved. By comparing stated intent with actual result, we can learn to gauge the relative effectiveness of each person in carrying out his intention.

In a well-coordinated individual, there is a very high correlation between intention and actual performance. This individual experiences a tremendous freedom of choice in terms of responses and is better able to respond freshly and creatively to each circumstance as it presents itself.

In an individual with poor coordination, there is often a practically irresistible response or pattern of responses to every circumstance which either stereotypes the response pattern or interferes with a fresh response to each new stimulus. This leads to a very low correlation between actual performance and intent.

In either case, by analyzing the motion performed, I can come to some conclusions about the thoughts and strategies which preceded them. In other words, if it is true that "by their actions, ye shall know them," then it is also true that by the manner of their actions ye shall "know" something of their thinking.

For example, let us look again at my touching my ear.

Suppose I announce that I am going to touch my ear, I must then decide which hand to use and which ear to touch. I then formulate my strategy for carrying out the action - which hand to use, which movement pathway to follow, how much force to use, etc. I then project the messages from my brain to the mechanisms involved, raise my left hand, and, with my index finger, touch my nose instead.

Because the degree of coordination in an individual is equal to the relative ability of that individual to conceive of an idea, and then to carry out that idea as conceived, by touching my nose after announcing my intention to touch my ear, we know that one of three things is true about me and my action.

Either I misrepresented my intention when I spoke, I have a great need of an anatomy lesson, or my coordination is seriously impaired.

Notice that, at this point and without further investigation, we cannot know which is true. But, we can "know" that there is a discrepancy between my stated intention and the action which I carried out.

There is, however, no discrepancy between the action carried out and the messages projected from the brain. In fact, the muscles, in the absence of any pathologic, organic condition, can only carry out the commands which they receive.

These commands represent the implementation of movement strategies conceived. While it is possible to change the messages projected to the muscles before they are sent out, there is no practical way to change them once they are sent. Because of this, we can trace a person's "thinking" back as far as the commands sent to the muscles.

Let us suppose that, in a lesson, a student is asked to begin walking without pulling his head back, and that the student agrees to do this. Then, if, as he actually begins to walk, he does pull his head back, we can only be certain that the commands to the muscles included the commands to pull his head back.

We cannot "know" with any certainty about the student's intent or whether or not the student actually projected the "Alexander orders." The student's thoughts are private and unknowable. If the student's response to the intention of walking was similar or identical to his habitual movement response in walking, we can infer that his habitual patterns of directive guidance dominated his relatively weak desire to change his manner of use in walking. We cannot know, however, whether or not he really tried to change his "thinking."

I remember one time I was teaching an introductory class and I asked a student to tell me out loud what she was intending to do as she tried to do on her own what she thought I had shown her. As she informed me she was going to move her head up, she pulled it back. As she told me she was going to let her body follow her head allowing her stature to lengthen, she began to collapse. The more she told me she was "thinking" about moving her head up and lengthening, the more she screwed herself down into the chair.

I urged her to continue for some time. I wanted to see if she would finally reach a point where this way of "moving up" felt like she was being squished. But, as she persisted (and shrank), she became more and more pleased with herself and confident that she was carrying out the "orders" she was speaking.[1]

---

1. By the way, the slump she created as a result of "moving up" was quite different from the slump she created when sitting casually. Therefore, it is unlikely that the slump of "moving up" was simply an increase of effort in her habitual response as is often claimed and assumed in such cases.

From this example, we can "know" that the commands which were going to her muscles were for her to pull her head back and press herself down.

How do we know this?

Because it is public and we can see it.

We can know that the final strategy which she turned into commands and carried out involved this backward and downward movement because muscles are activated by thoughts and the commands which activate the muscles must be connected to some form of planning. We can know that, in some way, she was thinking about "moving up," if only in her speech centers.

What we can't know is the private maze of strategies, intentions, concepts, and commands which turned her stated desire into a contradictory action.

As teachers, we can, at best, only make conjectures about these things, and we often have to, in order to construct appropriate teaching strategies. There is no way, however, in which we can say that we "know" what the student was thinking. We can only know what is publicly available - the movement

From the movement, we can work backwards to "know" something of the commands which initiated the movement. From the commands, we can work backwards to "know" something of the final decisions which led to the commands. With each backwards step, however, the variables increase, the connections become more tenuous, and the thinking more private.

If the process of learning this work can be seen as a battle between being trapped by one's habitual movement and being free to design appropriate responses at will, I do not believe that this "battle" will ever be won on the basis of movement correction, reflex initiation, or postural change. I believe that it must be won on the basis of how the student has trained himself to think.

If the student's thinking is sound, then satisfactory movement must follow.

CHAPTER 9

FEELINGS AND THE TIME LINE

The last topic we need to discuss from a physiological point of view before we look more closely at Alexander's work is the whole issue of our feeling sense with regards to movement. One of the most important and most difficult decisions a student has to make in this work is to decide the relative importance of our feeling sense with regard to our patterns of directive guidance.[1]

What do we mean by feelings with regard to movement? Are feelings in this sense the same as emotions? Do they make an effective tool for guidance? When do feelings occur? And so forth.

The list of questions regarding feelings in this work is quite long. Once again, the way in which these questions are answered will determine much of what you think the work is and how it is to be accomplished. As I have noted, the subject is so large it is probably worth two or three books in itself. What I propose to do in this chapter is present certain physiologic facts which serve as the basis for my own answers to these questions. As I go, I will try to demonstrate the relevance of this information with respect to the work

Like the chapter on muscles, the information may seem so technical that it may intimidate you. There is no need for any of this material to do that, even if you find yourself re-reading sections many times. Almost everyone has to read this kind of material many times and give it much thought before they can understand it. If you keep at it, however, I believe that when you are finished you will be well rewarded.

One way to look at how we are made is to see ourselves divided into two large divisions. In their book *Illustrated Physiology*, Callander and McNaught call these two divisions meta-systems because meta-systems themselves are made up of systems of organs in the body.

The first of these meta-systems is called the Vegetative System. It is made up of the digestive, respiratory, excretory, transport, and endocrine systems. The function of the Vegetative System is to keep us alive.

---

1. The discussion of the role of feelings and sensory appreciation in this work is important but extremely controversial. It would be inappropriate in this or any other introductory book to deal with this controversy in a manner befitting the importance of the controvers, and I hope that the balance of all my other writings will address this discussion more fairly and commpletely.

In this chapter I intend to present the distillation of the argument which makes the most sense to me. Because I will do this in a straightforward manner, I anticipate that the presentation of this particular aspect of what I teach might serve as a target point for the rejection of this appraoch as a whole.

While I respect one's right to reject this approach, I would ask the indulgence of anyone who is a strong proponent of any the other points of view about the importance of the feeling sense (or any other topic, for that matter) that they may suspend their final judgement about what is said now so that I may present a simple introductory argument here, and a more complete one elsewhere.

The second meta-system is called the Master Tissues. It is made up of the nervous system, skeleton, and musculature. The function of the Master Tissues is to receive information, analyze it, and formulate a response.

In very simple terms, the Vegetative System creates and sustains life, and the Master Tissues meta-system carries the Vegetative System around, acquires required resources, and generally keeps the Vegetative System out of harm's way.

Clearly, of the two meta-systems, the one most involved with Alexander's work is the Master Tissues. We have talked before about the muscles and bones. It is time now to look more closely at the nervous system to see if we can shed some more light on the role of feelings in guidance.

There are many ways to divide the nervous system.

One of the most common ways is to divide it into three parts: the Central Nervous System, the Peripheral Nervous System, and the Autonomic Nervous System. In this scheme, the Autonomic Nervous System deals with the Vegetative Meta-System, the Peripheral Nervous System deals with the Locomotive aspect of the Master Tissues, and the Central Nervous System organizes and mediates the responses to and from both.

While of value to know, this particular model of seeing the nervous system doesn't really advance our practical understanding. But, if we focus in on how the Central Nervous System deals with messages to and from both of the other systems, a very valuable way of looking at the nervous system presents itself.

The nervous system can be thought of as consisting of three parts:

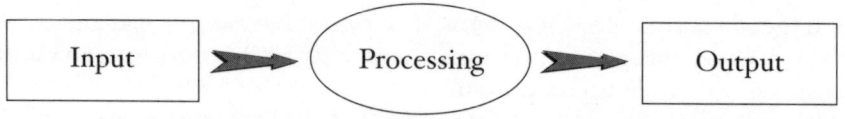

This includes a part for taking in information (Input), a part for correlating that information and formulating a response (Processing), and a part for carrying that response to the end organs, usually muscles, which will, make the response (Output).

We've already talked a little about these last two parts of this model in the preceding chapter.

As we saw, the "brain" processes the information available to it, makes a decision about what to do, and then sends the commands to the muscles to be carried out. Except in very special circumstances, once the commands reach the motor cortex of the brain - or, as I prefer to call it, the Out Chute - the action to be carried out cannot be changed. You can send a second counteractive command very soon after, but the initial, action itself cannot be changed. Therefore, if we are ever going to have an effect on changing our actions, the change must take place in our manner of processing commands.

But what about the parts of our nervous system which provide input? What role does the Input portion of our model play in the processing of commands?

When we think of the mechanisms of input in our nervous system, we most often think of the five senses: sight, taste, sound, smell, and touch. All of these senses deal predominantly with information which is external to us. They provide a means of understanding something about the world in which we find ourselves.

The last of these senses - touch - has a second role as well. The mechanisms by which we are able to sense a great deal of information about those things with which we come into contact is very similar to the mechanisms which we use to come into contact with ourselves. This process of self-sensing is called proprioception.

There are many different kinds of proprioception.[1] Through proprioception, we are able to sense hot and cold within us. We are able to distinguish between light and heavy touch. We are able to feel pain. We are able to sense pressure at joints. We are able to detect the amount of contraction or stretching in our muscles.

The proprioceptive sense which seems to be of the most interest to students of Alexander is the kinesthetic sense. For the most part, the usage of this term has become so generalized and misapplied that it is in danger of becoming a meaningless term.

Strictly speaking, kinesthesia is a part of what is called the position sense.[2] The position sense is made up of two parts: static position recognition and kinesthesia.

The static position recognition sense is that sense which registers the part to part relationships of bones to one another at the joints. Mungo Douglas talks about the importance of this function of muscles, this relationing of parts to parts at joints. In his paper "Re-orientation of the View Point upon the Study of Anatomy," Dr. Douglas tells us that "the function of muscle is twofold: to perform movements of parts about joints and [to] maintain relations of parts to parts."[3] The static position recognition sense is the feeling sense which informs us about these relationships.

---

1. Just as there are many kinds of exteroception, or sensing of our external environment. One of my favorites is called stereoognosis. This is the sense which allows us to identify an object which we hold in our hands by the sense of feeling its shape. In this regard, someone who holds an object in his hand and who can correctly identify it, but who refuses to believe his identification until he can actually see the object, is said to be a stereoagnostic.

2. Guyton, Arthur C., *Textbook of Medical Physiology*, 6th edition, W. B. Saunders Company, Philadelphia, London, and Toronto, p. 607

3. Jones, Frank Pierce, *Body Awareness in Action*, Schocken Books, New York, p. 60

Kinesthesia, on the other hand, merely informs us about the rate at which any given movement is performed.

The easiest way to identify and understand this static position recognition sense is to take one of your hands and hold it back behind your head so that none of your fingers are touching one another nor anything else. Then make a concerted effort to wiggle your fingers in such a way that you might confuse yourself about where your fingers are in relation to one another. Then, after a little while, stop.

If you will continue to hold your fingers "still," after a few moments you should begin to develop a kind of "picture" of how your fingers are arranged with respect to one another. For most people, in a very short time, it is almost as though they can "see" their fingers.

This ability to sense the relationships of the joints of your fingers without looking at them is technically called the static position recognition sense (although most refer to it as kinesthesia). The reason why these senses have such a strong visual component is that they share common neural pathways with the vision pathways in our brain.

After my students have done this little exercise, I then challenge them to do the same sort of thing in trying to "sense" where their heads are in relation to their bodies. In this experiment, wiggling and shaking of your head is optional. But, even without shaking your head, everyone to some degree should be able to "see" the relationship of his or her head and neck in just the same sort of way as you were able to "see" your fingers. When one is first starting, this image is not usually so clear as the image of your fingers, but it can be developed with time and practice.

This particular way of sensing the relationship of one's head to one's body is the only reasonable way to sense this relationship. It is also the only genuine foundation for learning to perceive someone else's condition through the placement of your hands on them.

The capacity to sense oneself in this way is a very valuable tool for the student and a necessary one for the teacher.

There are a number of other facts about the feeling senses which make up the input portion of our nervous system model, which will have great importance in assigning a value and a role to the use of these feeling senses in guiding our movements.

First of all, sensory organs, like muscles and other nerves, have a threshold for becoming active. In other words, a certain amount of stimulus is required before the sensory organ will fire.

It's a little like tickling someone who doesn't want to admit that he is ticklish. As you start tickling your victim, he may be able to hold still. If you keep it up, eventually he won't be able to control himself any longer and may start laughing or squirming or both.

In a similar way, there is a build-up of stimulation at one (and often more) of the sensory receptor organs until the threshold amount is reached. The sensory organ then sends off a message back to the brain that it is being tickled or stretched or compressed or made hot or hurt or whatever the particular job of reporting might be for that particular sensor. If this threshold limit is not reached, the sensor remains "silent" and no information is sent to the brain.

The second thing to remember about the feeling sense is that there is constantly a tremendous amount of information going into the processing part of the central nervous system all of the time.

Depopoulos and Ibernagl claim in their *Color Atlas of Physiology* that the number of bits of information which reaches the thalamus, a kind of central switch board to the higher centers of the brain, is about one billion bits each second, every second. The thalamus, in turn, passes along for recognition less than a hundred of these bits each second and herein lies some of the basis of the kind of misapprehension which Alexander called faulty sensory appreciation.

Often in this work, people get the impression that their teachers are saying that their feelings are unreliable.

If we take feelings to be the input part of the system, unless there is something organically wrong with the system, then our feelings are always reliable because our feelings, in this sense, are just the raw data going into the brain for processing. In the absence of disease or damage to the sensory mechanism, there can be no unreliability of the feeling sense.

It is what we make of this raw data - how we sort out which hundred pieces of information we will pay attention to each second, and how we choose which nine hundred, ninety-nine million, nine hundred, ninety-nine thousand, nine hundred bits to throw away - which will determine, in large part, the interpretation we will put upon our experience of our feeling senses.[1]

The first rule that is observed in "deciding" which bits of information to keep and which to ignore is based on survival. We register the most basic information on the priority of need.

If we have hurt ourselves, the information passes through the system quickly on the fastest nerves to make us aware of a problem to which we may need to respond. Similarly, as we swim along underwater, the relative need for another breath created by the oxygen debt of our activity is increasingly apparent.

So, the first rule of attention can be summarized as: any information which relates directly to the survival and well-being of our mechanism immediately has a higher priority than any other information.

This constitutes a kind of first rule about passing information on.

The first rule for excluding information is that any pattern of information which is constant and unchanging is more likely to be ignored.

---

1 There is no question that our appreciation of our feeling sense can become more and more reliable with increasing Alexander work and understanding of ourselves. To suggest, or even to imply, however, that this increase in feeling sense accuracy is due to some change in the input apparatus, that the feeling sense mechanism undergoes some kind of

In the first place, the amount of information sent to the brain is greatest at the moment of change - the point at which the threshold of sensor distortion is reached - and begins to reduce thereafter. Also, when dealing with the perception of movement, studies show that the understanding of movement is created by the successive firing of different receptors whose firing thresholds correspond to different joint positions through the movement. Lastly, as your system becomes accustomed to the stimuli provided by a particular condition, the persistence of the stimuli creates a context in which the relative importance of the stimuli diminishes. Therefore, one is more likely to register change than stasis.

In a similar way, to the degree we are able to direct our attention, we are able to shape the information we perceive.

Our concepts create certain kinds of filters which also seem to be in operation in determining which bits of information are saved and which are discarded. In other words, to some degree, we eliminate some information on the basis of disinterest or conflict, and pass along other information which conforms to our beliefs.

Anyone who has ever taken or taught an Alexander class in which students' impressions are solicited has probably seen this kind of denial at work. The most striking of this kind of experience has happened to me twice in my teaching career. On both occasions I have been working with someone on the activity of standing up from a chair. On both occasions, each student has argued with me vigorously about whether or not, after having left the chair, he was standing.

During the first incident, I was working with a student in my customary manner. All was going well until I asked him to stand. Throughout the entire movement from seated to standing, major transformations took place throughout his entire body. Once he had reached an easy and upright condition on his feet, he was hardly recognizable as the same person.

While I'm sure he got a tremendous surprise during this experience, I got an even bigger one when I asked him what he noticed about himself as he was standing there. The student assured me that he was not standing at all. When I casually remarked that he looked like he was standing to me, he told me that he didn't care what it looked like, he wasn't stand-

---

system "rewiring" which pops into and out of existence as an individual passes back and forth between accurate and inaccurate reportage of experiences is absurd.

Yet, this is precisely the position that is taken by anyone who claims that the feeling sense itself is unreliable and needs to be fixed.

The information being brought to the brain from our input mechanism, the feeling sense, is always accurate and reliable. It is the way in which we process this information which has become unreliable and which requires our attention.

There is no need to give proper kinesthetic experiences to any student because students already have them.

If we claim to be giving the kinesthetic experience associated with the correct way to move, then we have fallen into the trap of teaching the "right" way to perform an activity and we are guilty of a very sophisticated, but genuine, form of end-gaining.

Our attention in lessons should be directed instead to the training of students' minds to process protocols properly. If we do this, the increase in the reliability of their interpretation of their feeling sense will be unavoidable.

ing. When I asked him directly if he was standing, he told me, "Of course not. I can't stand like this!"

I realized, of course, that his feeling sense data was so different having moved in this new way that he couldn't match what he was experiencing with what he expected to feel in carrying out the movement of standing. What surprised me was that no amount of questioning or coaxing on my part could elicit any response from him except a firm and definite denial that he was standing. When I asked him what he was doing if he was not seated or standing, he said, "I don't know, but I'm not standing."

Once I became convinced that the student was not joking, I allowed the argument to go on to see how long he would insist he was not standing.

When I asked him about what he felt as he moved, he could talk about the feeling sense associated with some, but not all, of the events which took place as he came up out of the chair. When I asked him if he was still seated, he told me he was not. When I asked him if he had to look up at me to see my face when he was seated, he said, "Yes." When I asked him if he was looking up to see my face now, he replied, "No, I'm looking down at you." When I asked him if he was standing, he said, "No, I am not!"

I even invited the other members of the class to confirm or deny my contention that the student was standing. Not only did he not believe his classmates when they told him he was standing, but he argued with them as well, turning bright red from the exertion. After twenty minutes, it became clear to me that the argument was not going to stop of its own accord, so I asked the student to do what he needed to do to stand.

He promptly sat down and stood up again, this time more in accordance with his habitual manner of standing. I then asked him if he was standing and he said that he was. On questioning, however, he could not tell me what he had done to change from his previously unidentified condition to standing, nor could he be convinced that he had been standing before.

On the second occasion that this kind of experience occurred, I allowed the arguing to go on only long enough for the rest of the class to be satisfied that their classmate was convinced that he wasn't standing in spite of his present position. I allowed the argument to continue until it was clear to everyone that his carrying on about not standing was a demonstration of great internal distress and not a practical joke.

I asked him if he remembered the story I had told about the previous incident and he did. When I asked him if he thought that story was in any way relevant, he replied, "I don't know. I just know that I am not standing. I can't stand like this!" When I asked him to do what he would need to do to stand, rather than sitting down again and popping up, he merely collapsed into a much more familiar condition of slumping, breathed a sigh of relief and announced, "Now! Now I am standing!"

In both cases, both students had to have received, from their feeling sense, information about performing the act of standing. They must have had pressure on their feet. They must have felt the absence of pressure on their bottoms and backs of their legs as they lifted up off of the chairs.

They must have felt the multiple changes in joint degree, angulation, and rate of change consistent with the motion which they performed. But, because this act (and the feelings generated by the act) was so different from their usual way of standing, these sensations were edited out to some degree, and those sensations which got through were subjected to the most intense form of denial.

The distress and conflict which each student felt was genuine. The only difference for them and what most people experience in a lesson was one of degree. Still, the capacity for separating out unwanted bits of information and for denying inconsistent information remained powerful and real. In fact, recently I was joking in class with the second student about that particular experience to make a point. We all joked and laughed and enjoyed the relevance of the story to the question we were discussing, but, as I started to continue on with the next part of the lecture, the student said softly, "But I wasn't standing."

Part of what lies at the heart of this denial is the reliance we make upon our feelings to act as a kind of anchor for our impressions about ourselves. We use our interpretations of our feeling sense to judge our condition, to evaluate our performance of activities, and to act as a model for projected future performances. In fact, much of the teaching which is done in the performing arts and in athletics is based on developing the ability to reproduce a "feeling" in order to reproduce a sound, a movement, or a stroke.

This process of organizing responses to match a "feeling" as a means of directive guidance is the one which Alexander believed to be in place in himself and, upon early observation, which he believed to be nearly universal. He also, at one point, believed his reliance upon untrustworthy feelings for guidance was the source of his difficulties and the stumbling block which prevented him from being able to change the use of himself in activities. He, like many others, sought to retrain this manner of guidance to make it reliable once more. But, unlike many others, in the end, he rejected the guidance of even a trustworthy feeling sense because of its impracticality and irrelevance.[1]

In the first place, in order for reliance upon feeling to have value as a form of guidance, two things must be true: first, "feelings" must be free from imperfection and they must be unchanging in value and second, the feelings must come before the movements which create them.

As we have seen above, the probability of those bits of information which get through to our planning centers being free from the imperfection of editing is very low. We usually have too much investment in what we think is right to pay attention without censorship. Even if we had complete integrity with regard to what we perceived, the sheer volume of

---

1. For a more complete discussion, see Volume I of The Alexander Commentaries.

information would require massive amounts of exclusion which would tend, at least statistically, to minimize our chances of perfect assimilation of feeling sense fact. Even if we could somehow organize ourselves and act on the basis of the entire Input mechanism alone, perhaps we could, in the absence of disease or injury, meet the first half of the first requirement. But we could never-never-never-never-never-never-ever meet the second half because feelings are not absolute!

In order for feelings to be absolute, there would have to be some absolute zero point[1] of feeling with regard to every posture and motion. One does not have to investigate very long to find that such a concept is preposterous.

You can line up a dozen adults and ask them to stand straight and tall and you are liable to see a dozen different solutions to the problem You can ask a dozen dancers to plie and you will see a dozen ways to bend the ankles, hips, and knees. If you were to ask these same dancers for a more complex movement or a combination of movements, the variations would be greater.

In each of us, these elusive "zero points" are constantly changing through the influence of many different factors from outside and from within. Rather than having any innate and absolute value structure with regard to posture, movement and the feelings which movements engender, we are all subject to the constant reappraisal and redefinition of a relative, though shockingly conservative, value structure with regard to the interpretation of feelings.

Often when teaching a beginning class, at least one of the students will have the movement behavior of pulling his head and body very far backward and down, creating a very compressed posture with the appearance of "falling" to the rear as he walks. When one works with such students and begins to prevent this excessive backward movement, they will then begin to walk around with a lessened backward slump. Inevitably, when questioned about what they are feeling, they will reply that the teacher has tipped them overly forward. Many will claim that they are falling for-

---

1. When I use the term "zero point," I mean that posture or positioning of the body parts which satisfies the conditions determined by the individual for the performance of a given activity.

If we were to ask a person to sit in a chair, he would perform a certain movement behavior which would satisfy the "feeling coordinates" established for sitting in a chair. In effect, he would then be at the "zero point" for that activity.

If we were then to ask him to sit up straight in the chair, he would compare his present movement behavior to the "feeling coordinates" he had established for the movement behavior of sitting up straight in a chair.

If his zero point for sitting up straight in a chair matched the zero point for sitting in a chair, he would probably reply to our request that he already was sitting up straight in the chair.

If the "feeling coordinates" for the two activities did not match, he would then have to move away from the zero point for sitting in a chair until he had achieved a movement behavior which conformed with the zero point for sitting up straight in a chair.

It is important to see that while a zero point has a fixed value for a given activity, this value is actually relative. In other words, your zero points are determined by your interpretations of, and the values derived from, your prior experiences, which, in turn, are colored by your belief systems. As such, all of these values and interpretations may change with further changes in experience or concept.

ward, and, occasionally, the sensation of "falling forward" will be so pronounced that they will refuse to walk.

What has happened in these cases is that these people have come to place their zero values upon the sensations generated by the movements which create the appearance of falling backwards. When they move in this falling backward way, the feeling sense impressions which they receive tell them that they are standing up in a normal, natural way. When they move in such a way that their bodies are less backward, rather than experiencing themselves as moving away from their distorted postures and more towards a condition of less distortion, they experience themselves as moving too far forward of the "normal, natural way" of standing.

Because their feeling sense appreciation has become comfortable with their distorted zero point postures, and because they are now moving away from a "normal, natural way" of walking, they experience themselves as falling forward in spite of their continued, and still pronounced, backward leans.

While these people are claiming to be "falling forward" while walking, it will be clear to any outside observer that they are continuing movement patterns which still have the appearance of falling backwards, only to a lesser degree.

If the interpretation of our feeling sense was based on any absolute scale, the combination of still moving as though one were "falling backwards" and feeling like one was "falling forwards" would not be possible. Such a conclusion could only be reached if our feeling sense interpretation was relative and based on our impressions of past experiences and the conclusions which those impressions caused us to reach.

Based on the experience of teaching thousands of students, I can say without a doubt that this kind of relative value scale has proven universal and without counter-example. All of our values with regard to feeling sense interpretation are subject to this kind of distortion.

Because our sensory appreciations are relative and dependent upon impressions from past performances, they would make a poor choice as an objective source of guidance. Still, many people choose to try and retrain their feeling sense interpretation as a guide.

They do this because they believe that their dissatisfaction in themselves and their manner of performance is due to a loss of reliability, and not to the nature of the procedures performed. These people believe that if they could only acquire accurate sensory impressions, then they could continue with their present form of guidance and direction. "Surely," they reason, "fixing the value and reliability of the data and its interpretation would be an easier and more cost effective process for change than dismantling the whole operation."

There is no question that this way of making a change would be easier. The only problem with it is it can't work.

It can't work because it is not possible for our feeling sense interpretations to serve as a source of guidance. It can't be done.

It can't be done because that is not the way in which we are made.

Perhaps the easiest way to understand why it is impossible to use our sensory appreciation as a direct means of directive guidance is to take a look at the nature of feelings with respect to the time line.

One of the great difficulties in creating a model is that you must make choices which clearly alter the nature of what you are observing.

One of the clear characteristics about the way in which we respond to stimuli and carry out behavior is that it is continuous. With regard to the process of making any given movement, however, there seem to be four different kinds of activity involved.[1]

First, there is the movement itself. Second, there is the feeling associated with the movement Third, there is the process of planning the movement And, lastly, there is the "thinking" which is involved in projecting the commands created by the planning for the purpose of directing the movement In other words, by "thinking," I mean the actual process by which we are able to project the messages from the brain to the mechanisms involved. Because of the continuous nature of these interactions, these four aspects of the performance of a given movement can be thought of as appearing on the same circle in this fashion:

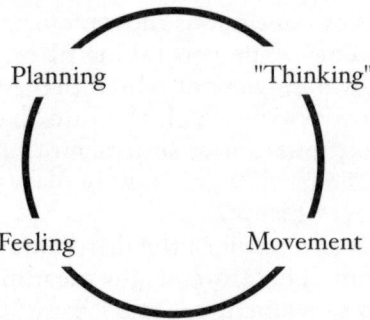

Planning   "Thinking"

Feeling   Movement

When I speak of creating a time line, I mean the placement of these four aspects of a movement into a straight line by which the causal relationships of each of the aspects is kept intact with regard to the performance of a specific, single activity. The time line is what would happen if one were to cut this continuous circle and stretch it out into a single line of events. In fact, one of my favorite classroom tasks is to ask my students where they would divide this circle.

The usual guesses divide the circle either between three o'clock or six o'clock.

---

1 In the discussion that follows, by "feeling" or "feelings," I will usually mean the feeling sense interpretation of the raw data sent through the input mechanism. This usage of the term "feelings" should convey both the data and the impressions derived from the data. I will try to use the term "feeling sense" when referring to the data alone.

In a similar way, the use of the term movement in this discussion is intended to refer to volitional movement, movements which we plan in response to stimuli. The issue of the role of reflexive actions and their relevance to conscious guidance and control is beyond the scope of this book.

Those choosing three o'clock do so because they say that with respect to a movement, the movement itself is the most important starting point. The ones who choose six say that, because they habitually guide themselves by feelings, any movement would begin with the feelings with which they guide themselves.

Both of these answers are good and clearly reflect a given point of view and, in fact, I agree with the reasoning of one of them, but I come to a very different answer in the end.

When considering a movement and when trying to find a way to interrupt this on-going cycle of stimulus and response meaningfully, I believe that it is important to start with the movement itself. Then, one has to look at the temporal relationships involved.

When we were looking at what caused feeling sense input, we saw that movement caused different sensory receptors to fire at different times. Without the movement, these receptors would not be activated. In this way, it can be seen that the predominant experience which reaches us with regard to any movement is the sense of change created by the successive firings of different sensory receptors. Because these firings were caused by the movement, the "feeling" of a given movement is engendered by the movement itself and hence, can happen only after the movement has taken place.

Even in those cases of continuous movement, when the experience is of "feeling the movement" while it is taking place, the movement which one is feeling is actually a movement which preceded the present movement. It is only the speed with which the information is transmitted in the presence of the continuation of similar motion that creates the illusion of feeling a movement while it is taking place.

Feelings, therefore, are history.

They take place only as a result of the distortions of the sensory organs caused by the movement. Therefore, in any meaningful time line, feelings with regard to a given movement can only happen after the movement.

But, if feelings can only follow and be created by movement, then what creates movement?

As we have seen, muscular contraction creates movement.

But what creates the muscular contraction?

The messages projected from the brain to the mechanism involved create the muscular contractions. These messages are initiated by the process I call "thinking", the initial projection of the commands which, in turn, become messages projected from the brain to the mechanism involved.

The creation of the commands of "thinking" is the function of planning. In planning, we formulate strategies as a response to the stimulus which presently has our attention. In turn, we translate these strategies into the commands of "thinking" and these projected commands are turned into our specific movement response.

When seen in this way, it is clear that the planning which creates the commands precedes the "thinking" or projection of those commands. It is the process of projecting those commands, the process of "thinking", which directly precedes the messages from the brain to the mechanism involved. The movement is determined by these messages. Once these messages reach the Out Chute, the motor cortex of the brain, they cannot be changed thereafter. The movement, in turn, distorts the sense organs, causing them to fire which creates the feeling of the movement. The feeling of movement can only come after the movement in time.

As a result of this reasoning, I cut the circle listed above at nine o'clock which yields the following formula for a time line with respect to any given movement:

$$P \Longrightarrow \text{"t"} \Longrightarrow M \Longrightarrow F$$

where P (planning) is the creation of the protocol to be followed in the performance of a given activity, "t" ("thinking") is the projection of the protocol, M (movement) is the realization of the protocol, and F (feeling) is the product of the movement.

When one understands the relationship of feelings to the time line, one immediately understands the bankruptcy of using feelings, trustworthy or otherwise, as the source of directive guidance.

Feelings can only happen after the movement.

You can't use something which hasn't happened to create itself.

And yet, in class, we seem to try to use this strategy all the time.

A student who is having a lesson while beginning to walk will often remain standing still long after the teacher has given the suggestion to move. On questioning, the student will often reveal that he was trying to "feel" that smooth sense of gliding which he had had in a previous lesson. He is convinced that that particular feeling is what he wants and he will wait until it happens before he begins to move. Consequently, he will stand rooted to that spot forever (or at least until the teacher devises a way to move him or gives up on trying to find such a way).

Even though standing still has no chance to create the feeling he desires, a student will persist in this behavior, convinced that he is trying every conceivable way to get that feeling back. The one thing the student won't do in this situation to get back the feeling of walking that he liked is to begin walking, the only procedure that has a chance to produce the effect he desires.

A student caught in this dilemma has misunderstood the time line and the causal relationships between movements and feelings.

And, even if he does move, his movement is unlikely to reproduce the "feeling" he desires because his interpretations of his feelings are not absolute. They change with time, concept, and changes of motion.

As the performance of a given activity changes, the feeling sense associated with the performance of that activity changes. In addition, the interpretation of the generated feeling sense changes.

About the only feeling I have ever had in this work which has seemed consistent, is that sense of emptiness, of ease, which accompanies a more efficiently performed movement. And yet, many times I have had a clear sense of stiffness or artificiality or being pumped up like a cast-iron pot-bellied stove or being twisted into grotesque deformities or being in acute pain during a lesson, only to turn and see that Marjorie is pleased with my progress.

The interpretations of feelings, even properly administered feelings, change through time, experience, understanding, and changes in concept and movement. Therefore our "feelings" are not absolute.

If you divide the time line circle at six o'clock and begin your time line with feelings, you are left with only two choices.

If you believe that feelings can lead directly to movements, if you take the statement that your movements are guided by your feelings literally, then you will try to proceed through the time line circle counter-clock-wise.

Creating a time line in this manner would yield the formula:

$$F \implies M \implies \text{"}t\text{"} \implies P$$

While I must admit that I have quite often seen students remember a feeling they would like to have and start moving a long, long, long, long, long, long, long time before they begin to do a process of constructive "thinking," it seems patently absurd that projecting thoughts could lead to planning, and even more absurd that planning, in turn, could lead to the kinds of feelings which are generated by movements.

It is not possible.

This is precisely why the student standing around, waiting for the feeling of walking more easily to happen before he moves, is being so silly.

Feelings are the product of movements. Feelings can only be history. They cannot be the direct source of guidance.

You can't use something which hasn't happened yet to create itself.

The other choice left to someone who is beginning his time line with feelings is to proceed in a more logical clockwise fashion:

$$F \implies P \implies \text{"}t\text{"} \implies M$$

In this scheme, it can be argued that feelings are being used as the raw data to create the planning which then proceeds in a normal fashion to the movement.

While there can be no doubt that the feedback created by feelings contributes to the process of planning, placing the emphasis on feelings as the starting point is filled with problems.

First of all, a feeling is the product of a movement. No matter how trustworthy it may be, by putting one's attention onto a feeling in order to plan a protocol in order to project appropriate commands in order to realize the appropriate movement to produce the appropriate feeling means that one's attention is focused on the product one wishes to achieve. The last time I looked, putting one's attention on, and working towards, the product one wished to achieve was called end-gaining.

In fact, any process designed to retrain feelings to achieve politically-correct postural responses, reflex and otherwise, in order that these responses may be repeated at will is nothing more than an increasingly sophisticated form of end-gaining.

Secondly, if one begins with feeling as a starting point, there is no chance of improvement because the specific feelings which are generated by a specific motion cannot change. Just as the movement which occurs is determined by the projected messages which create it, the feeling sense input is determined by the movement which occurs.

You cannot change the movement once the motor commands reach the motor cortex. You cannot change the input data once the movement has occurred. The only way in which change could occur in this scenario would be to change the interpretation of the data which comes in.

Willfully changing the interpretation of data to fit one's needs and concepts makes experience irrelevant. For all of its shortcomings, there is something reasonable and nice about using the sense data generated by an experience to evaluate the experience.

Most people, though, find it more comforting to change their interpretation of events to fit their needs and concepts. As a result, rather than being based on what happened, their interpretation of an experience is independent of the actual experience itself. The need for the preservation of their prejudices and filters which allow them to operate constantly in the "right" is so great that the entire operation of the universe bends and twists itself to conform to their beliefs. Or so it seems to them.

You know these people.

These are the people who never let reality get in the way of their opinions.

The problem with willfully changing your interpretation of the feeling sense data is that you obliterate the causal relationship between movements and the feeling sense data they generate which decreases the accuracy and value of your interpretation of the data.

The feeling sense data produced by a movement always has a direct correspondence to the movement performed. It is this direct correspondence which makes interpretation valuable.

If you are going to change the interpretation of your feeling sense to fit your needs and concepts, you don't need this work or any other work to make those changes. You can make those changes on your own because you are intentionally divorcing your actions from your experience of your actions.

Most importantly in this regard, beginning your time line with feelings is problematic because feelings are not in charge of creating the protocols of response. Your planning is. Even if your proposed movement were to have a one-to-one correspondence with the feeling you wish to generate, the execution of that movement must still pass through the planning and "thinking" stage before it can be performed.

Feelings do not produce movements: movements produce feelings.

While there can be a volitional movement which is not preceded by a feeling sense impression, as in the case of doing some action for the first time, there cannot be a volitional movement which is not preceded by a thought.

There is no such thing as an Immaculate Contraction.

When planning leads to "thinking" and "thinking" leads to movement, the movement creates the changes which create the feeling sense of movement. These impressions go into the brain via the input system for processing. There, these impressions may form part of the basis for planning a response, but so do many other things.

Past experiences, education, training, inspirational readings, the amount of space you have available, your present level of conditioning, rules of etiquette - all of these things will help determine whether or not you will knock the creep, who just hit you, on his ass.

In effect, your feelings become part of a much larger data base from which you will make your plan of response. While your feeling sense and your interpretation of your feeling sense may contribute to the protocol's formation, your capacity to plan comes from a much larger pool of resources.

In my opinion, the starting point of any response is the planning process which is performed to create the protocol for carrying out that response. As such, I place planning at the beginning of my time line. This is the point of initiation and the point which I believe has the most importance.

If you think you are starting with your feelings or even being guided by them, you are only fooling yourself.

When Alexander admitted that he had not thought out how he had directed himself, he decided that he had relied on his feelings to guide himself. He had no proof of this. It was just his supposition.

He then set out on what seemed to him to be a reasonable course of action to make this means of guidance trustworthy again. He found, to his surprise, that this process of guidance didn't work.

As we follow his narrative through "Evolution of a Technique," we see that he abandons efforts to make his feelings a trustworthy source of guidance. He abandoned these efforts because his feelings did not prove to be the actual source of his directive guidance when he passed through the critical moment and went into activity.

Feelings are, without a doubt, an important tool to use to judge the quality of a past performance, and this is a task for which they are well suited. A past performance is a thing of history just as feelings are history themselves.

When Alexander sought to find a way to change his responses in the on-going future, he found that feelings, as creatures of the past, contained neither predictive value nor future imperatives. He found that his responses were organized in a way which was not solely dependent upon feelings but was governed by other principles instead. After learning these principles and how they worked, he devised techniques for retraining his thinking so that his responses could be raised to a constructive, conscious level of planning and execution.

It is these techniques of retraining a person's thinking which create the value which we seek in Alexander's work today. These are the tools which he created and employed to fashion the person of achievement and control which he became and which we choose to emulate.

Once, after he had possessed these "secrets" of knowledge and discipline, Alexander was faced with an inquiry from someone still bound to the fruitless task of making his feelings more reliable in order to improve his manner of self-guidance. You can almost hear Alexander smile when you read his reply to this student: "When the time comes that you can trust your feeling, you won't want to use it."[1]

From this it is clear that Alexander thought that the processes of directive guidance that we would use to retrain our sensory appreciation would be superior and preferable to our former manner of directive guidance.

If we are ever to complete our task successfully, if we are ever to do what Alexander did, then we must find out about those processes which Alexander thought we would prefer to use. We must come to understand what they are, their importance, how they came about, how they operate, and how we can use them for our own benefit.

Having learned the nature and role of feelings with regard to the process of directive guidance, we must put aside our fascination with the past and look ahead to how we can shape our futures. We must recognize the effort to retrain our feelings as a source of reliable guidance for the false trail that it is, and learn to accept that there are processes for changing our manner of directive guidance which will make the accurate retraining of our feelings unavoidable. We must continue to seek these processes which will retrain our manner of thinking and which will provide a basis for constructive change in our lives.

In order to do this, we must first come to understand the true nature of the transactions involved in the problem which Alexander solved, the problem which troubles us still.

1. Maisel, Edward, ed., *The Resurrection of the Body*, Shambala Publications, Boston & London, 1986, p.11

CHAPTER 10

OUR HABITUAL PATTERNS OF DIRECTIVE GUIDANCE

When Alexander began looking at what he used to direct his own use, he first believed that he relied upon his feelings for his source of direction. He wrote, "I had never thought of how I directed the use of myself, but that I used myself habitually in the way that felt natural to me. In other words, I, like everyone else, depended upon 'feeling' for the direction of my use."[1] When he tried to retrain this process of direction, he gradually came to see that the actual source of guidance within him was something else entirely. Consequently, what he had to learn in order to make changes in the use of himself in activity changed as well.

Rather than merely recalibrating the existing mechanism which he believed to be the source of his guidance, he had to discover the actual nature of how he sent himself into activity. He came to see that his habitual patterns of responses to stimuli were not entities in themselves but the direct results of commands which he was constantly giving to himself. These commands, based on his values and beliefs, became the practically irresistible basis for all of his responses.

In a similar way, we, too, have set convictions about who we are and how we work.

We have turned these convictions into commands which we project as we enter into movement. It is not so much that we have a way of responding to stimuli which is fixed and habitual, but that we have made decisions which are fixed and set about how we should respond to stimuli. The commands associated with those decisions are the ones which we habitually invoke. Once called upon, once these habitual commands reach the Out Chute of the motor cortex in our brains, the movement behavior associated with those commands cannot be stopped

To the outside observer, our public behavior appears to be habits of movement, but, from our understanding of the relationship between movement and thought, it is clear that these movement behavior patterns are actually the products of certain "habits" of thought.

There are certain thoughts which precede and accompany every movement.

These thoughts can occur on many levels. They range from the simple conviction we may have about what is required to initiate any movement to the most intricate of gestural protocols such as weaving or surgery.

---

1. Alexander, F. M_ The Use of the Self, Centerline Press, Long Beach, Ca., pp. 20-21

These thoughts, these practical expressions of our beliefs and values, become the commands which generate the realization of our beliefs.

If we are going to move, there has to be both planning and thinking which precede the movement.

When we perform acts which are common and familiar, we call upon the storehouse of information we have developed with regard to movement. We call forth protocols which we have used before.

Rather than going through the hassle of "re-inventing the wheel" each time we move, we tend to generalize circumstances as much as possible in order to label the task in some familiar way. This allows us to re-issue the commands of previous protocols with only a superficial sense of their appropriateness in a given situation.

These commands of previous protocols are like the initial programming in computer software. Certain set values and conditions are built into the starting point of each piece of software. This is called the default setting. If you turn the computer on without making any changes in the programming, the printer will print out the default material just as it appears in the software.

If you begin an activity or a movement without making any changes in the commands which have been issued previously and which remain in place, your responses will be the same responses as before because every movement performed has a one-to-one correspondence to the commands which create it.

These commands of previous protocols are present in every activity. They determine the nature and quality of our movements. They are the stuff with which we forge our characters and shape our lives. They are always in place. They are always active. It is only with the greatest of disciplined efforts that we can learn to escape their domination.

We can think of these commands of previous protocols, from which we draw the design of our common responses, as our habitual patterns of directive guidance.

For the Most part, the development of these habitual patterns of directive guidance, occurs without notice. The major reason for this is that many of these decisions and the commands which they engender occur at a very early age.

I remember sitting in the Dallas airport a few years ago, waiting for my flight, and watching an infant who was lying on his back in an infant carrier.

As I watched, I was fascinated by the movement of his legs.

His left leg was curled around in that circular progression of joints so typical of young babies as he played with his foot with both hands. What made his behavior so fascinating was that, at the same time, his right leg was being held out to the side, in a straight line, at a 45 degree angle up and out from his hip. He was repeatedly snapping his lower leg in a near-perfect point, like a ballet dancer, alternating from a straight leg to a fully flexed knee.

Here was this young boy with one leg in a near-perfect, motionless but continuous circle and the other leg in a near-perfect, but constantly changing and repeating, series of angles and lines.

I watched him for a while to see how long this would continue.

As with any infant, there would be times that his attention would be caught up in the noises around him, but, for the most part, he performed this activity for over fifteen minutes before curiosity led me to interview his mother. I'll never forget what she said, nor how she said it.

"Moving like that seems to be his favorite thing to do. He'll just sit and do it for hours. I don't know why he does it. It just seems like one day he decided that that was what he wanted to do, and he's done it ever since.

"We've tried to get him to stop. We've even tried to get him to change legs, but he's made up his mind that this is the way to do it and so, do it he does."

I don't have any better idea why he does this behavior than his mother did, but I believe that somehow, somewhere, he got excited about moving his legs in this way and sent out the commands required to do it.

And he continued to send them out.

This behavior and the feelings they generated had now come to play a central part in his world. They will probably play a central role in his world for a long time to come.

I would love to be able to watch this child periodically over the next twenty to thirty years to be able to watch what progression of behavior, if any, occurs as a result of this favorite way of moving. I would love to see what becomes of this behavior. I would love to see whether it remains overt or whether it becomes modified to something more acceptable or whether it serves as his identifying choreographic style as a world famous dancer or whether it just gets dropped altogether.

I don't know why he decided to behave this way, but I am sure that he decided to do it. I am also sure that this movement behavior will remain enforced until he decides to change it, if he can.

All movement behavior comes from the commands which represent the realization of the strategies required to make the ideas generated during the planning stage happen.

Once used, these movement behaviors have a strong tendency to be repeated. The sources of these ideas, however, are not always as mysterious as with our little Texan.

The most commonly cited source of movement ideas for young people is imitation of the movement patterns of others. For the many reasons involved, a person may adopt any of a number of movement characteristics from any of a number of people.

I know that in my own case, years ago I saw a picture of Bob Cousy[1] standing with a basketball resting on his hip. To balance this action, his hip was slung out to the side and his body appeared to be dropped down into his other hip. Anyone who knows this picture and who has seen me standing casually (with or without a basketball) will readily see that this picture, along with a dash of hero worship, provided the basis for my stance.

And the source of our imitation does not have to be famous people or unusual actions.

One day I was walking in Lincoln, Nebraska, with my best friend.

As we were walking north on Thirteenth Street, we saw coming towards us a boy and his parents. They were walking three abreast with the young boy in the middle, holding his parents' hands.

The mother, standing to the boy's right, walked with a characteristic swinging of her stiffened right leg in a wide arc. The father, on the boy's left, walked with a very strong collapse into his left leg and hip. The boy, walking between them and keeping in perfect step with each parent, had a pronounced swing of his right leg and a marked collapse on his left.

Both my friend and I were convinced that the other had arranged this piece of street theatre as a kind of practical joke. We couldn't believe that any kind of behavior which was that clear and obvious a demonstration of the principles of imitation could be true. I have since seen at least four other similar familial trios, but never one so striking as that first time.

And not all of a young child's decisions are based on simple imitation.

Most of the unusual behaviors that I see in my classes and my clinic come from the strategies devised to respond to some perception of a problem in the real world. Sometimes these strategies are in response to mistaken perceptions, as we will point out again later, but, quite often, they represent solutions to problems, solutions which can be seen as nothing less than brilliant.

A couple of years ago, some of my colleagues brought their very young daughter to see me in my clinic to consult with me about an abnormality which had appeared in her walking gait.

It seemed that with each step of her left leg there was an added motion of her upper leg outward which was not present when she moved her right leg. I no longer remember what made me think of it, but I suddenly remembered where I had seen her use this motion before. To test my theory, I took the little girl out to a nearby set of stairs and asked her to climb up them.

When I let her go up on the left side of the stairs, she went up them easily. She would lift her left thigh up, place her left knee on the next tread, and push herself up to the next level.

When I forced her to move to the right side of the stairway, she hesitated.

When I forced her to begin her climb with her right leg, she was unable to figure out a way to go up the stairs.

---

1. Bob Cousy was a guard who played basketball for Holy Cross and the Boston Celtics. Cousy is credited with elevating the importance of dribbling and passing skills in professional basketball, and was the first superstar of the Celtic dynasty.

For her, the process of going upstairs was something which was performed by getting as far to the left as possible and by getting your left knee over the tread and wedging yourself up with your knee. On the face of it, this seems like fairly bizarre behavior, but, with a little more information, it can be seen for the clever solution that it was.

This little girl and her parents live in a beautiful home which has a stairway near the front door. The most striking aspect of this stairway is that it is a spiral stairway which turns to the left as you face it from below. Because of the space in which it is built, the top of the step nearest to the axis of the stairway is a considerably shorter distance to cover for a little person than the much larger right side of the stairway. For this reason, the left side of the stairway is the most efficient pathway for a little person to go up. Therefore, the strategy which makes the most sense on this little girl's "significant" stairway is for her to go up the stairs on the left side.

This strategy for placing herself to the left on her significant staircase had become generalized in her mind as part of the necessary protocol for climbing all stairways. By forcing her away from her customary side of climbing, even on a non-spiral staircase, I created a conflict between her task of climbing these stairs and the protocol requirements she believed were necessary for climbing any stairs.

More importantly, I wouldn't let her perform the act of climbing stairs by lifting her left leg.

From the very first time she began climbing stairs, placing her left knee on top of the step and pushing down on the knee to lever the rest of her up to the top of the step was the only way to do it. This way of climbing was how she had learned to go up stairs. There was a time when she was unable to get her knee up that high, but, one day she could, and from that day onward, the act of climbing stairs started with the command, "Put your left knee up on top of the step, etc."

By the time her parents brought her in for consultation, she was tall enough to easily bring her knee over the top of the step. Instead of bringing her leg up just enough to clear the tread, she still brought her leg up to the angulation which she originally needed to cover the distance. This caused a gap of many inches between her knee and the top of the step before she put her knee down on the step. In spite of the fact that this caused extra work and movement, she could not be talked into raising her leg a little less when she began climbing the stairs. For her, bringing her knee up to begin climbing stairs was a distance which was measured in personal joint angulation, not inches of stairway.

The problem in her walking gait was caused by the generalization of this stair climbing strategy to the use of her legs in walking.

The movement which seemed odd and out of place as she walked was actually a very small firing of the outside muscles of her left hip as she began to move her left leg in walking. This movement was, of course, the very first part of the movement required to put her knee up on the step.

It is as though she made the decision that if moving her left leg outward to go up stairs was so successful, maybe she should include that outward movement every time she moved her left leg. As she got tall enough to walk up stairs, and she developed a different strategy for performing this important, liberating task, the older strategy of climbing up the stairs on hands and knees became less important and was relegated to a position of relative abandonment.

The strategies and movements related to the new activity of walking up and down the stairs have come to be more dominant. The decisions and commands which were associated with her former stair climbing behavior have become overridden with new commands and decisions.

I would be willing to bet, however, that if we were to ask this little girl to climb stairs on her hands and knees, today or in the future, she would probably go to the left side of the stairs and raise her left knee upward to begin. I would bet she would begin this way even though she would probably not be able to tell us why she did it.

In addition, I would bet that whenever she enters a time of increased conflict or stress, that small excess movement of her left leg outward as she begins a step will reappear and increase in her walking. She, like everyone else, would find herself caught up in the reason for repeating these familiar movements based on previously issued commands: she has used the commands before, she has had some success with them, and she is still alive.[1]

If there are thoughts or strategies that have worked for you in the past, or have seemed to work for you in the past, you will tend to use them again and again.

The most common example of this is that of the baseball player who adjusted his cap, stepped up to the plate, tapped the plate once, took two short practice swings, and then got a hit. You can be certain that the next time he comes up to the plate, he will adjust his cap, tap the plate once, and take two short practice swings. If he gets another hit, he will be following this procedure for a very, very long time.

---

1. It might be of some interest to readers that this little girl's mother and I recently put this wager to the test and asked the little girl if she would walk up some stairs for us on her hands and knees.

When she climbed the stairs on this day, she did not go to the left.

Prior to the test, however, she had been modelling her behaviour after some other older youngsters palying on these same steps. All of the older youngsters had used the middle of the steps in their playing. When she climbed the steps for us she also used the middle of the steps.

When I said I would take this bet I did not intend to imply that the little girl would be necessarily locked into a left-sided ascent. There are plenty of other factors and decisions (such as imitating the older children she had most recently been playing with) which could dominate this early behavior. My willingness to wager reflects only the belief that her past performance and decisions would weight the probability of choices in favor of a left-sided approach. In spite of the last experiment, if someone would give me the right odds and circumstances, I would still be inclined to take the bet.

On the other hand, the excessive movement of her left hip muscles outward does appear to continue to be increased during times of increased stress.

And, even if he doesn't get a hit the next time, he is liable to go hitless for thirty attempts or more before he changes this ritual.

About the only way to change this ritual would be if he forgets how to do it during his current batting slump or if he doesn't do it one time and gets another hit anyway.

But, this really doesn't present a counter-example to my argument.

Rather than becoming free of the first ritual, he is almost certain to adopt the "new" ritual which he performed before he got this latest hit.

Consequently, a real or imagined success which is assigned to a protocol for real or imagined reasons is a strong factor in the retention of a protocol.

It is not the most important factor, however.

If the thoughts and strategies which you have used in the past worked AND you are still breathing, you will use them again because they have acquired what I call Survival Value.

There is somewhere within us the knowledge that, if we do something wrong, we could die.

The first thing we check after almost any event is whether or not we are still alive.[1] If we are still alive, then the actions which we carried out during the event are seen as promoting survival. It is this aspect of protocols acquiring Survival Value which makes change so difficult.

Why would one forsake behaviors which have worked in the past and which have demonstrated survival capacity for any new and untried behavior? We come to the conclusion that those ways of being and doing things which we have used in the past have proven to be of value. The greatest proof we have is that we are still alive. Consequently, any change from our past procedures threatens our sense of what we believe we have done in the past to remain alive.

In class and in the office, I constantly kid my clients about why the process of change is taking longer than they would like it to. I say to them, "Why are you so discouraged about how long this is taking? All we're trying to do is change everything about you."

One of the most important things which we are trying to change is this conviction that there is a causal, immediate, and non-trivial relationship between the way in which we have always done things and the fact that we are still alive.

During a skiing lesson this winter, my instructor was making exactly this point.

He told me that what makes skiing so hard to learn is that everything you need to do to ski well and safely is the opposite of the way that it seems it should be.[2]

---

1. As experience and security become more commonplace these little processes of life verification become so "automatic" that they are rarely acknowledged, but they still occur. For most of us, it requires some special event to make us respond in this way overtly.

2. Anyone who does not downhill ski and who is still unconvinced about the close relationship of learning new and different activities to a sense of survival is encouraged to

On your first day of skiing, there you are poised at the top of the terrifyingly steep bunny hill.

You are about to tilt forward in a death-defying act. As you start your horrifying descent, your immediate reaction is to lean back on your skis, lean back towards the upper part of the hill, and to turn your body away from the direction in which you are falling down the slope.

The person you are with, who is trying to teach you how to ski, then insists that you should bring your weight forward, place it over the downhill ski, and keep your upper body turned facing downhill.

This places you in a conflict worse than the little girl's when I wouldn't let her use her left leg first to climb stairs. At least she was standing still when her ideas wouldn't work.

There you are, hurtling down some mountain, and everything you have ever learned or believed is telling you that what is being asked of you can't be done. The decisions, strategies, and commands which have served you well before and which have always kept you alive in the past now threaten to send you over some cliff or, at least, into some snow bank.

My instructor then told me about the most amazing skiing lesson he had ever taught.

A man who appeared to be in his late thirties came in for his first lesson on his first day of skiing. Because the man valued instruction, he had set up a two-hour lesson.

The instructor very carefully explained what his student should do to ski and explained that his instructions would all seem wrong but that they needed to be done anyway.

As the two of them started skiing, the new student did everything the instructor asked of him almost as soon as he asked for it and without variation. Consequently, the new student began to progress dramatically.

As the student progressed, the instructor took his beginner on increasingly difficult terrain, first to see if he could handle it, and then to see just how far he could go. Even though the lesson took slightly more than the scheduled two hours, by the end of his first lesson, the "beginner" was expertly skiing the most difficult terrain available.

The somewhat astonished instructor then told his student what he had accomplished and asked him if he knew of any reason why he had done so well and learned so quickly. The student laughed and explained.

The reason why this student had time to be skiing was because he had recently retired from the air force where he had been a test pilot for fighter planes for over twenty years. As such, of course, his coordination and conditioning were very high.

More importantly, though, the ex-pilot credited his training.

At very high speeds, certain maneuvers which he performed in his jet plane produced tremendous amounts of pressure and disorientation. In fact, some maneuvers create such pressure that it is almost a certainty that

the start skiing. Anyone who learned to downhill ski as an adult, or at least as someone old enough to have acquired the wisdom of fear before starting, is encouraged to remember their early experiences.

pilot will "black-out" while performing them. When this happens the disorientation can be almost complete. It is very common upon regaining consciousness for the pilot not to know where the ground is, or, worse, have a very strong conviction about where the ground is which is wrong.

When this happens, the pilot has to learn to put aside his conviction about the ground's location and go through a particular protocol for reading his instruments. Then, he must ignore his belief about his orientation and make the maneuvers appropriate to what his instruments say even when they are different from his "feelings."

The former pilot said flying his plane according to the panel and against what he believed is the scariest thing he had ever learned to do, but it saved his life many, many times. So, when the ski instructor asked him to ignore his convictions and "throw his body down the hill," he relied on his training and his confidence in the instructor and simply did as he was told.

Because he did what he was told, and because he received good instruction, and because he had a high degree of fitness and coordination, he became an expert skier on his very first day.

In a way, though, there is no difference between our new skier, our little girl, and what they both did.

Both had developed behavior response patterns which had served them well. Both had employed these response patterns and were still breathing. Both would be likely, when faced with new activities or experiences, to rely upon these response patterns and the patterns of thoughts and commands which engendered these patterns because they wanted to continue to survive.

The only difference between them was the sophistication of their different strategies and the realities of the dangers which they faced.

The little girl's strategy was appropriately childish, based on a child's perception and formulation of the problem. The pilot's procedures were based on a process of reasoning nearly as sophisticated as the planes which he flew.

Still, both people at the critical moment of going from planning through "thinking" and, hence, into activity, reverted back to the commands and procedures which they had used before, and which, after using, had kept them alive.

So, the first value we place upon any given response pattern is its Survival Value.

To us, a good response pattern is any pattern which we use, and afterwards we are still alive.

The second major determining factor in the persistence of a given response pattern is what I call Virtue Points.

Any strategy which has Survival Value and which either becomes associated with a positive result and/or praise from a "significant other" earns Virtue Points. The greater the positive outcome and/or the greater the praise, the greater the number of Virtue Points a given strategy will receive. The greater the number of Virtue Points which accrue to any given strategy which has Survival Value, the more difficult it is to deny or move away from that strategy. [1]

One day in class, I was talking about the fun I was having teaching myself to shoot baskets more efficiently. The class decided that what they wanted to do next was to have a lesson learning to shoot a basketball. We all went out to the court and worked on the process of learning a new skill.

Most of the class members, by following instructions, began having a certain degree of success which surprised and delighted them.

One person, however, continued to miss every shot.

Finally, when I tossed him the ball and began saying out loud the commands he should be thinking to increase the probability of his success as I had done before with him and everyone else, he very clearly ignored what I was saying, looked down at the ground next to his right foot, and threw the ball towards the basket

The absolute worst of all possible consequences occurred.

The ball went in the basket!

From that point on, there was nothing that I could say or do which would stop him from looking at the ground near his right foot just before he released his shot. He had come to associate successful shooting of a basketball with moving his eyes and head away from the basket just before he let go of the ball.

The fact that he never made another shot when he did this did not dissuade him from the practice.

A discussion of what was involved in the process of shooting and the strategies most likely to enhance the probability of making a shot provided complete and total theoretical agreement about what was required. It did not, however, prevent him from looking away as he shot

The student had confused the coincidence of making a basket while looking away from the basket with the belief that there was a causal relationship between the two events. There was now within him a conviction that to make a basket required looking away just before you released the ball.

When he had first shot the ball at the basket and looked at the basket, he had no success at all even though he had followed the instructions as best he could. The one time he looked away out of desperation and frustration before he shot the ball was the only time the ball went in.

The ball went in. He was still alive. His classmates cheered.

---

1. We can see that in all of our previous examples both Survival Value and Virtue Points were involved.

The little girl achieved the ability to move between levels of her house without being carried. In addition, she received the praise of her parents for being such a big girl. The batter went on a hitting streak "because' of his ritual and perhaps, as a result, was able to date the groupie of his choice. The test pilot lived long enough to learn to ski in a day.

It is important to see that Survival Value and Virtue Points are difficult to separate. In most cases, it is the Virtue Points which will determine the staying power of a given strategy, but it must never be forgotten that the depth of these decisions to persist in a strategy is as strong as survival itself.

That settled it!

He became convinced that this procedure of looking down and to the right of his feet, away from the basket, was the way shooting baskets had to be done.

The fact that he never made another basket was not enough reason for him to change the way he looked away every time he shot the ball. The fact that the ball's going into the basket that one time had everything to do with the distance, direction, and pathway in which he threw the ball and had nothing to do with looking away was not enough reason for him to change his "proven" procedure. The fact that there is nearly universal agreement among the experts that the best way to enhance the probability of putting the ball in the basket is by looking at the basket in order to solve the equation each time for determining the proper distance, direction and pathway of flight in which to throw the ball - even this was not enough reason for him to change.

The fact remained that he had looked away. He had shot the ball. The ball went into the basket. He was alive. His classmates had cheered.

Don't confuse him with the facts!

His mind is made up!

Looking away from the basket and down and to the right as you get ready to shoot is how shooting baskets is best done!

Now, every time the stimulus for shooting a basket comes to his mind, he calls forth from his storehouse of directive guidance commands the commands which were present the one time he enjoyed success. These commands include the commands associated with creating the downward and rightward look in the sequence of events which precede shooting the ball. Unless he makes a very determined effort to change these commands, to escape the tyranny of their dominance, they will always remain in place and in charge.

As a result, until he disciplines himself to make the changes required, he will always look away before he shoots.[1]

Armed with these concepts of Survival Value and Virtue Points, it might be advantageous to look again at the behaviors of some people we saw earlier.

Do you remember our marching cadet?

This was the fellow who walked in such a bizarre way because he was trying to avoid stepping on the heels of the cadet marching in front of him, thirty years after the cadet in front of him had left.

While he was in military school, he had had a number of problems. One of these problems was this problem of hitting the heels of the guy marching in front of him during close order drill. He told me that not only did the guys who were getting their heels clipped give him a hard time, but he was constantly being harassed by the instructors and commandant

---

1. By the way, I recently asked this same student in a class to pantomime shooting a basketball, and every time I asked him to do it, he still looked down and to the right.

I'm sure he was under such pressure to come up with a solution that he never heard the solutions offered to him by his instructors. When he finally came upon this bizarre strategy for walking and he stopped hitting the other cadet's heels, I'll bet he was swimming in Virtue Points (not to mention the "Survival Value" of not getting beaten up any more by his classmates).

In fact, the strength of the Virtue Points was so great that thirty years after he had last marched in close order drill he still walked the same way to avoid the heels of the cadet marching in front of him.

Then there was the little girl who was using the muscular overcontraction of her muscles to "keep the world from falling apart."

There is no doubt that she was under a lot of pressure in her parental home. Her perception of her world was that it was falling apart. On one level, the holding together of the world by proxy, by holding her own joints together, was a brilliant kind of solution.

Within her home, she was in a relatively powerless position. Within her home, there was little she could do to change her parents, their behavior in general, or their behavior towards one another.

She did have some control over her muscles, however.

By intentionally keeping her muscles tied together, she could be exerting her will in the kind of omnipotent way that only children really believe in, forcing the world to conform to her desires.

As long as her parents stayed together, she received Virtue Points for having brought it about. If they had broken up, she would initially have been consoled by having kept them together for so long and then she probably would have redoubled her efforts to keep the "world" from falling apart any further.

Both of these people continued to carry on behavior which was initiated by commands which were created by planning in response to specific problems from very long ago.

From another point of view, however, neither behavior made sense.

If the cadet had been able to follow the directions of his drill instructors, the problem of hitting the other person's heels would not have come up. But, his condition of general coordination was already so bad by the time he went away to school, that the only solution which worked was to exaggerate his movement faults further still.

When I asked him to show me how he walked before he went to military school, he immediately started walking, but in a different pattern of malcoordination, one which featured a throwing forward of his feet.

The point to be taken away from this is two-fold.

First, the commands which were required to create this older way of walking were already in place and ready to be used. These particular commands, which were part of his patterns of directive guidance for his older way of walking, were ready to be used instantaneously.

Second, the commands which created his non-heel-kicking walk were based on altering the older sets of commands to accomplish the immediate goal at hand. Not only were the patterns of directive guidance which he had learned to use in walking still intact and ready to be used, but they remained used in his newer form of walking. The difference in appearance between the two gaits was due to adding in more muscular effort in the second way of walking. This only served to distort further the misshapenness of the preceding walk rather than bringing about a more efficient and effective way of walking.

The little girl's behavior of clamping down on her muscles to keep the world from falling apart makes even less sense.

But, from the very first day she tried it, the world didn't fall apart.

Every time there was a family crisis, she increased her efforts to meet the needs of the crisis and the world didn't fall apart again. Even on those occasions when events didn't turn out in the way that she wanted, she experienced relief and satisfaction in the knowledge that her efforts had prevented them from being worse.

This strategy for survival had progressed to the point that, by the time she came into my office for treatment, her sense of "zero muscular effort" for movement involved such a powerful and continuous pulling of her muscles against herself that she was creating an overuse syndrome degeneration[1] in herself while living a relatively sedentary life.

There is no more probable causal relationship between her holding her own muscles tightly and her life crises working out satisfactorily than there is with our friend looking away before he shoots baskets. Yet, neither has a greater conviction than the other about the necessity for carrying out their incidental behaviors as a means of achieving their ends.

This is the trap that became the problem that Alexander solved.

Like all of these people, all of us are trapped in the dominance of the procedures which we have used before.[2]

We have performed certain acts and enjoyed certain successes and drawn certain conclusions about the causal interrelationships of the way we do things to the success we enjoy.

As long as we remain alive, we will always have the sense that the way we have performed our activities promotes survival. This, in itself, is enough incentive to continue with our activities as we have always done them.

In addition to this incentive, we have Virtue Points heaped upon us as we grow up.

The acceptance of these Virtue Points creates an even closer connection between how we do things and receiving what we want. Even in those cases in which there is no actual, causal relationship between the

---

1. An overuse syndrome degeneration is the name given to the degeneration of the quality of the tissues, particularly bone and cartilage, of the joints involved in the overuse syndrome. The deterioration is caused by small but constant amounts of distressful pressure on the joints caused by muscular overcontraction. This diagnosis seems to be the new and chic way to talk about mild injuries and distortions in joint tissues due to "wear and tear."

2. A much more thorough discussion of these last points can be found in Volume I of The Alexander Commentaries in the section on the Three Universal Delusions.

little "rituals" we perform and the success that we enjoy, we have come to believe that there is.

Similarly, we delude ourselves about being in control of these relationships and ourselves.

We believe that the outcome of the events which have occurred was based on our intention, rather than the actions caused by carrying out our habitual patterns of thought and analysis. In my parental home we acknowledged this "truth" by saying, "If it happened that way, it was because we planned it that way."

Our problem is that through the course of growing up, we have adopted certain strategies and behaviors which we keep in place and carry out as best we can fit them to our perceived needs at any given time. These strategies and behaviors have come about often in a haphazard way without regard for planning or efficiency. In those cases where this kind of training has proven sufficient for us to become the kind of people we want to be, to achieve the goals we have set for our lives, and to acquire all of our desires, there is no need for any other form of organizing our thoughts. This kind of haphazard, happy outcome, however, is usually the exception and not the rule.

The problem is that, all too often, we, like the basketball player, mistake the fact of a success for the "fact" that our success was based on what we believed we had done. We have the belief that the success of our ventures is always due to the planning and execution of our response design as we conceived it.

As long as things are going well, this mistaken evaluation remains harmless.

It is when things do not go well that problems occur.

If we believe that what we do is the genuine cause of our success when it is not the genuine cause, we create a problem for ourselves when faced with failure. In such cases, we often believe that our only course of action is to increase the amount of effort used to do the things we did before to create future success. This is what the little girl did by tightening her muscles even more.

Even when we are given appropriate "corrections," as our marching cadet was, the probability for genuine success and change remains slight because the corrections will be carried out with the faulty habitual commands already in place. We will continue to work on the corrections with our faulty habitual commands until our experience satisfies the distorted zero points of our distorted conceptions of movement and self, or until we believe the person correcting us is satisfied.

There is no question that our cadet was satisfied and pleased by his final movement solutions for the problem of walking. He was even proud. So proud in fact, that he continued this brand of walking as a kind of kinetic badge of courage long after the need for the solution had graduated and disappeared.

And what if the individual has been given appropriate corrections? What if the individual has decided that he will stay with the "thinking" required to bring about the commands required to bring about the appropriate and changed behavior which he desires? What if he has decided not to be concerned about whether or not this new behavior feels right, and is only concerned that he is carrying out his new commands for movement?

He will find that his "mind" is not the superior directive agent. He will find that his reliance upon his past patterns of directive guidance is practically irresistible. He will find that these patterns of directive guidance dominate all of his activities and the manner in which they are performed. He will find that the jumbled genesis of these concepts of guidance was formed without much regard for cause and effect, but rather had to do with survival and praise. He will find that he is unable to change because, rather than having trained his mind to guide his actions, the commands associated with his prior actions have come to "train" his mind. He will find that he has come to believe that his mind is still in charge when, in fact, it is the habitual pattern inmates who are running the directive guidance asylum.

He will find that his problem is that he is unable to change his response to stimuli because the commands associated with his previous responses are not the servant to his intentions and desires, but have become the masters of his response.

If we are ever to change successfully, we must learn to train our minds to subjugate our previous protocols of directive guidance. We must train our minds to operate on principles of directive guidance which are conscious, flexible, and themselves subject to evaluation and change. We must train our minds to the point that we can continuously overcome the dominance of these habitual patterns of directive guidance and escape their habitual tyranny.

This is precisely what Alexander did and what he encourages us to do.

For those of us who are satisfied with the results which we have achieved through the continuous employment of our habitual patterns of directive guidance, there is no need to go through the training required to reorganize one's thoughts in a more constructive way.

But, for those of us who believe that we can become a little bit better, happier, and more fulfilled, for those of us who want more and who are willing to pay the cost of becoming more, these instinctive, subconscious, and unreasoned patterns of directive guidance which are responsible for initiating our usual responses are not good enough.

We must learn to find a way to bring these patterns of guidance up to a level of consciousness and understanding where we can hope to make a change, and free ourselves of the dominance of these old habitual patterns of thought.

The only way we will ever effectively change the manner of our response to stimuli is to discover a way to challenge the dominance of these habitual patterns of directive guidance.

We must re-evaluate all of our pet strategies and ways of doing things, no matter how much Survival Value or how many Virtue Points they may have accrued. We must learn to overcome our universal delusions. We must put aside our reliance upon correction as a restorative procedure, and learn to trust in something other than our feelings as a guide for our movement behavior. We must learn to identify and overcome our incorrect conceptions and fixed ideas, and substitute for them an understanding of the ways in which we are made and the ways in which we work. We must carry out the same procedures that Alexander did when he was faced with this new information.

We must find a way to probate man's supreme inheritance, the power of his conscious mind to acquire complete control of his potentialities, or we will be forever left in the muddle that Alexander described.

PRINCIPLES WHICH PROVIDE A SOLUTION

CHAPTER 11

THE THREE PART PROCESS FOR PROTOCOL DESIGN

In the first chapter of *The Use of the Self* Alexander describes the experiences and decisions he went through in gaining his ability to change the use of himself in activity.

I believe that this chapter is the most important document in all of the literature which pertains to the Alexander Technique.

It is in this chapter that Alexander provides a blueprint for change. Here, an answer can be found in black and white to all of the questions about what Alexander did to improve himself. This chapter sets out clearly and in sequence all of the stages that Alexander went through in his own development.

For many years now I have watched myself, my fellow classmates, and my students as they learn this work and I have seen this same sequence of events repeated again and again. This has led me to postulate that everyone learns this work in the same stages and in the same sequence.

Having reached this hypothesis, I have then based a part of my analysis of a student's condition upon matching his interests, actions, and understanding with the sequence of events in this chapter. By comparing the kinds of issues each student has and talks about with the appropriate point in Alexander's own development, I then design my lessons to help the student reach the next point of development in Alexander's story. By doing this, I have enjoyed a very satisfactory degree of success and efficiency in teaching.

Although I have found many students who could "read ahead" and give Alexander Answers with regard to points of understanding beyond their own experience, I have never observed any student who has owned any of these ideas out of sequence. [1,2]

---

1 The term Alexander Answers comes from a workshop that Marjorie Barstow taught in Boston in 1975. To find out what kind of a background the students had in the work, she began the workshop by asking a series of questions about Alexander and his procedures. Whether the people in the workshop didn't know the answers or whether they were just nervous about speaking out in front of strangers, no one said anything. After a while, Marjorie turned to Ed Maisel who was in attendance and asked him, "Well, Ed. How would you answer these questions?" To which he replied, "Oh, no. Don't ask me. I already know all of the Alexander Answers."

2 In the Basic Principles class, the concept of "Owning an Idea" is reserved for that knowledge over which one has so much understanding and command that one's ability to

Another aspect of this chapter which is important to keep in mind while reading is an aspect of style which I call narrative integrity.

Alexander writes this chapter as though it is in a kind of past present tense. Although he is writing about events which had occurred in the past, he writes about each stage of understanding with the command of knowledge appropriate to that stage. Perhaps it is his sensitivity as an actor which leads him to show us what happened as it happened rather than tell us about it after it had happened.

He does this by making each point of understanding as real and as limited as once it was.

Like the actor who "knows" it is only Polonius and not his uncle behind the arras, and who yet thrusts his fatal blow with the present time conviction that he is avenging the death of his character's father, Alexander shares each discovery, each belief, as it occurred to him and as he believed it to be true at that time.

This authenticity to the truth of each moment and step, even when it did not speak well of him, is what I mean when I say that in this chapter Alexander displays an incredible and illuminating style of narrative integrity.

While the use of this conceit creates a teaching document of unsurpassed power, it has also served as a source of confusion to those students who did not understand the author's style or intent.

Most books of this nature are written in a straightforward essay style. With an essay, it is common practice to extract bits and pieces of the authors argument, and to represent these pieces as some significant portion of the argument as a whole. In fact, Alexander tells us that we can't avoid being drawn to those particular bits and pieces which conform to our preconceived values and ideas.[1]

Because of our preference for passages which confirm our present prejudices, any kind of dogmatic use of aphorisms is usually a risky proposition. It is much more risky in this particular chapter because the author is not writing with the omniscience of the essayist, but with the peculiar momentary blindness of an individual presently caught up in a given set of events.

To understand what Alexander is trying to say in this chapter, one must not only understand each part of the story, but must understand how the parts relate and how subsequent events either confirm or deny impressions and conclusions which had been previously reached.

---

convey the information is independent of circumstances. If you own an idea, there is nothing anyone can say or do which will confuse you about it. An owned idea is one which has a practical basis and one in which you have complete understanding and confidence. It is more than the ability to recite words at will. It is the certainty about your experience of the ideas involved which allows you to articulate the concept in your own way in any situation. Because of its basis in practical reality, an owned idea is the antithesis of an Alexander Answer.

1 The pertinent section in the literature is the beginning of the chapter from *Constructive Conscious Control of the Individual* entitled, "Incorrect Conception," perhaps the second most important document in the literature, particularly pp. 126-128 in the 1985 Centerline Press edition.

When reading Alexander's narrative, I believe that it is important to apply this same overview process, this peculiar skill of the actor, to see the immediate section of the text as it relates to other sections and the whole piece simultaneously. This is important because I believe that Alexander's background as an actor led him to write with the assumption that the reader would employ this manner of study in his reading. To this end, I advise my students to beware the temptation to pick off some small piece of Alexander's writing and to brandish it as an answer of any kind.

This warning is nowhere as important as it is in this chapter.

The need for this kind of comprehensive approach to the study of Alexander's writings and the need for developing the tools necessary to accomplish this type of study provided the fuel for the creation of both my Basic Principles course and the writing of The Alexander Commentaries. The first volume of this series is devoted to this first chapter in Alexander's third book. It provides an investigation of Alexander's description of his experiences in much greater detail than is appropriate here.

In this section, we will look at the four parts of the procedural puzzle which comprise the cornerstones of the foundation of Alexander's technique for change. While the discussion will necessarily be more brief than it deserves, I believe the reader will come into possession of all the tools required to overcome the problems caused by his own habitual patterns of directive guidance and to achieve a satisfactory source of direction for the use of himself in activity.

In the first half of "The Evolution of a Technique," Alexander concerns himself with what we might call the more physical aspects of his use. He discovers his harmful tendencies in speech. He associates these tendencies with the shortening of his stature. He learns the importance of moving his head not just forward, but forward and up. He discovers the close connection between use and functioning. He finds out that the misuse of his vocal mechanism is associated with a misuse of his other parts in the actions attendant to the process of speaking. Finally, it gradually dawns upon him that these individual wrong uses actually constitute a habitual wrong use of his mechanism as a whole.

Further, he recognizes that the strength of this harmful manner of response was not only due to the fact that it was habitual, but that he had cultivated it as well.

The influence of this cultivated habitual use, therefore, acted as an almost irresistible stimulus to me to use myself in the wrong way I was accustomed to; this stimulus to general wrong use was far stronger than the stimulus of my desire to employ the new use of my head and neck, and I now saw that it was this influence which led me, as soon as I stood up to recite, to put my head in the opposite direction to that which I desired.[1]

All of Alexander's discoveries to this point were important and helpful. The succeeding discoveries could not have occurred without them. But, at this point, when Alexander discovered the practically irresistible influence of these cultivated habits upon the manner of his response to stimuli, he reached the most important turning point in his investigation.

It was at this point that his investigation turned from the discovery of the appropriate correction for a faulty mechanical event to the investigation of the means by which all mechanical events are directed. He turned from looking at how the different parts of our mechanism interacted (a subject which he knew well) to the search for the source of guidance for all events. It was at this point that Alexander wrote what I take to be the most important sentence in all of his work.

For, it is at this point, the point at which Alexander understood the importance and power of his cultivated habits - after he had understood the mechanical imperatives involved in the interaction of his body parts in movement, after he had understood the importance of forward and up, lengthening the stature and so forth, after he had already enjoyed a gratifying degree of success in overcoming his original problem - it is after all of this that he writes, "I now had proof of one thing at least, that all of my efforts up till now to improve the use of myself in reciting had been misdirected."[2,3]

Alexander now understood that his efforts had been misdirected because the key to improving the use of one's self in activity has to do with understanding and learning to operate the means of directive guidance which creates responses in the individual.

All of Alexander's previous efforts gave him the tools and skills with which to proceed, but it was this investigation of the means of controlling the patterns of directive guidance, not just controlling his physical responses, which he recognized as being of the utmost importance.

It was the process of raising this source of control from the instinctive on to the conscious plane which now formed the central focus of Alexander's story and work.

1. Most of the quotes in this section will be from "Evolution of a Technique" from *The Use of the Self*. Consequently, I will merely identify the page numbers rather than use a more standard footnote format. Also, I will list both the 1986 Maisel and 1985 Centerline Press pages in that order. I regret I do not have a Gollancz edition as well, but I believe everyone will be able to follow along quite easily with this system. pp. 148-149 (p. 19)

2. p. 149 (p. 19)

3. I always feel it is important at this point in my classes to go over the difference between "misdirected" and "wasted." Alexander does not suggest that all of his effort and insight and training prior to this time was wasted. In fact, he makes it very clear that he benefitted greatly from all of those experiences. There is no question that he (or any other student) would benefit from the kinds of constructive changes in postural and movement behavior which Alexander describes before this point in the chapter. These kinds of beneficial changes happen daily and may very well satisfy the student in search of relief or improved performance. If, however, the goal of the student or the teacher is to improve the use of the individual in activities as a general discipline and principle, then efforts focused on the more physical aspects of the training will be efforts, like Alexander's, which will have been misdirected.

As we talked about before, Alexander's first efforts dealt with "feeling" as a source of direction.

When he looked around for the source of his direction in activity, being guided by feeling seemed to provide the only answer which he could initially find. As he looked further, he found that there was a discrepancy between what he thought he was doing and what he actually did. As he watched others, he found this same sort of discrepancy. The only difference he could find between himself and other people was one of degree.

In fact, he discovered that our "instinctive control and direction of use had become so unsatisfactory, and the associated feeling so untrustworthy as a guide, that it could lead us to do the very opposite of what we wished or thought we were doing." [1]

It was at this point that he started his search for a means to restore trustworthiness of feeling as a guide.

In this search, three points in particular impressed him. Firstly, by observing that he did not move his head as he intended, he had proof that his actions were being misdirected and that the misdirection was associated with his untrustworthy feelings. Second, this misdirection was in place and functioning seemingly on its own and, together with the untrustworthy feelings associated with it, made up his habitual use of himself. Third this instinctive misdirection which was associated with the wrong use of his head and neck and which led to the wrong habitual use of himself was initiated by the decision to use his voice. In other words, this misdirection was his instinctive reaction to the stimulus to use his voice.

When he thought about that last point, he decided that if the misdirection came as a reaction to the decision to use his voice, and if he could find a way to stop this physical reaction which started with the wrong habitual use of his head and neck, he would be stopping his whole unsatisfactory reaction at its source.

Once his initial, harmful reaction was stopped, he could then look for a direction of himself which would guarantee an improved use of his head and neck. He believed that the manner of guiding himself in activity associated with a new and improved use of his head and neck would provide a satisfactory use of himself in reaction to the stimulus to speak.

As with all of Alexander's decisions, conclusions, and discoveries, these ideas led to a period of practical investigation. As Frank Jones points out, there is no "mere theorizing" in Alexander's work. All of Alexander's theories "were derived from his own experience in establishing a degree of conscious control over his own stereotyped behavior." [2]

Every conclusion which Alexander reached and espoused was the result of empirical investigation.

---

1. p. 151 (p. 23)
2. Jones, Frank Pierce, Body Awareness in Action, Schocken Press, New York, 1976, p. 28

The experiments which Alexander performed in response to his new reasoning led to two major conclusions: the first dealt with the appropriateness of feeling as a guide and the second set out a plan for creating appropriate responses to stimuli.

"In the work that followed I came to see that to get a direction of my use which would ensure [a] satisfactory reaction, I must cease to rely upon the feeling associated with my instinctive direction..."[1]

After reading this passage, there can be no question about the percentage of guidance associated with previous feelings which Alexander believes should be used in planning a response to stimuli.

The percentage to be used is zero.

"I must cease to rely upon the feeling associated with my instinctive direction." If Alexander had still been interested in the process of making feelings more trustworthy again for the purpose of directive guidance, we would expect this sentence to be finished in this manner: "I must cease to rely upon the feeling associated with my instinctive direction and in its place employ the feeling associated with my newly retrained and trustworthy sense of direction."

But, this isn't the case at all.

What Alexander says is "that to get a direction of my use which would ensure [a] satisfactory reaction, I must cease to rely upon the feeling associated with my instinctive direction, and in its place employ my reasoning processes."[2]

This is the first time that Alexander suggests the replacement of the means of direction associated with impressions supplied by the feeling sense with a new direction which relies on the reasoning processes.

In this sentence, he outlines a particular three part process for designing protocols of response to stimuli. It is this switch from the use of his previous instinctive process of guidance to a means of guidance which is not associated with feeling at an which provides the first cornerstone of the foundation for the process of change we all seek in his work.

"In short," Alexander wrote, "I concluded that if I were ever able to react satisfactorily to the stimulus to use my voice, I must replace my old, instinctive (unreasoned) direction of myself by a new, conscious (reasoned) direction." [3]

He decided he must replace the old manner of directing himself which was associated with feelings of all degrees of trustworthiness; and replace it with a manner of directing himself which was based on his reasoning. Any directive guidance based on his reasoning would necessarily be divorced from his feelings in any direct or causal way.

---

1. pp. 152-153 (p. 25)
2. pp. 152-153 (p. 25)
3. p. 153 (p. 25)

If Alexander was ever to get a direction of his use which would ensure a satisfactory reaction, he must employ his reasoning processes:

1) to analyze the conditions of use present;

2) to select (reason out) the means whereby a more satisfactory use could be brought about;

3) to project consciously the directions required for putting these means into effect.

In my classes, we generalize these three rules and call this the Three Part Process for Protocol Design.[1]

If I am going to perform any activity, I must create a protocol for carrying out that activity One of the sources I can always call upon are the old protocols I have stored within me.

The trouble with this, of course, is by responding with past protocols I am more likely than not going to be distancing myself from where I presently am and what is actually going on now. If I respond with past protocols, at least some part of me will be responding to what went on before, the conditions past rather than the conditions present.

By employing the Three Part Process for Protocol Design, I am placing myself squarely in the present. I am looking at the conditions which are present and not at what the present conditions remind me of.

Because I am looking at the conditions which are present, I can create a response which is tailor-made to the actual situation. I can reason out what procedure or procedures are appropriate to the given situation and then carry out those procedures.

Whenever I think of the freshness of experience implied by this process of analysis and selection, I am always reminded of watching Marjorie Barstow bake bread. I have personally known Marjorie to bake bread hundreds of times, and even a cursory knowledge of her lifestyle would lead one to conclude that this is a procedure which she has carried out thousands of times Still, every time I have watched her, she has followed the same procedure. One of the first things she does is get out her favorite cookbook and read about how to bake bread.

I suspect that the steps the book suggests are relatively similar to the steps suggested the last time she read the book, but she reads it just the same anyway. Then she consults her shelves or her memory to see what flours she has on hand and decides what adjustments she will have to make to the recipe as a result. Then, step by step, consulting the book, she repeats a procedure she has followed hundreds of times.

I suspect that there have been times when, due to lack of time, she has not formally checked the cookbook. And there have been times when she has used a different book to make a new and different kind of bread. But, I have never watched her bake bread when she hasn't followed this procedure.

---

1. The general statement of this process would be 1) analyze the conditions present, 2) select the appropriate means you have reasoned out whereby you can gain your end, and 3) project consciously the directions required for putting these means into effect.

I don't believe that she looks up how to bake bread every time because she is forgetful or doesn't remember. I believe she looks up how to bake bread because she has learned to appreciate the value of the process of applying an appropriate protocol to the baking of bread - an appropriate protocol which is repeatable, consistent, and can account for the conditions present

In class, we often talk about the direct relationship of such appropriate protocols to the probability of success.

In our efforts to succeed, we are so accustomed to keeping our attention on the goal we wish to gain that we lose sight of this important relationship. We misdirect our attention by thinking of the product or goal we wish to achieve rather than the process which we would use to achieve our desired end. By placing our attention on the process of selecting and carrying out appropriate protocols, we enhance the probability of our success because the more appropriate the protocol is to the realization of a given end, the more likely the end will be reached.

In fact, if the end is attainable and the protocol being used is appropriate to the attainment of that end, then, by continuing with the carrying out of the protocol, achieving one's goal is unavoidable.

Conversely, if the process we have chosen to pursue is inappropriate to the attainment of our goal, the probability of our enjoying success approaches zero.

It's not precisely zero because if it is possible to select an inappropriate process, it's also possible that one might make just the right number of mistakes in just the right sequence to enjoy success in spite of one's intentions. As a friend of mine who has caught the flavor of this kind of success of errors is fond of saying, "Even a blind squirrel finds a nut now and then."

Do you remember our friend, the basketball shooter?

There is no way in the world that not looking at the basket before shooting is a successenhancing strategy. Yet, as chance or the capricious gods would have it, the one time he looked away before he shot, everything else went right and the ball went in.

The danger of relying on repetition of the procedures believed to have been used in prior successes, rather than an analysis of the conditions present and their relationship to an appropriate protocol, is that the actual cause of one's success might never be found. If, on the other hand, one is constantly disciplining oneself to carry out the analysis of the conditions present and the evaluation of the appropriateness of the means selected to gain one's end, then one will experience a constantly improving sense of causal relationships and an increasing ability to select appropriate means.

The very last part of this plan is one I like to test my students out on during classroom presentations.

As I write the plan out on the board I say, "The three parts of this Process for Protocol Design are to 1) analyze the conditions present, 2) select an appropriate means whereby the goal can be achieved, and 3) project consciously the directions required for carrying out the_____."

In almost every class, someone will be taken in by the hypnotic recitation of the first part of these rules and fill in the blank with "the ends you wish to achieve" or some such phrase.

The idea of keeping your attention strictly on the end you wish to gain instead of the means by which you can gain it is so strong that, given the chance, we slip back into that kind of thinking in the performance of our given activities as easily as my students do in class recitation.

The whole key to this Three Part Process for Protocol Design, and the first key to the retraining of one's mind in this work, is learning to direct one's attention away from the goal one wishes to achieve in activity as well as the feelings that such attainment provides. This will allow us to focus our attention on the recognition and execution of the steps to be performed to achieve our goals.

If the end you wish to gain is achievable and the process you are employing to achieve that goal is appropriate, then, by continuing with the carrying out of the protocol, achieving your goal will be unavoidable.

CHAPTER 12

WITHOUT ATTEMPTING TO "DO" THEM

By the introduction of the Three Part Process of Protocol Design, Alexander had now created a way to discover an appropriate protocol for every act he would choose to perform. He figured that he had now found the answer to all of his problems. He thought that all he had to do was carry out this process as he performed every act.

He was confident that he "should be guided by [his] reasoning rather than by his feeling when it came to putting this [strategy] into action, and that [his] 'mind' was the superior and more effective directing agent."[1]

When he began to experiment to prove this hypothesis, however, he discovered a remarkable thing. He found that he could think about these new procedures to improve his use of himself in speaking only as long as he didn't try to speak. "At the critical moment when [he] attempted to gain [his] end by means which were contrary to those associated with [his] old habits of use [his] instinctive direction dominated [his] reasoning direction."[2]

When he began to make a response to the stimulus to speak, he found that his old habitual patterns of directive guidance were still in place, still sending out commands to his motor mechanism, and still dominating the relatively weaker influence of his newly reasoned out protocols of response. "This meant that the old instinctive direction which, associated with untrustworthy feeling, had been the controlling factor up to that moment in the building up of [his] wrong habitual use, still controlled the manner of [his] response, with the inevitable result that [his] old wrong habitual use was again brought into play."[3]

Alexander discovered that as soon as he received the stimulus to speak, he tried to 'do' something to speak. As soon as he tried to do something to speak, he invoked the habitual patterns of directive guidance by which he did everything. As soon as these commands went out, he responded by moving in his old habitual manner because the commands which were sent out most strongly were the commands which created his old habitual patterns of movement.

In order to overcome this difficulty, Alexander wrote, "If I was ever to be able to change my habitual use and dominate my instinctive direction, it would be necessary for me to make the experience of receiving the stimulus to speak and of refusing to do anything immediately in response."[4]

---

1. p. 153 (p. 26)
2. p. 154 (p. 26)
3. p. 154 (p. 27)
4.. p. 154 (p. 27)

In other words, his problem began when he received a stimulus to perform an activity. As soon as this happened, he tried to do the activity immediately. As soon as he tried to do the activity immediately, even when his activity was to change his manner of use, he called forth the directive guidance commands which brought about his old movement responses.

If he was ever to succeed in making changes, he had to find a way to stop this chain of events. He had to find a way to "drive a wedge between stimulus and response."[1] As long as he responded immediately to the stimulus, his chosen manner of responding was guaranteed to be directed by his old means of directing himself. If he was ever to succeed in making the changes he desired, he had to find a way to prevent his immediate response to stimuli.

The response which he had to prevent was not really the change in relationship of his head to his body which initiated his wrong habitual use, but the thinking which created this response. In other words, he had to devise a new procedure by which he could train himself to be able to receive a stimulus without making any response so that he could finally free himself from his old manner of misdirection.

He called this new procedure inhibition.[2]

In class, there are three points which I make about inhibition which would be of value for us to pursue at this time.

First of all, inhibition is a mental discipline and not a physical action or movement.

There is a strong tendency in all of us to respond immediately to every stimulus we receive. In fact, one of the prevailing beliefs about thought and movement is that you cannot have a thought without a movement. Whether or not this is clinically true, it is a belief which is put to practical use in sports all of the time.

---

1. Marjory Barlow in a lecture at the 2nd International Congress in Brighton.

2. At one point in time, it was very chic to engage in involved discussions as to the relative appropriateness of the term inhibition.

On the side of using the term, inhibition is the correct physiologic term to describe the prevention of a given response. This is the way the term is used by Sherrington in one of the most quoted (and least understood) passages in the literature that "to refrain from an act is no less an act than to commit one, because inhibition is co-equally with excitation a nervous activity."

The argument against the term had to do with the popularizing of the Freudian concept of inhibition as repression of behavior. Some teachers and critics have expressed concerns at great length and with great passion that there was a danger in encouraging people to learn to "inhibit" because they might confuse Alexander's intent with Freud's bane and do themselves irreparable harm

I hope we have finally outgrown this argument.

The confusion of a single response to a single stimulus with a whole class of behavioral interpretations and responses is the kind of error in perspective which could only be made by someone who is looking for trouble. A simple examination of the differences in the order of magnitude between the two concepts should be enough to eliminate all argument.

As for the danger of confusing a student by creating an unwanted association of a given term with his previous knowledge and understanding, I have never yet encountered a concept in this work which did not confuse a student by creating an unwanted association.

Almost all sporting events have an offensive aspect, in which one tries to score, and a defensive aspect, in which one tries to prevent the opponent from scoring.

When one is first learning a sport or playing against someone who is learning a sport, it is often possible to go directly for one's offensive goal and enjoy great success. The other player often does not have the skill, strength, or experience to defend a direct approach.

As players grow in skill, however, and become more evenly matched, these direct, straightforward strategies become more easily defended. As a result, it often becomes necessary to practice deception in the gaining of an offensive objective.

To do this, the offensive player makes a move or moves designed to make his opponent believe and react to one offensive plan, when, in fact, as soon as the defensive player reacts to the first plan, a different strategy is implemented. This kind of indirect procedure is called a fake or feint and is just as much a part of sports such as fencing, cycling, and chess, as it is a part of team sports like basketball and football.

If we look at the procedures involved, however, we will see that one of the reasons why a "fake" works is this very issue of the immediacy of response to a thought.

What the offensive player wants to create in his opponent is the thought that the offensive player, for example, is going to run to the left. If he can do this, the defender is more likely to react in a way which would defend a run to the left. Often, this simple reaction commits the defensive player for enough time and distance defending the imagined run to the left that he is unable to respond to the actual run to the right quickly enough.

A lot of young players never fully understand that the intent of a "fake" is to create a thought in the defender to which the defender will react. Too often, they simply try to create the reaction. This has the tendency to slow down the offensive player so much that there is not enough time to initiate the second strategy. The best offensive players simply create the idea of the "fake" in the mind of the defender and let the defender take care of the reaction. The only time these players get into trouble is when their reaction times are so fast that they don't allow enough time for the defender to take himself out of the play.

The defender, on the other hand, is taught procedures and protocols which minimize the probability of being deceived.

When trying to make a tackle in American football, for example, a defender is taught to pay no attention to the head, arms, and legs of the runner, but to target himself on the numbers of the offensive player's jersey. Relentlessly, continuously, and under control, the defender should decrease the distance between himself and the offensive player's torso. As one of my coaches used to say, "Don't try to figure out which way his arms and legs are going. Just follow his body. Don't worry about his arms and legs. Tackle his body. Wherever he goes, you can be pretty sure he's going to take his body with him."

Properly focused, the defender does not have room for any other distracting thought to mislead him.

The good defender sees the fakes made by the offensive player but he trains himself not to react to them. He trains himself to react only to the protocol he has reasoned out to be appropriate to his task. As a result, and in spite of the efforts of the offensive player, the wrong thought cannot occur. The immediate reaction to the wrong thought cannot happen. The offensive strategy of a fake will not be effective in such a case.

In a similar way, in the practice of inhibition, one learns to make the experience of receiving a stimulus and then refusing to do anything immediately in response.

Just as the stimulus caused by an offensive "fake" creates an "automatic and appropriate" response in the unwary defender, there is an "automatic and appropriate" response built into every stimulus we receive. If we continue to respond to each stimulus immediately, we will not only be doomed to responding in our habitual way by use of our habitual misdirection, but we will be committed to a manner and type of response which may or may not be appropriate to the actual conditions present.

I find that a great number of my clients and students are constantly "faked out" by life, because they respond immediately to what they believe is happening before they have taken the time to investigate what is really going on.

What they need to learn to do is to apply the mental discipline of inhibition so that they can prevent their immediate commitment to a stereotyped reaction, analyze the conditions present, select an appropriate means whereby they can reach their ends, consciously project the directions required to bring about their means, and thereby respond more appropriately to every stimulus.

As a general practice, I think that we would be wise if we would restrict our use of the technical term "inhibition" to making the experience of receiving a stimulus and of refusing to do anything immediately in response.

Very often you can hear people talk about "practicing inhibition" by deciding to stand up from a chair and then "inhibiting" themselves by staying on the chair. The problem with this claim is that what these people are actually doing by staying on the chair is Preventing the performance of standing up, and, as I understand this work, there is a difference between inhibition and the prevention of a given activity.

Inhibition is a technical term which refers to a mental discipline applied immediately upon the receipt of a stimulus. Inhibition is a process which is applied to each stimulus. Behavior which is more complex than a single stimulus is just too complex a behavior for the application of the technical term "inhibition." [1]

---

1. In the Basic Principles class, the confusion created by the use of one term to mean two different kinds or sizes of events is an example of the problem we call Order of

In the example above, there is much too much time between the decision to stand up and the later decision to stay seated for the term "immediately" to apply. By the time someone has decided to stand up from a chair, done the constructive thinking required, changed his mind, and decided not to get up, it seems to be pretty late in the game to apply the term "immediately" to the person's responses.

The only way that "immediately" would apply, in this instance, is if the individual had really decided to pretend to get out of the chair and remain sitting still instead. If this was the case, however, then the goal of the individual would have been to remain seated in the first place, and there wouldn't have been any 'prevention of activity' at all.

The process of inhibition is something which is intended to occur with respect to each and every stimulus. It is a skill which is immediate and singular. When we start talking about multiple stimuli or chains of events with multiple stimuli, the order of magnitude of our consideration is much larger than inhibition can be. You can practice inhibition on each stimulus individually, but not in groups of two or more. This kind of grouping of stimuli is just too big to apply inhibition appropriately.

The intent of inhibition is to make a constructive dissociation between the reception of a stimulus and any kind of response. Once this dissociation has occurred, there will be enough time to plan and direct a more appropriate response.

If one were to receive a stimulus and respond immediately, the chances of responding in a way other than one's usual manner of response would be vanishingly small. As Alexander points out, an immediate response would not allow for enough time to project the directions for the new use sufficiently to dominate the directions for the old use. Therefore, the process of inhibition needs to happen immediately, as soon as the stimulus to perform an activity comes. In this way, the practice of inhibition is coupled to the reception of a stimulus and is not intended to be applied to larger behavioral units.

Furthermore, the fact that one practices inhibition with regard to the reception of a particular stimulus has no bearing whatsoever on whether or not the activity related to that stimulus will be performed.

If I am practicing inhibition and I decide to stand up from a chair, I will make the experience of receiving the stimulus to get out of the chair

---

Magnitude.

The concept of Order of Magnitude problems comes from the experience of looking through a microscope at a drop of water using magnifying lenses of varying sizes. As each different objective swings into place, the previously viewed animals and objects "disappear" from view and new animals and objects "take their place." The fact is that all of the animals and objects were there all of the time. It's just that the vast differences in size make it seem as though the objects being viewed appear and disappear depending on the level at which one is looking.

In a similar way, there are different levels involved in many complex subjects such as movement behavior. Sometimes the confusion that students experience is in unwittingly trying to apply the same terms and lines of reasoning to more than one level of behavior at the same time. It would be like trying to see all of the different levels in the microscope at one time. It can't work.

When students begin to restrict their usage of terms and the logic of their arguments to one level at a time, they find that many of their confusions disappear.

and refusing to do anything immediately in response. If I do this, then I have practiced inhibition already. After that, it doesn't matter what I do, because inhibition is a mental discipline, not a physical action or movement.

If I am sitting on a chair and decide to stand up, and upon receiving this stimulus I refuse to do anything immediately in response, then I will have successfully practiced inhibition. I will have been successful not because I stayed on the chair, but because I will have performed the mental discipline required.

If I am sitting on a chair and decide to stand up, and upon receiving this stimulus I refuse to do anything immediately in response, and then, while continuing to refuse to do anything immediately in response, I project the directions for the new use in an appropriate way and stand up, I will still have successfully practiced inhibition because I will have performed the mental discipline required.

And the same would be true if I had followed all of these procedures and raised my hand instead.

Whether or not I am successfully practicing inhibition has little or nothing to do with what activities I do or do not perform. It has everything to do with whether or not I make the experience of receiving a stimulus and of refusing to do anything immediately in response.

For these reasons, I instruct my students to restrict their usage of the term "inhibition" to the practice of this mental discipline and to talk about a "prevention of an activity" to describe a failure to make any particular gestural response.

The last point I like to make about the practice of inhibition is that because inhibition is a mental skill, there is nothing to "do" to practice it

There is no action, movement, or lack of movement which has anything to do with the process of inhibition. It is a mental discipline by which we can gain the time necessary to accomplish the thinking required to dominate our old manner of habitual misdirection.

There is nothing to 'do' to inhibit.

Whenever I think about this 'problem' of what to 'do' to inhibit, I am reminded of a student I had in my Basic Principles course in Washington, D. C. in 1988.

One weekend she came in determined to get an answer to her question. When I called on her, she asked, "What do you have to 'do' to inhibit?" When I told her that you have to make the experience of receiving a stimulus and refusing to do anything immediately in response, she said, "Yes, I know that. But, what do you have to 'do' to inhibit?"

After several rounds of her asking the same question and my giving the same answer, it quickly became apparent that repeating my previous answer was not going to satisfy her. Usually when an appropriate answer fails to satisfy a student, you can be pretty sure that the student is asking a different question than the one you are answering.

When I listened to her question again, I realized that she had meant the word "do" literally. She wanted to know what she had to "do" in order not to "do" what she ordinarily "did" in activity.

Trying to find out what to "do" in order "not to 'do' what you ordinarily "do" is missing the point.

In inhibition, we are not concerned with the actions one does or does not perform as much as we are concerned with the way in which one performs them. The point of the Alexander Technique is not to get better by substituting "appropriate" movements performed in an habitual manner for "inappropriate" movements performed in an habitual manner. The point of the Alexander Technique is to learn how to discipline oneself to acquire a conscious guidance and control of one's potentialities, thereby freeing oneself from the tyranny of habitual misdirection.

There is a way in which asking "What can I 'do' to inhibit?" is like asking, "What can I eat to lose weight?" The initiation of the activity in question is almost certain to doom the project.

When I finally figured out what she was asking, I gave her an answer that she understood, but didn't believe.

I told her that inhibition is a mental skill. I told her that there is no action, movement, or lack of movement which has anything to do with the process of inhibition. I told her that inhibition is a mental discipline by which we can gain the time necessary to accomplish the thinking required to dominate our old manner of habitual misdirection. As a result, there is nothing to "do" to inhibit.

And how did I know she didn't believe me?

Because for the next few months, every time we had a seminar, she would ask me a new question. And, every time we examined the new question closely, it always turned out to be the same question: "What do you have to 'do' to inhibit?" In fact, the next year in class she asked me the same question again.

"What do you have to 'do' to inhibit?"

Nothing.

Inhibition is a mental skill, a mental discipline by which we can gain the time necessary to accomplish the thinking required to dominate our old manner of habitual misdirection.

There is nothing to "do" to inhibit.

This definition of inhibition led Alexander to another long period of practical investigation.

For many people, the prospect of yet another "long period of investigation" is incredibly disappointing. In our increasingly instant, microwaveable society, we seem to be caught up in finding the quickest answer to solving problems, the short cut.

I am on record in many places as saying that the exacting, straightforward, complete performance of any given task is almost always the short cut, but my point here is slightly different and probably more important.

Much is said about the amount of work Alexander performed to "discover" this work. It is often suggested that because Alexander did all of this work, succeeding generations of students won't have to. This argument has always had a sort of Christian flavor to it, as if Alexander had figuratively "died" upon the "cross" of his experimentation for us, so that, by learning the truths of his conclusions, we can avoid the arduousness of his task.

While I can see the marketing value of offering a thirty-lesson course of study to learn the work instead of presenting it as an on-going process of self-discipline and training which can only be acquired through hard work over a period of many, many years, I have often believed that the myth that our tasks in learning this work will be shorter and easier for having been done by others before us is extremely misleading.

If we are to "do what [Alexander] did," then we must do what he did.

These long periods of experimentation which Alexander performed yielded not only conclusions and understandings, but skills necessary for the learning of the work.

Even as early on in the investigation of the work as failing to notice his harmful tendencies of misuse in his ordinary speaking, Alexander attributed his failure to the lack of "experience in the kind of observation necessary to enable me to detect anything wrong in the way I used myself in speaking."[1] Alexander's skill of observing himself accurately came from the actual practice of observation which his investigation required

Alexander could not develop these skills without practice, and neither can we.

Nowhere is this rule of skill acquisition through practice more apparent than in those skills required to retrain one's thinking.

From the very first day of class, students want to know if they are "doing the Alexander Technique right." Most teachers jump on the last part of this question and chastise their students about their desire to be right. This criticism has some merit, of course, but teachers might serve their students better by paying more attention to the first part of their students' desires.

In order to learn this work, we are all going to have to come to grips with our desire to "do."

This desire to "do" was what fueled Alexander's immediate responses to stimuli and caused him to appreciate the need for inhibition. The procedure that he used to overcome this desire and to reach the next level of his investigation is, however, a procedure that we must all use if we are to learn his work. It is the procedure to which we must all constantly return if we are to continue in our process of improvement.

"I therefore decided to confine my work to giving myself directions for the new 'means-whereby,' instead of actually trying to do them or to relate them to the 'end' of speaking."[2]

---

1. p. 142 (p. 10)
2. p. 154 (p. 27-28)

Alexander explains in a footnote that, by the term "means-whereby," he is referring to the "reasoned means to the gaining of an end" which includes both the "inhibition of [his] habitual use" and "the conscious projection of the new directions necessary to the performance of the different acts involved."[1] In other words, during this next stage of his own development, he simply gave himself the directions for carrying out the act of speaking and did not try to put these directions into practice.

Usually, after much brow-beating, I can get my best students to try this procedure of projecting directions without attempting to "do" them for minutes on end in class. Rarely, I can convince them of its value sufficiently to get them to do it on their own. But, the importance of carrying out this procedure is demonstrated by the amount of time that Alexander did it himself.

He told us that, in his work periods, he would give these directions for "long periods together, for successive days and weeks and sometimes even months without attempting to 'do' them."[2] If we are to gain the same abilities and skills as Alexander, then we will have to invest in the same kinds of practice that he did.

The way that most of my students apply these procedures is with a process we call Dr. Connie's How-To Chart.

After being frustrated with not knowing "how to think," and feeling a little guilty about not "thinking" all of the time, Dr. Amundson devised a little procedure for herself to try every morning. She decided that when she got up in the mornings, she would continue with her usual activities, but, for just five minutes every day, she would project her directions without attempting to "do" them.

Sometimes she would simply lie in bed and project her directions. Sometimes she would exercise. Sometimes she would put in a load of laundry.

The nature of her activity wasn't important.

What was important was that she made a deal with herself that, whatever she did, for a short period of time, every day, she would give her directions without attempting to 'do' them. She figured that if F. M. could do this for months at a time, she could manage five minutes a day. Further, if she did it in the mornings, her obligation would be finished and she wouldn't feel guilty if she didn't "think" for the rest of the day.

When she started this experiment, she did have trouble projecting her orders for five whole minutes at a time. She would become distracted or bored or just plain tired of "thinking" in this way. As time went by and she practiced every morning, she noticed that she had another problem: she couldn't quit after just five minutes.

As time went by, she noticed she was getting more done when she first got up. The quality of her work was improving. And, every time she looked at the clock to see how much time was left to go, she had already exceeded her five minutes, often by large amounts of time. More to the

---

1. p. 154 (p. 27-28)
2. p. 155 (p. 28)

point, she found it harder and harder not to "think" in this way at other times as well.

My favorite place to perform this procedure is when I am using a rowing machine.

I know that I am going to be there for a given period of time. Because of the repetitive nature of the machine, I can be reasonably assured that no major crises of decision are going to occur. I simply practice giving my directions without attempting to "do" them as I continue to row away.

As a result of these practice times and all the other times I project these orders without attempting to "do" them, the nature of my thinking processes has radically changed. The freedom initiated by the process of inhibition has been enlarged by the skills learned in this new procedure. Now I can not only receive a stimulus and refuse to do anything immediately in response, but I can continuously project specific stimuli for movements which I do not carry out

This process of projecting directions without attempting to "do" them is not the "Alexander Technique," nor is it the whole of the process required, but it is a skill which we all must acquire if we are ever to learn this work.

Alexander does not tell us that it is the information which he gained from this particular practice which was of value but "the experience [which he] gained in giving these directions which] proved of great value when the time came ... to consider how to put (these directions) into practice.[1] By performing this process for considerable amounts of time and with great discipline, by projecting his directive guidance commands without attempting to 'do' them, or even to relate them to the end he wished to gain, he acquired the skills necessary to learn about and perform his work. Further, without these skills, he could not have gone on to acquire the skill of Additive Thinking or have been able to carry out the Five Part Plan.

Alexander needed to acquire these skills to develop and learn the work. We will need to learn these same skills if we are to learn how to do the work, too.

There is no short cut.

There are no steps to which we can give lip service or which we can eliminate.

We must learn to acquire each skill for implementing the work, just as surely as we must acquire an understanding of each transaction involved, if we are ever to be able to do what Alexander did.

---

1.   pp. 154-155 (p. 28)

CHAPTER 13

THE PRINCIPLE OF ADDITIVE THINKING

As Alexander practiced both the skills of inhibition and of giving his directions without attempting to "do" them, through the experience he gained, he began to acquire a new mental skill, a skill which I call the Principle of Additive Thinking.

Formally stated, through his experience of projecting his "directions" without attempting to "do" them, Alexander learned:

1)   that before attempting to "do" even the first part of the new "means-whereby" which [he] had decided to employ in order to gain [his] end.... [he] must give the directions preparatory to the doing of this first part very many times;

2)   that [he] must continue to give the directions preparatory to the doing of the first part while [he] gave the directions preparatory to the doing of the second part.

3)   that [he] must continue to give the directions preparatory to the doing of the first and second parts while [he] gave the directions preparatory to the doing of the third part; and so on for the doing of the fourth and other parts as required.[1]

The importance of learning how to do this particular procedure cannot be overemphasized.

It took Alexander most of his narrative to get to the point where he had forsaken directive guidance by any form of feeling for the directive guidance of his reasoning processes. The first procedure which he introduced for the implementation of this new source of directive guidance, the Three Part Process of Protocol Design, was not entirely new or unique to his work, nor did it require specialized skills.

While analyzing the conditions present, selecting appropriate procedures for gaining an end, and then thinking about the process you wish to perform instead of the product you wish to gain is not commonly employed, it certainly does not require a knowledge of Alexander and his work to be used.

In fact, most good, modern athletic training and coaching programs use this very design as a basis for their procedures.

It is only when Alexander begins to apply his new skills of constructive dissociation through inhibition and the projection of the orders without attempting to "do" them, and then organizes his thought processes according to the Principle of Additive Thinking, that he begins to suggest procedures which are truly contrary to any procedure "in which man's instinctive processes have been drilled." [2]

---

1. p. 155 (p. 28)
2. p. 160 (p. 35)

It is inappropriate in an introductory text to discuss the topic of Additive Thinking fully in the manner which it deserves. That discussion is more appropriately performed elsewhere. There are, however, a number of points in that discussion which I believe will be of value to mention.

First of all, it is important to remember that the discovery of how one's thinking may be organized additively was a direct result of the skills acquired in the carrying out of the experiments in inhibition and projecting directions without attempting to "do" them. These skills in thinking can only be acquired by carrying out that kind of disciplined practice for prolonged periods of time. These particular skills are necessary to the understanding and implementation of the new principle of Additive Thinking.

Secondly in class we have found that the nature of this process of Additive Thinking can be summarized in three words. Additive Thinking is repetitive, additive, and successive.

That the process of Additive Thinking is repetitive is obvious from the very first part of the procedure that Alexander describes. He tells us that, "I must give the directions preparatory to the doing of this first part very many times." Even if one were to give only one of the directions necessary to the doing of a given activity before beginning that activity, one must give that direction very many times. Therefore, the first characteristic of Additive Thinking is that it is repetitive.

The second characteristic of Additive Thinking is that it is additive.

When one progresses to the giving of the directions preparatory to the doing of the second part of a protocol for the performance of a given activity, one CONTINUES to give the directions for the first part WHILE adding in the directions for this second part of the protocol.

In this way, the repetitive aspect of this manner of thinking is emphasized, and the additive nature of this manner of thought can be seen.

To "think" in this manner, one CONTINUES to repeat the directions which have gone before as the new directions are added in. One CONTINUES to repeat and give the directions preparatory to the doing of the first part of the protocol as one ADDS IN the directions preparatory to the doing of the second part of the protocol. Then one CONTINUES to repeat and give the directions preparatory to the doing of the first and second parts of the protocol as one ADDS IN the directions preparatory to the doing of the third part. Then one CONTINUES to give the directions preparatory to the doing of the first, second, and third parts as one ADDS IN the directions preparatory to the doing of the fourth part, and so on.

In this way the process of Additive Thinking can be seen as both repetitive and additive.

The third aspect of the process of Additive Thinking is at least as important as the other two. Additive Thinking is successive, i.e., it occurs in a sequence.

Every movement which we perform is sequential. Like a well-made play, it has a beginning, a middle, and an end. Similarly, the "thinking" which produces such a movement is sequential as well. If it were not, the order of the firing of the muscles and the movement that these firings caused would be "out-of-sequence" for the intended movement. In a large sense, this is what we mean when we say that a movement is mal-coordinated.

The only way the movement performed can match the movement which was intended is for the sequence of the commands projected to the muscles to match the sequences required to perform the intended movement. Once one has decided on what movement to perform, and analyzed the conditions present, and reasoned out an appropriate protocol for response, then the sequence of the "thinking" which is projected must match the sequence of the protocol.

Therefore, the process of Additive Thinking is repetitive, additive, and successive.

Alexander tells us that even after he had become familiar with this process of combining the giving of directions, it was still necessary to "continue this process [of training my thinking] in my practice for a considerable time before actually attempting to employ the new 'means-whereby' for the purpose of speaking." [1]

Even after he had spent all of those days and weeks and months, in practice, leading up to this procedural discovery, he had to continue to practice it - without attempting to "do" anything - for a considerable time "before attempting to employ the new 'means-whereby' for the purpose of speaking." Even after all the practice required to create this new procedure, he had to practice this new process of thinking for a considerable time before putting it to use.

This manner of thought takes time and practice to develop.

It took Alexander a considerable amount of time and practice to develop it and there is general agreement that he was a genius. Therefore, it is likely that it will take us a considerable amount of time and practice to develop it for ourselves.

Alexander told us that "anyone who carries (these new thinking processes) out faithfully while trying to gain an end will find that he is acquiring a new experience in what he calls 'thinking.'"[2] The new practitioner will be acquiring a new experience in thinking because this part of Alexander's technique, the Principle of Additive Thinking, requires the creation and implementation of an entirely new and different way of organizing and sending out movement protocol commands.

---

1. p. 155 (p. 28)
2. The quotation marks are Alexander's.

Because Additive Thinking is a new skill, it will take time to learn. It took Alexander time to learn it. It took everyone who came after Alexander time to learn it. It will take you time to learn it.

It will also take time for you to refine it.

If we think of someone who has become a concert pianist, we can ask the question: When did this person learn to play the piano? The only answer which makes any sense is the moment when the relationship between striking the keys to make a sound was established. Everything which came after that moment was a refinement and development of first learning to play.

It will take time for you to refine your ability to do this thinking just as it did Alexander and me and everyone else.

It will take time and practice.

There is a step in the development of your ability to think in this manner which will probably prove most difficult. By saying this, I am not trying to cloud your thought with negative ideas. I am merely passing on what Alexander told us was true of every student he had ever known. In fact, this step is so important, I believe that it is one of the distinguishing differences which makes this work a skill to be acquired rather than information to be learned.

Usually the most important stage in learning information is the step from not having the information to having it We can think of this as the step from zero to one where zero represents the stage of ignorance with regard to the information and one represents the stage of possession of the information.

In the acquisition of a skill to be performed, there are often many different bits or pieces of information required to perform the skill, but the possession of this information does not mean that the skill has been acquired. There is a tremendous difference between having word perfect recall of an accurate book on the skills of bronco-busting and surviving an actual ride on one of these horses in a rodeo.

The acquisition of a skill has to do with the ability to be in Practical possession of one bit of significant information, and then being able to add to it succeeding bits of significant information in a practical manner.

In this way, the most important step in the acquisition of a skill is not simply coming into possession of new information, the step from zero to one, but the ability to add, in a constructive way, each successive new step to the ability you already had. In other words, the most important step in the acquisition of a skill is not the step from zero to one, but rather the step from one to two.

Similarly, the most difficult step to learn to add in while practicing the Principle of Additive Thinking is also the step from one to two rather than the step from zero to one.

Alexander tells us that anyone can project one direction. Anyone can focus their mind repetitively on just one of these directions. It is the next step when one tries "to continue to give this direction as we project the second" [1] wherein the difficulty begins.

To be able to do this requires a new and different process of thought. Once you have learned to accomplish this step of being able to continue to project one direction while projecting the second, however, you will have created within yourself the template for each succeeding stage of development. Once you have taught yourself how to continue to project one direction while projecting the second, you can more easily learn to continue to project the first two as you add in a third, and each succeeding, direction.

In time, you will acquire the skill and ability to project all of the directions necessary for improving the use of yourself as you proceed to gain your end.

I have known many students to reach this point in their training only to become discouraged at how slowly progress is initially made. I don't know why. I mean all that is required to proceed to the next level of development is a skill in a manner of directive thought which is contrary to any manner of directive thought which has been used previously throughout all of evolution.

In addition, Alexander points out in his narrative that every student he has ever known has stumbled when coming up against this very point.

I do not know precisely what this kind of thinking is. Nor do I know precisely what changes take place in the organization of one's thoughts for this additive ability to take place. I do know that every one of my students who has taken this challenge, and worked on this skill in the way that Alexander describes, has acquired the ability to think additively.

Some a little slow. Some a little fast.

Everyone to only a very small capacity in the beginning.

But, every student who has ever taken this challenge and passed through the step from one (the ability to give one direction) to two (the ability to continue to give the first direction while giving the second) has, over time and with practice, acquired a constantly increasing capacity to do this kind of thinking in a successful way with very gratifying results.

Once Alexander had worked on this skill for several periods of considerable time, he "believed [that he] had practised the 'means-whereby' long enough, and [he] started to employ them for the purpose of speaking." [1]

The only problem he had at this point was that he failed more often than he succeeded.

He was frustrated by this turn of events because he knew he was attempting to prevent his habitual responses. He knew he was saying his directions repeatedly. He thought he was doing everything that he

---

1. p. 155 (p. 29)
1. pp. 155-156 (p. 29)

believed he should in the way that he should, and still he did not enjoy success.

He was doing everything as it seemed he should, but he still continued to fail at a very high rate.

Most of us can relate personally to this experience in learning this work, but, in order to solve this new dilemma, Alexander did something most of us would avoid. He went back to the beginning and reconsidered everything once more.

Upon reflection, he saw that the times that he failed were those times in which he had failed to prevent the dominance[1] of his wrong use. This was because the instinctive direction which he had formerly used still dominated his conscious reasoning direction.[2] Because of the faith he had in his reasoning and the new means for change which his reasoning suggested, he looked elsewhere for the cause of his failures.

First, like all of us, he blamed himself as though his personal shortcomings were the root cause of his lack of success. When he found that this contention did not have the power to advance his investigation even if it were true, he looked elsewhere for the source of his continuing failures.

The only other possible cause for his failures which he could think of would be if, at the critical moment of taking his planning into movement, he had failed to continue with his intention to change his manner of use in the performance of his activities. He wondered if, instead of "continuing to project the directions [he had reasoned out] in their proper sequence," he reverted to the instinctive misdirection of [his] old habitual use," his old habitual pattern of directive guidance.

In spite of his "feeling" or believing he had stopped using these old command protocols, he discovered through further investigation that he did. in fact, revert to his old habitual patterns of directive guidance as he went into activity.

---

1. A number of people have criticized me for introducing what they see as a concept of conflict which is implied by my use of the verb "to dominate". Apparently, they are in possession of a kinder, gentler consciousness and manner of thought which they feel is threatened by these terms of conflict. Further, they say to me that by introducing this idea of conflict into my work, I doom my students to a much darker view of the world, and thereby they miss all that the world can be.

Whether or not my students are doomed is an issue I will put aside for the moment long enough to say this: I did not introduce the concept of dominance; Alexander did.

Almost every idea which I put forward in any of my efforts can be found somewhere in the literature of this work. As a matter of fact, I very seriously doubt if you could find an original idea or concept in this whole book.

For the last twenty years, I have tried to learn or discover something new which Alexander did not know or write about. I have never learned, said, or seen anything of value in this work which could not be found somewhere in Alexander's writings.

This is why I urge everyone who is interested in learning this work to study Alexander's writings unceasingly. They are a resource whose depth and value may never be fully appreciated because the understanding that they represent and convey are so far beyond the ways in which we ordinarily think.

2. These two sentences (lines 605 - 612 in the Maisel edition) report the final major change in understanding which Alexander shares in his narrative. It is without question the most important step he takes in his journey. For having abandoned the pursuit of kinesthetic reeducation as his means of change, he finally puts aside consideration of habitual wrong use as the dominating force within him. At last he sees that what domi-

Upon further reflection, Alexander saw that this dominance of misdirection could hardly have been otherwise. This process of instinctive direction is the only direction which any of us have ever used. In addition, this mode of directing himself had become so familiar that it now felt "natural and right."

Moreover, by disciplining himself to project conscious directions in a sequence, he was trying to follow a new and different process of guidance in which none of us have very much experience at all. In this way, the power of the racial inheritance of instinctive direction was made greater by the racial inexperience of projecting directions consciously, particularly directions in a sequence.[1]

In order to succeed against the strength of these tendencies, Alexander decided that first he needed to close any remaining loopholes in his plan for change and then develop a new procedure which would make the implementation of his new plan a success.

When Alexander had finally seen the importance and inherent difficulty of the task, it led him to see the final obstacle which he had erected in his own way.

He writes to us, "I had recognized much earlier that I ought not to trust to my feeling for the direction of my use, but I had never fully realized all that this implied." [2]

He had failed to recognize that because his standards for judgment were based on his familiar sense of what felt right, the attempt to apply these standards of judgment immediately in any meaningful way would doom his efforts to change from the outset.

Obviously, any new use must feel different from the old, and if the old use felt right, the new use was bound to feel wrong. I now had to face the fact that in all my attempts during these past months I had been trying to employ a new use of myself which was bound to feel wrong, at the same time trusting to my feeling of what was right to tell me whether I was employing it or not.[3]

---

nates his actions is not any set pattern of physical response, but his manner of directing himself in activity.

When he is dominated by misdirection, he is unable to change as he desires. To the degree he is able to dominate his instinctive manner of direction with his new and reasoned conscious direction, he will succeed.

Some have questioned my judgment that this step is the most important step in the journey. My only defense is that Alexander thought it was so important that he wrote "and this was of the utmost importance" in reference to this step.

Careful study of Alexander's writing shows that, as a writer, he was precise, conservative, and economical. I know his sentences are often long and complex but the concepts conveyed are just as often immense and simultaneous. For a writer such as he was to take the time and space to leave a flashing neon day-glo trail marker like the phrase "and this was of the utmost importance" is sufficient proof to me of the tremendous importance of the step to which he refers.

1 It is clear from the context that Alexander's use of the term "racial" has more to do with the characteristics of the human species as a whole rather than the specifics of any subgroup.

2. p. 157 (p. 31)
3. p. 157-158 (p. 32)

The important issue with regards to feelings is not so much one of rel-ative trustworthiness as one of self -defeat caused by a reliance upon feel-ings and the reinitiation of instinctive misdirection which this reliance caused. Here he was trying to employ a new use in his activities "while for the purpose of this attempt [he] was actually bringing into play [his] old habitual use (by means of reverting) to [his] instinctive misdirection. Small wonder that this attempt had proved futile!" [1]

In order to employ a new use, Alexander decided that he must employ a new and reasoned manner of directing himself in activity. By allowing his interpretation of feeling to be a part of his efforts, he initiated (and reverted to) the old manner of direction associated with the act of reliance upon feeling for a guide.

As soon as this old manner of direction is initiated, its strength, with respect to the strength of the newer and weaker though reasoned direc-tion of himself, becomes practically irresistible. In other words, you can-not use the directions associated with your old manner of performing an activity in any way while installing a new manner of directing yourself without getting caught up in your old manner of direction.

Once your old manner of directing yourself is initiated, the game is over.

You can't use something to perform the act of not using it.

You can't use your old manner of directing your use in activity to pre-vent yourself from directing yourself in that way.

You can't even use your old manner of directing yourself in activity to judge how well you are directing yourself in your new way because your old manner of directing yourself is such a powerful influence that as soon as it is initiated, for whatever reason, any new means of direction you are trying to employ is liable to be dominated

To succeed, you must find a way to break this cycle. Finding a way to break this cycle became Alexander's goal.

> I now saw that if I was ever to succeed in making the changes in use I desired, I must subject the processes directing my use to a new experience, the experience, that is, of being dominated by reasoning instead of by feeling. [2]

To succeed, Alexander had to find a way of directing himself which did not touch upon or invite unwanted his old manner of directing himself in either the process of guidance or judgment. He had to find a way to guar-antee that he could discipline himself to use his new manner of direction throughout the performance of his activities. To succeed, he had to, "at all costs, work out some plan by which ... [his] instinctive reaction to the stimulus to gain (any) end remained inhibited, while [he] projected in their sequence the directions for the employment of the new use at the critical moment of gaining the end."[3]

---

1. p. 158 (p. 32)
2. p. 158 (p. 32)
3. p. 158 (p. 33)

CHAPTER 14

THE FIVE PART PLAN

The Five Part Plan For Projecting Directions is the name I have given to the procedure that Alexander worked out to ensure that his instinctive reaction remained inhibited. Formally written, it refers strictly to his metaphoric purpose of speaking. Here, we will present the more generalized form which we have adopted in my classes:

THE FIVE PART PLAN FOR PROJECTING DIRECTIONS

1)   inhibit any immediate response to the stimulus

2)   project in their sequence the directions for the primary control (Intrinsic Directions) and whatever significant Extrinsic Directions you have chosen

3)   continue to project these directions until you believe you are ready to take them into activity

4)   then, while continuing to project the directions for the new use, stop, reconsider your previous decision, and make a fresh decision then and there and

5)   either

a)   continue to project the directions for maintaining the new use and go on to gain your original end

b)   continue to project the directions for maintaining the new use and not go on to gain your original end

or

c)   continue to project the directions for maintaining the new use and go on to perform some entirely different activity.[2]

In class, we make three major points about this plan.

---

1. In my classes, we make a distinction between what we call Intrinsic and Extrinsic Directions.

The Intrinsic Directions are those directions which are intrinsic to the improvement of a person's use in any activity. More formally, we would call these directions the directions for the improvement of the use of the primary controlling factors in movement. The Intrinsic Directions most commonly attributed to Alexander are: let the neck be free, let the head go forward and up, and let the back broaden and lengthen. In every activity in which you want to improve your use, you must begin with the giving of the Intrinsic Directions.

The Extrinsic Directions are those directions which are specific to, and descriptive of, a given activity. An Extrinsic Direction for playing golf would very likely be to keep your eye on the ball. An Extrinsic Direction for walking might be to support your weight on one leg while you bring the other leg through.

There is a strong correspondence between Intrinsic Directions and relationing movements and between Extrinsic Directions and gestural movements.

2 In his book, Alexander listed these three possible responses in the order of not going on to gain the original end, going on to perform something else entirely, or going on to gain the original end. Through the years, my classes have learned this plan better when it has been presented in the sequence used above. In the discussion that follows, I hope to show a further practical advantage of this particular sequence.

First of all, I ask students, "How many steps are there in the Five Part Plan?"

By the point in the year when I ask this, the class is pretty well divided between those who are certain that I am testing their wills and confidence in their own knowledge by asking an obvious question with an obvious answer, and those who are certain that there is a trick to this question.

In this case, the tricksters won.

There are six steps to the Five Part Plan.

In this plan, and in the application of all of this work, the zero step or the step which precedes the usage of the procedure that Alexander outlined is that you must have a specific goal or activity. In order for Alexander to have the stimulus to speak, he must have the goal of speaking. In order for a student in a lesson to employ this information in walking, he must have the goal to walk.

The Alexander Technique is a practical skill which can be applied universally to all of your activities as you perform them. It is not a separate, pseudo-meditative mantra which magically transforms you at some later date if you repeat it repeatedly, even if you are receiving proper kinesthetic experience at the time.

The Alexander Technique is a means of disciplining your conscious mind so that you can acquire a constantly increasing ability to direct yourself in activity in increasingly constructive ways. It is a tool which must be specifically applied in "real" circumstances before it has any meaning whatsoever. When one takes "practicing" this work out of the realm of practical experimentation, serious problems occur.

In the first place, the causal relationship between thought and movement becomes obscured.

Thoughts are private and beyond external judgment. The need for lessons, as demonstrated by a diminished coordination, usually eliminates the probability that the student is capable of judging the quality and manner of his thoughts and directions on his own. By restricting one's practical investigation of this work to quiet periods of manipulative infusions of information - even in the presence of repeatedly projected directions - one loses any chance of objective criteria by which to judge accomplishment and understanding.

Secondly, the taking of students out of activity while teaching them avoids the central point of conflict - the critical moment of taking an idea into activity. This may very well rack up a number of impressive "movement" or "postural" victories, but these will be victories which will have little or no practical meaning.

A National Football League team might do very well indeed in a game against a local high school team. Playing against such a low level of opposition, however, they would risk acquiring bad habits and over-confidence. They might even be more easily defeated in a more meaningful game against another professional team. In fact, it has been demonstrated on many occasions and in many different sports that, if the calibre of opponents in practice is too low, athletes seem to hurt their chances for victory in the important contests.

The important task, and the only really valuable task in this work, is to gain the degree of conscious, mental discipline required to direct yourself effectively and with constant improvement of quality of performance in activity. No style points will be awarded for accomplishment in "thinking" while "sitting very still" in a chair.

This work is about being able to organize your mental activity so that you can perform meaningful activity free from the tyranny of habit. As Marjory Barlow would say, it is about "driving a wedge between stimulus and response." This space, this region between stimulus and response, is the battleground on which the victory of gaining conscious control[1] of the individual will be won. As Frank Jones says, "The Alexander Technique opens a window onto [this] little known area between stimulus and response and gives you the self-knowledge you need in order to change the pattern of your response." [2]

While there is some good which can be obtained by establishing some principles of this work in isolation from activities, the only truly meaningful work which can be done in lessons must be done by challenging students' responses as they approach and move through the critical moment into activity.

In order for there to be a critical moment, there must be a specific goal or activity to be performed.

---

1. Over the past few years, I have heard more and more people defining "conscious control" as the tool which Alexander used to change the use of himself in activity. To me, this usage has two problems.

First, by defining conscious control in this way, the term enters the panoply of conceptual misuse which is often perpetrated upon students by instructors and fellow students who have not done their homework. It becomes one of the "mysteries" of the work, because students can never find any procedural instructions for the use of this "tool." Then, when they do begin to read Alexander's writings, they become confused further still by trying to fit their acquired definition onto Alexander's actual usage leading them to conclude that Alexander wrote poorly.

Because Alexander's writings are so filled with information, experience, and ideas - much of which is contrary to the common experience - they can be a great challenge to read and to understand even when there is agreement of terms between the writer and the reader. Having two or more definitions for the same terms makes it practically impossible. And this is the second reason why defining conscious control as a method is problematic to me because this is the antithesis of what Alexander meant.

There is no such thing as a "conscious control" which you can use to improve your use in activity.

Conscious control is merely the condition which you can attain by following Alexander's procedures and learning to retrain your manner of thinking and directive guidance.

How do I know this is true?

Alexander told me so: "*In this connexion I wish it to be understood that throughout this book I use the term conscious guidance and control to indicate, primarily, a plane to be reached rather than a method of reaching it.*" (Alexander, F. M *Constructive Conscious Control of the Individual*, Centerline Press, Long Beach, Ca., 1985, p.10)

2 . Jones, Frank Pierce, *Body Awareness in Action*, Schocken Books, New York, 1976, p.4.

Therefore, the Five Part Plan for Projecting Directions has six steps, the zero step of which is:

0) have a specific goal or activity.

The second major point we make about the Five Part Plan comes from the fifth step.

All too often, students become seduced by what seems to be the importance of the three response options which Alexander describes in the fifth step.[1] Students sometimes approach these three options as though the secret to the work comes from trying to sneak up on yourself at the critical moment and fool yourself as to which action you will take.

If you know what to look for, you can watch students practicing "not going for their ends." They look a lot like people who sit very still with serious or worried looks on their faces.

Probably even funnier than these people are the ones who think or state that they intend to speak, and then lift their hands instead or perform some such "other end," usually by employing their old patterns of habitual use. Upon questioning, these students have assured me that, by going on to an end which is different from their original intention, they are building up a skill which will serve them well in their attempts to learn how to change the use of themselves in activity. "After all," they argue, "isn't this why Alexander was so specific in listing these three possibilities?"

It hurts me sometimes to have to crush this type of enthusiasm, but I have to tell them no. Alexander listed these three possibilities not because there is some inherent secret or magic formula involved. He listed them because at any given moment, for any given activity, for any given response, these are the only responses possible.

If I am standing and announce that I am going to start walking, there are only three possible responses I can make.

If I make my announcement and begin walking, we can all agree that I have gone on to gain my original end. If I make my announcement and remain standing still, then we can all agree that I have not gone on to my original end. If I make my announcement and begin singing or sitting or making a pizza, then we can all agree that I have changed my end and done something different.

But, once I have made my announcement, these are the only three outcomes possible.

Either I do what I say and gain my end, or I don't do anything and don't go on to gain my end, or I do something else entirely. There are no other choices.

The secret of the power and effectiveness of the Five Part Plan is not to be found in the game of Go On, Do Nothing, Or Do Something Else.

1. In the defense of students, it is important to note that this particular importance seems to be emphasized by Alexander as well in a subsequent paragraph. p. 160 (p. 35)

The secret is not in finding the appropriate way to fool yourself. The secret of the power and effectiveness of the Five Part Plan is to be found in the other half, the first half of both the fourth and fifth steps.

The power found in the first half of these steps is the third and most important point I make about the Five Part Plan in class.

When I give a quiz or exam over this material, I often ask students to write out the Five Part Plan and I tell them that the answer is worth ten points. I generally give one point each for listing: (o) have a goal or activity, (1) inhibit any immediate response, (2) project in their sequence the directions for the primary control in intrinsic directions, and whatever significant extrinsic directions you have chosen, (3) continue to project these directions until you believe you are ready to take them into activity, (4) stop, reconsider, and make a fresh decision, and (5) go on to make one of the only three responses possible. This, with the arguable exception of the fourth step, is the design which Alexander had used up to this point in time in his investigations.

What makes the Five Part Plan different and effective is the stipulation that, in the fourth step, one stops, reconsiders, and makes a fresh decision *"while continuing to project the directions for the new use."* What makes the Five Part Plan different and effective is the stipulation that after one has *continued to project his directions for the new use* and made a fresh decision, one either *continues to project the directions for maintaining the new use* and goes on to his original end, or one *continues to project the directions* for maintaining the new use and does not go on to his original end, or one *continues to project the directions for maintaining the new use* and does some other entirely different action.

What you do or don't do is not important! Continuing to project the directions for the new use is!!! [1]

This is the true source of power in the Five Part Plan for Projecting Protocols.

Alexander's procedure prior to the Five part Plan was very similar to the emasculated Five Part Plan without the continuation of the projection of directions which I listed above, and which most students use to answer the question on the quiz. Without the continuation of the projection of directions, this plan would be as effective as the adjective "emasculated" implies.

Even after he had developed the capacity to employ the Principle of Additive Thinking, and after he could give his directions in a repetitive, additive, and successive manner, Alexander found that when he tried to

---

1. The mathematically inclined will have already figured out that 40% of the value of the question is devoted to the continuation of the projection of directions for the new use in the last two steps, making the total value for Projecting the directions 60% of the total points awarded. If anything, this figure of 60% is a gross underestimate of the importance of "thinking" in learning and carrying out this work.

employ his new experience of "thinking" for the purpose of gaining his end, he "failed far more often than he succeeded." [1]

After going all the way back to the beginning and reconsidering his premises, and after deciding that his premises and procedures were sound, and after having excused himself for personal shortcomings, and after a long period of investigation, he "discovered that [he] gave all [his] directions for the new use in their sequence right up to the point when [he] tried to gain [his] end and speak, but that, at the critical moment when persistence in giving the new directions would have brought success, [he] reverted instead to the misdirection associated with [his] old wrong habitual use." [2]

It was this reversion to his old patterns of misdirection which caused his failures. It was the actions commanded by his old misdirection which prevented his success "at the critical moment when persistence in giving the new directions would have brought success." The Five Part Plan For Projecting Directions is the procedure which Alexander reasoned out to ensure that his "instinctive reaction to the stimulus to gain [his] end remained inhibited, while [he] projected in their sequence the directions for the employment of the new use at the critical moment of gaining that end. " [3]

The continuation of the projection of the directions up to, and through, the critical moment of making the decision to give consent and move into activity, is the difference in his procedure which provides the key for his success.

As Alexander points out, the change in procedure occurs at the critical moment.

In his other procedures, it was always at this point that the instinctive misdirection of his use came into play either by inattention, by the failure to project his new directions, by an unintentional invitation of his old misdirection through the employment of his feeling sense interpretation for either guidance or evaluation, or by a lack of discipline which resulted in a failure to continue to project the directions for the new use throughout the planning and actualization of the activity he wished to perform. By employing this new five part strategy, he believed he would be "subjecting [his] instinctive processes of direction to an experience contrary to any experience in which they had hitherto been drilled." [4] By employing this strategy, Alexander intended to retrain his manner of direction of himself to escape the dominance of his instinctive direction-ions.

"Up to [the] time (in which he adopted this new strategy) the stimulus of a decision to gain a certain end had always resulted in the Same habitual activity" [5] because the reaction to the stimulus had always involved

---

1. p. 156 (p. 29)
2. pp. 156-157 (p. 30)
3. p. 158 (p. 33)
4. p. 159 (p. 34)
5. p. 159 (pp. 34-35)

the projection of the instinctive direction for the use which [he] habitually employed for the gaining of that end."[1]

It is important to see once again that it is the commands associated
with his habitual patterns of directive guidance which engender his habitual use and not his "use" or his "habits" which generate his "thinking."
There is a causal relationship between habits and thoughts, but it is
always the thoughts which create the habits.

In practice, Alexander found this to be true, for "as long as the reasoned directions for the bringing about of new conditions of use were
consciously maintained, the stimulus of a decision to gain a certain end
would result in an activity differing from the old habitual activity." [2] In
other words, it is what we are thinking and how we are thinking it which
will determine what our actions and their probable outcome will be.

The importance of our mental landscape in shaping and determining
our relationship to the world and our actions within it has long been recognized in success education and motivational psychology. The value of
the creative use of our imagination as an organizing principle of our
thoughts and actions to direct us towards goals is beyond dispute.

What Alexander does in his work, however, is put aside the real but
limited value of administering these principles through the faculty of
"habit," and, in its place, gives us the tools to build a more specific, more
accurate, and more responsive means of employing our imagination
through the attainment of the condition of conscious control. These
tools, principles, procedures, and skills, which he acquired for himself
through a patient process of investigation and practice, provided the
material he needed to solve the problem of his own misdirection of himself in activity.

As he learned to apply these principles and procedures, he developed
the skills and experience necessary to attain a plane of conscious guidance
and control which, with time and practice, freed him from his throat and
vocal troubles and allowed him to become the person we respect and
choose to emulate today.

Let there be no doubt that the problem posed for us by the tyranny of
our habitual patterns of directive guidance and the habits of thought and
movement which they create is a mighty problem which will require
much discipline, diligence, and effort to overcome. But, let there be no
doubt whatsoever that the principles which Alexander discovered and
the procedures which he devised for the retraining of our "thinking," and
our manner of directive guidance, provide tools far stronger than the
problem posed by these habitual patterns of directive guidance.

These principles and procedures provide tools which only require
being used to provide a solution.

---

1. p. 159 (p. 35)
2. p. 159-160 (p. 35)

GENUINE TRUST

CHAPTER 15

"YOU COULD LOOK IT UP!"

"If I was ever to succeed in making the changes in use I desired, I must subject the processes directing my use to a new experience, the experience, that is, of being dominated by reasoning instead of by feeling." [1]
>   - F. M. Alexander

There are a lot of misconceptions about Alexander's work.

People in introductory lessons are often looking for the right way to stand or the way to get rid of their backaches. They are concerned that if they study this work, they won't be allowed to have emotions any more because Alexander was against feelings. In a life already crowded with too much to do, they worry out loud about how they will find time to think about each and every thing that they have to do each and every day.[2]

Once they get involved in the work, students start being worried about "doing it right." They become embroiled in debates about whether or not their feeling sense interpretation can ever become trustworthy again. They become overly concerned about the relationship of their heads to their bodies or practicing the correct positions or keeping their backs back or choosing the right chair.

Most of all, they become passionately concerned with which teachers are right and which are wrong and who is really doing the Alexander Technique and who is not. Alexandroids from all of the various tribes roll their eyes when they hear tales of the misguided and devil-spawned efforts of the shaman from the other tribes with the kind of prejudice which can only be achieved through profound ignorance and the certainty born of it.

No one can step forward to unite all of our efforts because we all have two basic and unshakable convictions deep within us. First, we all know - teachers and students alike - that none of us really know what the Alexander Technique is, or how to teach it. Second, we all believe that, if

---

1. As in the last chapter, I will footnote all of the quotes from "Evolution of a Technique" listing both the Maisel and Centerline page numbers. This quote is from p. 158 (p. 32)

2. When I think about this complaint, I always remember the chairman of a theatre department in the Midwest who complained that if he wasn't allowed to have his "habits" each day, such as shaving his face in the same particular way, his life would become so cluttered with making decisions about what to do next that he would not have time to get on with it.

What has always made this plea so poignant to me is that, as far as I could tell by polite examination, the man wore a full beard and didn't shave at all.

we step forward and admit that we don't know what it is, some great disaster, real or imagined, will befall us.

I don't know what the Alexander Technique is.

I have spent the better part of the last two decades trying to find out. I have worked with a large number and wide variety of teachers for over three thousand hours of instruction, visited and observed a number of training centers, trained to be a teacher both formally and as an apprentice, taught several thousand different students for a total of several thousand hours of teaching, observed several thousand more students being taught, closely read a lot of books, written a few, gone to chiropractic school, synthesized a new neuromuscular re-education technique for rehabilitation and performance enhancement, provided thousands of treatments to hundreds of patients, attended a number of political meetings, been threatened with a few law suits if I tried to teach this work in certain parts of the country, gone to two International Congresses, helped found a center for the study of the Alexander Technique, taken on some apprentices to train, made a lot of friends, made some enemies, too, spent countless hours talking with Marj and Frank, spent many hours talking with everyone else, and worked unceasingly on my own thinking and use.

I have even given lessons to my parents.

But I don't know what the Alexander Technique is.

I only know what I have experienced and learned and thought about and listened to and judged. I have been ignorant, opinionated, mystified, justified, outraged, entranced, elated, depressed, bored, weary, wired, vexed, patient, frustrated, high, disappointed, and just plain wrong. I have never taken anything in this work at face value, and the only thing which has come easily is a feeling that my shortcomings in the work were due to some irredeemable failing in myself.

When it became clear to me that I was not going to learn this work overnight and that, as a teaching partner in training classes, I had earned people wanting to work with anyone else because of the quality of my hands, I asked myself, "What is it that I can do?"

I couldn't feel anything in a lesson. I couldn't see anything in other lessons. I couldn't understand what people were nodding their heads about knowingly. I couldn't even guess what I was supposed to be doing with my hands while teaching someone else, even when I could feel my hands on the other person's neck.

But, as I took stock of myself, I recognized that there were three things that I could do.

I could read, I could think, and I could persevere.[1]

---

[1] With regard to the importance of perseverance, the words of Calvin Coolidge come to mind. "Nothing in the world can take the place of persistence. Talent will not; nothing is more common than unsuccessful men with talent. Genius will not; unrewarded genius is almost a proverb. Education will not; the world is full of educated derelicts. Persistence and determination alone are omnipotent."

Being able to read didn't seem like such a big advantage when I began. I remember reading the books over and over again without much effect.

Realizing that I wasn't retaining much of what I had read, I began to apply some of the skills I had been taught as a young actor, and the study techniques I had picked up by osmosis from my parents. Consequently, I wrote out longhand, verbatim, all of Alexander's books. Three times. Each. I still didn't retain as much as I believed that I should, but I was starting to see some of the larger strokes on the canvas which Alexander painted.

While engaged in this process, I went to study with Frank Pierce Jones. Although the study was for less than a calendar year, I had over fifty lessons with Frank and many more hours of discussion, camaraderie. and mutual respect with another person for whom reading, thinking, and diligent effort held a high value.

This part of my training was balanced by my on-going training with Marjorie Barstow. Marjorie's practical experimentation and sense of adventure continually reminded me that there was more to life, and to me, than just the things I was able to do well.

So, I stretched out and tried to challenge myself in those aspects of this work at which I wasn't very good. I "sensed" myself in a lesson and tried to find a way to express what I sensed. I talked about what I saw or didn't see in other people's lessons. I continued to put my hands on other people, even when they grimaced or my hands shook. Marjorie's smile, patience, and encouragement kept me going even as these experiences continued to pile up in the disaster column.

I persevered.

And when I began my student teaching - always supervised, always approved,[1] - there were near constant phone calls of questions, desperation, or triumph. There always seemed to be a subtle hint, or a penetrating question, or a gentle laugh which told me that I was all right, that I had done well or done poorly, and that my task was to learn from all that I had done.

Then there were the times I lived in Lincoln in the big white house on the corner with the barn in back. There were the days we would get up and make breakfast, talk about Alexander or discuss some point from his work, clean up the dishes, go into the library and talk some more until lunch, make lunch and eat it, and clean up, and return to the library to continue the argument until dinner was prepared and eaten and washed up after and put away, only to retire to a cozy fire in the library to talk some more. And there were all of those other days when business would prevent us from making a day of this kind of pursuit and it only seemed like we talked forever. And there were the nights that I took one or more of Alexander's books to bed with me, sure that one of us was wrong, only to find that it was me.

I read. I thought. I persevered

---

1. And in the beginning there were a number of times when Marjorie said, no, I wasn't ready to do a certain project or go up to the next level of challenge.

And because I did all of these things, I began to change. Not so that anyone noticed. Except subtly perhaps.

And I learned. And I grew.

I didn't know what the Alexander Technique was, but I was starting to get some ideas.

These ideas began to come into my teaching.

If good teaching relied on a keen eye, soft, knowledgeable hands, and easy social skills alone, then I was in big trouble.

If somehow I could learn to incorporate what I did well into the process of teaching, if my reading, thinking, and perseverance had something to do with this work, then maybe I could give my students something of enough value while these other skills had time to develop.

I often feel that I should apologize to those first few thousand people I worked with, or at least pay them something, because they were the ones who helped me learn how to teach. But, when I remember that a number of them are still active in this work, and that some of them have become excellent teachers in their own right, and that all of my students got some information and experience which was of value to them along with a smile, I decide that it was okay that I wasn't a perfect teacher when I started.[1]

Just like I'm not a perfect teacher now.

You see, I don't know what the Alexander Technique is.

I only know what I've concluded from my practice, experience, learning, reflection, experimentation, and efforts. That's all anyone's conception can be and all that everyone else's understanding is as well. Just like I taught my first students what I know and what I do and what makes sense to me, everyone else teaches what they know and what they do and what makes sense to them.

None of us know what the Alexander Technique is. We only know what the Alexander Technique is to each and every one of us.

If this work was about natural aptitude, I would have been out of luck. If this work was about kinesthetic awareness or good hands, after twenty years of lessons and practice, I might be able to sneak by. If this work was about being able to reproduce what was being done in class quietly, efficiently and just like the teacher, I might as well have given up before I started. Everything I needed to know about not conforming, about not going along to get along, and about not submitting to authority on its own whim and for its own sake, I learned in kindergarten.

But, if this work was about the ideas that Alexander discovered and the procedures that he designed and the disciplined experimentation that he encouraged, I had a chance. But where was I to find verification for this belief?

There were so many different teachers and so many different answers. The answers conflicted with and opposed each other so much, it was clear that they couldn't all be right. And if they couldn't all be right, which

---

1. One of the things that made me and a lot of my colleagues feel better when we were getting ready to graduate from Chiropractic school was to be reminded that a doctor doesn't graduate and go into perfect. A doctor graduates and goes into practice.

ones were right and which ones weren't and how could you tell and what is the Alexander Technique anyway? If Alexander was the source for all of this, how did he answer questions about what the work is?

Every source I have ever read, researched, asked, or consulted about how Alexander answered questions about the work has given me the same answer. Whenever Alexander was asked questions about the work, he told his students to read his books.

This recommendation on his part has been characterized as everything from a labor saving device to a Machiavellian avoidance of discussions. Still, the fact remains that when Alexander was asked questions about the work, he told his students to read his books. He told them that all of the answers to all of their questions could be found there. What if his recommendation to read his books as an answer to questions about the technique was simply good advice and not the kind of crafty or lazy evasion it is often characterized as being?

It was obvious that I would never have the experience of working with F. M., but this was okay, because working with F. M. would have only been just a different kind of practical experience. But, even though I could never work with F. M., I had equal opportunity and access to the answers about the work which he gave to his students: I could always read his books.

I believe that Alexander told his students to read his books because he knew that the answers to their questions were there.

If the answer to the question "What is the Alexander Technique?" can be found in Alexander's books as I believe it can, I still don't know what the Alexander Technique is because I don't have sufficient command of all of the books as yet. I know that some of you in reading this book or taking my classes would be kind enough to dispute this claim, but I know how much is left undone. While I believe I have an excellent command of the nearly two hundred pages of the Alexander Technique literature which I have brought up to the levels of my standards, and while I believe that an argument could be made for the relative value of these two hundred pages, the majority of Alexander's writings remains unowned by me.

I will never forget how devastating it was to my belief structure in this work to find the sentence that contained "all my efforts up till now to improve the use of myself in reciting had been misdirected." [1] Once I found this sentence and began to apply it in a meaningful way to my understanding of Alexander's narrative, everything about my understanding of Alexander's work changed.

There is no way for me to know whether or not another sentence as important and as devastating as that one was isn't lurking out there in the tall grass waiting to prove all of my efforts wrong. It may be. I don't know. I'm not sure.

---

1. p. 149 (p. 19)

The only thing I can guarantee, however, is that I will not fence off my present understanding into some kind of gamey preserve of "what I believe" in the hope that no one else will find the smoking gun of an undiscovered conceptual heffalump. I will be out there in the bushes looking for the one sentence or phrase which will demonstrate my own misdirection, so that I can enjoy at least as much success as Alexander did when he proved himself wrong so many times.

I don't know what the Alexander Technique is.

No one does.

But, I do know where to look for it. I am going to look for it in the very place Alexander told me to look: in his books.

When I look in his books and when I match what I've learned with what I've done and what I've thought and what I've seen and what I've believed and what I've had proven wrong, I will come up with an answer to the question, "What is the Alexander Technique?"

In my books and in my classes, I will keep putting forth the best answer I have to that question at any given moment. I will keep saying what I believe is true as clearly and as loudly as I can. Not because I think I am "right" or that my answer is the only way. I will keep putting forward what I think as loudly and as clearly as I can because, by my being as clear and honest as I can about all that I have learned and thought, you, as my colleague, will have the best chance to learn from me and to teach me all that you can.

I don't know what the Alexander Technique is.

No one does, but it doesn't matter.

I still have a lot more information about who we are and how we work than my students, and they can benefit greatly from all that I can share with them.

I don't have to have all of the answers. I don't even have to be right as long as my procedures are genuine and authentic to Alexander's work, and as long as I keep pursuing his process of investigation, and as long as I don't allow myself to settle for any quick or final answer. Like Alexander, I must be "willing to 'accept amendments' or even to alter one or another of [my] premises if new evidence should cause me] to do so." [1]

All any of us as teachers and students will ever have is our best understanding at any given time. If we could all just learn to accept our ignorance and celebrate each other's efforts and ideas, we would spend less time squabbling among one another, and more time learning what we all have to share.

1. Jones, Frank Pierce, Body Awareness in Action, Schocken Books, New York, 1976, p. 28

CHAPTER 16

GENUINE TRUST

When I look at what Alexander said in his books, I am most impressed with what he said about the importance of relying on one's reasoning as a source of guidance rather than on one's feeling sense interpretation. The "mysteries" surrounding this issue must make up over half of the questions I am asked in teaching. In watching people's reactions while I answer these questions, I have begun to notice certain common, horrified responses.

People are so accustomed to being "guided by feelings" and then judging the results immediately upon the completion of a given act (or sooner) as a further addendum to their guidance protocols that they become quite uncomfortable with the suggestion that they stop, slow down, and see what they are really doing.

After much beating and sufficient practical demonstration, they will eventually put aside their Feeling Guidance Mode and try to "think" a little. After telling them repeatedly that using their feeling sense interpretation to judge their actions only reinitiates their habitual misdirection (a point which is greatly reinforced by their continued lack of success in making the changes they desire), students will begin to consider eliminating this final loophole in their means of directive guidance.

But, what finally, really makes students begin to shake, hold up crucifixes in front of me, and run screaming from the room, however, is when I ask them to take the final step. Almost none of my students are willing to stop judging the success of their performances as a way of deciding whether or not to change their directive guidance procedures, and even fewer are willing to rely completely on their reasoning processes to bring them safely to their ends.

When Alexander admits that he had failed to realize all of the implications of not trusting to his feeling sense, he begins a section of his story whose importance cannot be overemphasized.

Because of its long term familiarity, and because of how well it matched his "zero points" for a given activity, the sensory experience associated with his old use would not only FEEL RIGHT to Alexander when he moved in a familiar way, but performing the act in this way would be judged by him, as BEING RIGHT.

The sensory experience associated with his new use would be generated by different actions, thereby exciting different static position recognition sensors. As a result, performing actions with his new use would necessarily send back different feeling sense data to his central nervous system. This would enhance the probability that performing a given act in this new way would feel different from performing it in the customary way.[1]

Because the act would "feel" different when performed in this new way, and because the judgment of "feeling" associated with performing the act in the old way was that the old way WAS RIGHT, performing the act in this new way can only be judged as BEING WRONG.

It is not simply enough to recognize that the movement performed in this way would FEEL wrong. Feeling in these cases is only the means to the reaching of a moral decision. We leap from the "feeling right"-ness of an action to the conclusion that we ourselves ARE RIGHT.

Because our new manner of movement is being judged against the zero points of previous performances, and because we have invested our relative scale of feeling sense interpretation with a tremendous moral value, any new movement which does not match up with the feeling sense of previous performances not only FEELS wrong, but is judged to BE WRONG.

When Alexander looked further, he saw that for months he had been trying to employ his new use while at the same time relying upon his old misdirection and manner of use to judge his success.

In the process of using his old misdirection to judge the quality and nature of his performance, he reinitiated a reliance upon his old misdirection as his source of directive guidance. When he tried to project his new manner of directive guidance in an effort to overcome the dominance of his old mariner, he put his old manner of directive guidance in charge of the process of judging his success. When he gave to his old misdirection the power to decide which commands would be implemented, he was actually reinitiating his old misdirection as a means of deciding which manner of direction, the new or the old, would be initiated!

I understand the "English" penchant for understatement, but to describe the nature of this circumstance as a "small wonder" that the attempt proved futile does not even begin to cover the dimensions of this disastrous arrangement.

Alexander was using his old misdirection and manner of use to judge his success in carrying out the directions required for his new use. By relying on the old misdirection to judge his immediate successes, he brought his old manner of misdirection into play. Of course he failed more often than not in changing the manner of his use!

---

1. It is important to note that this is only a probability. I have taught a large number of introductory lessons in which the change in appearance and manner of movement in an individual has been dramatic enough to elicit gasps of surprise and amazement from the other students in the class only to have the individual having the lesson report that he felt about the same. In these cases, the students who are having the lesson notice very few, if any, differences as a result of my manipulations, even though the changes were dramatic enough to evoke responses from the rest of the class.

Consider for a moment the strength of the ruling conceptual monarchy in an individual who can undergo transformational experiences which go undetected by his feeling sense interpretation.

By bringing into operation the very thing he was trying to prevent from operating, he was guaranteeing the enduring success of his continual failure.

It was at this point that Alexander took the step which sounds the death knell for any consideration of kinesthetic reeducation. It was at this juncture that Alexander points out the need to rely on his reasoning as a source and means of guidance as well as the folly of pouring investments of time and energy into the pursuit of an increasingly trustworthy sensory appreciation.

> If I ever was to succeed in making the changes in use I desired, I must subject the processes directing my new use to a new experience, the experience, that is, *of being dominated by reasoning instead of by feeling.*[1]

What would be the purpose of developing an increasingly reliable sensory appreciation if, in order to do this work, you are not going to use it?

Alexander said we must be "Dominated by reasoning instead of by feeling." The issue here is not one of reliability. It is a matter of choosing what you will use to guide the processes directing your use: (left hand) Reasoning or (right hand) Feeling. Alexander makes the answer so clear we don't even have to Score this Decision. All we have to do is read!

> If I was ever to succeed in making the changes in use I desired, I must subject the processes directing my use to a new experience, the experience, that is, of being dominated by reasoning instead of by feeling.

The correct answer according to Alexander is (left hand) Reasoning!

The quality of the appreciation of feeling is not the issue, because feeling is not going to be used.

It won't be used for guidance.

It won't be used for judgment.

It won't be used at all.

As for the wisdom of putting your efforts into retraining your feelings, between (left hand) Genius and (right hand) Idiot, how would you Score someone who put all of his efforts into perfecting a tool he will never profitably use?

And, someone who is doing anything special or extra to retrain his feeling sense appreciation is making an even worse choice in how to spend his time and energy than the previous question implies, because, by carrying out Alexander's actual procedures, you can't help but increase the trustworthiness of your feelings.

It's unavoidable.

---

1. p. 158 (p. 32) My italics.

Some people direct all of their efforts to improve the trustworthiness of their feeling sense as a guide in spite of the fact that Alexander says we must no longer rely on our feelings in this way. Moreover, if these same people would simply follow the procedures which Alexander advocates, they would be unable to avoid the satisfaction of retraining their feelings anyway.

Remember, refinement is not really the same thing as change. There is a difference between genuine change and refinement. Making your feeling sense more trustworthy would only be an attempt at refining an already existing manner of direction. As such, it is just an attempt to get better without having to change, and Alexander says that we must make a fundamental change in the way we direct ourselves if we are to succeed.

Between Genius and Idiot, how would you Score someone who spent all of his time trying to acquire a certain capacity which cannot achieve his goals, when, by investing his time more wisely in a different procedure, he could not avoid reaching his goals and, as a by-product, could not avoid acquiring more of the previously desired improvement in his faulty sensory appreciation than his initial efforts could achieve?

When I think of people like this who dedicatedly throw themselves into a project which logically carries the seeds of its own destruction, I am reminded of a fellow I once met at school.

One day at the University of Cincinnati, I was sitting with my friend Richard in the commuter lounge trying to prepare for a test. One of the local pests, one of those people whose reasoning goes something like, "I don't want to study, so why should you have to?", came up to us and began talking. After many subtle hints and a few direct requests for him to leave, it became clear that a more powerful tool was required to pry him loose from our company. So I turned to him and said, "Don't you realize that we have to study now because there isn't enough time to study now even if we did study now?"

While he was trying to pick his way through that question, Richard, who was somewhat of a whiz at math picked up the dissertation without losing a beat. "You see, if we start with the simple fact that there are only 168 hours in a week..." he began, and the chase was on.

For the next hour or so, we "proved" to our unwanted guest that when all of the aspects of living were assigned time values and added together, one would need over 180 hours each week just to live, sleep, eat, etc. Because of this, an intelligent person would quickly see that to then add study time onto this excessive figure would make the time requirements of living even more impossible.

Consequently, there wasn't enough time to study and to live so that was why we had to study now because there wasn't enough time anyway. In fact, there wasn't any time at all. Because there wasn't any time at all, time didn't exist. Consequently, because time didn't exist, it wasn't possible to study at all because there wasn't any time at all to study.

We watched his eyes continue to widen as he took in more and more of the "truths" we were sharing with him. When we had finished, he just sat there in silence and we began to be concerned that we had gone too far and he would be angry at us for teasing him. But, as he sat there, a little flicker began to glow in the back of his eyes. As he chewed on what we had said, you could see this glow growing into a purpose, and the purpose into a mission.

"Thanks, guys" he said, "I never understood any of this before. Somebody's got to tell the others."

While we weren't sure just who the "others" were, we told him that, because we had to study, we didn't have time to tell them, but that we thought that he would be the perfect messenger.

"Do you really think I could do it?" he asked

"Sure, with a little training," was our reply. So, for the next half hour, we "trained" him in how to give our presentation and he left.

Richard and I figured that there really wasn't any harm done. We had needed a study break. We had had some creative fun. We had gotten rid of a study impediment who wouldn't take "please leave" for an answer. And we figured that our friend would surely wise up or be wised up by the first person to whom he showed our presentation.

But, for the next several weeks. he could be seen constantly, all over the student union, "proving" to people that there wasn't enough time to study. When the next grades came out, he didn't do too well. Instead of serving as a warning that he should reconsider wasting what little time there was and get back to work on his books, his poor performance only served to reinforce his conviction that his mission was justified.

We had thought that the first person who heard this presentation would laugh so hard and so loud that our timeless friend would wake up and understand that it was all a little joke. Apparently, though, no one laughed. In fact, whenever he made a presentation, his audience sat spellbound and intrigued.

I don't know what became of our friend.

After a while, both Richard and I began to notice that we didn't see him around any more. I suppose we were concerned that we had caused him more harm than we intended when his crusade got out of hand, but, as freshmen in college I think we were more concerned about the laughs that we got and the fascination that we experienced at how long our little "experiment" continued. Besides, every time either one of us had run into him, he had always come up and thanked us again for showing him the truth and changing his life. He certainly seemed to be happier whenever we saw him after our little talk.

While his constant gratitude in the face of what appeared to be a major interruption of his college career made me feel guilty at times in later years, I have always preferred to believe that this fellow eventually went into sales. With the practice and the skills he had developed in putting across the load of manure we had given him for a "presentation", I have always believed that, as a salesman, he would have enjoyed great success in his life regardless of the company or the product.

Alexander decided that he must dominate his process of directing his use by reasoning. He decided that he must stop using his feelings, trustworthy and otherwise, as a source of guidance or as a means of judging his performance in the moment, because either procedure would initiate his old habitual patterns of directive guidance and misdirection.

This meant that I must be prepared to carry on with any procedure I had reasoned out as best for my purpose, even though that procedure might feel wrong.[1]

Because the carrying out of the procedure would FEEL WRONG and because Alexander, like all of us, assigned a moral value with regard to his identity based on his feelings, then, FEELING WRONG in the carrying out of a procedure under a new manner of directive guidance would mean that he WAS WRONG in doing the procedure in that way.

If Alexander was ever to be successful in changing his manner of use in activity, then he must put aside all of his judgments based on feeling, and stay with the procedures he had reasoned out as being best for his purpose even when his feelings were screaming out that he WAS WRONG. Even when his feelings were confusing him with sensations of pain or of cramping or of being pulled out of shape or of being overly lengthened or of pleasure or of ease or of lightness, he must stay with the procedures he had reasoned out as being best for his purpose.

In order to change, Alexander decided that he must stay with the procedures he had reasoned out as being best for his purpose even when his feelings were screaming out that if he continued in this new and different manner that he would die.

This sense of mortal danger is the aspect of the concept of Survival Value that is the hardest to see and understand.

When we have performed an activity in a given way and afterwards we are alive, then we assign a Survival Value to that particular way of doing that activity. The Survival Value that gets assigned to any particular way of performing an activity is that we are alive BECAUSE we did the activity in that particular way. If we ever try to perform that activity in any other way, we experience that change as a way of tempting fate and increasing the chances that we may die.

In this light, the choice about whether to change or not becomes clear.

If we perform the activity the old way, we know we will live. If we change and try to perform the activity in a new and different way, we might die. The familiar way of performing an activity is a known and proven quantity. We have always done things that way and we are still alive. The new manner of performing the activity is untried, and, if we do it that way, we may die. The old way meant life. The new way might mean that we will die. While there is no way to be certain that we will die by

---

1. p. 158 (p. 32)

performing an activity in a new way, there is no way to be certain that we won't.

Why take chances?

This is the chain of reasoning that we all go through on some basic level as we first approach changing the manner in which we direct ourselves in activity. Many will think I have exaggerated my claims or overstated my contention. "Surely," they might argue, "our persistence in our familiar means of direction and guidance is not so fixed as that." But, before you dismiss my claim too quickly, I would like to ask you about some observations I have made.

Have you ever tried to get a child to change the way he or she does something? No matter how often the child fails, there is almost no way to get that child to give up a familiar procedure even if the child knows that that procedure has failed before.

No matter how often students claim in class that they are going to do their "thinking" and not start getting out of a chair by pulling their heads back as they have always done before, you could probably throw away your nut cracker if you would just place a walnut on the back of a student's neck as he begins to stand.

When you watch a friend who stumbles from one bad relationship to another, who promises to reform, and who is back in the bars on Saturday night, you begin to get a sense of the power of what Alexander called the "lure of the familiar." [1]

How can you account for this die-hard persistence in the face of failure and the certain knowledge that the cause of the failure lay within each person and only needed a redirected effort to change?

What if the power which fueled the persistence of these people came from a concern that if they tried to do things in a new and different way, they might die? What if their persistence in the carrying out of strategies and behaviors which guaranteed failure came from a belief that, although they might continue to fail by continuing with their old ways of doing things, at least they weren't dead? As a clinician, a counselor, and a friend, I cannot tell you how many times I have heard someone tell me that, "Things may be bad at home, but at least I'm still alive."

The consequences of changing any particular procedure may seem trivial to an outside observer, but the threat to the feeling sense interpretation of the person involved and to the sense of self generated by that interpretive continuum all too often becomes a matter of life and death to the person involved.

I once worked with plumber named Ray in Pennsylvania. He was standing and ready to walk. I was standing behind him, and using my hands to guide the relationship of his head to his body as he began to walk. Everything went well until he began to lower his leg to take a step.

As he lowered his leg, Ray began to shriek screechingly, as if he were in great and mortal pain. He stopped lowering his leg, raised his knee once more, and placed his foot down, next to his other foot, as it had

---

1. Maisel, Edward ed., The Resurrection of the Body, Shambala Publications, Boston & London, 1986, p. 11.

been before. When I asked him why he had screamed, he didn't know what I was talking about. He didn't even know he had screamed.

When he started to walk again, he screamed once more as he lowered his leg, he picked it back up, and he placed it quietly next to his other foot once more.

Every time he tried to lower his leg to take a step, he screamed. Every time he returned his foot to its starting position, he was quiet. Every time I asked him why he had screamed, he didn't know or remember that he had screamed.

Although we worked together on taking that first step for more than a dozen attempts, he was never able to put his foot down anywhere but the place where it had started without screaming. When he tried to take a step, he screamed every time. Because of the overwhelming nature of the feeling sense experience and its implications to everything he believed, he was never able to overcome the "horror" of this different way of stepping. For the whole class, he was never able to complete his first step.

Ray's scream and his inability to take a step while being guided happened no matter with which foot he started. He was always able to walk without incident if he wasn't guided. But, if I helped him, he would scream.

If you had just heard the scream alone, outside of the context of a class, you would have been convinced that the screamer was in fear of his life. And he was!

Ray had "always" walked in the way that was familiar to him and he was still alive. With the use of my voice and my hands, I was asking him to walk in a new and different way. By asking him to walk in a new and different way, I was creating a threat to the very foundation of his existence.

No wonder he screamed!

I am only surprised that more students don't.

By doing familiar or even untried activities in familiar and approved ways, we guarantee that we will still be alive when we are finished.

By trying something new, we relinquish our sense of control, and we feel like anything can happen. The way we do things and the values and beliefs which underlie and create those processes are as much a part of us as the color of our hair. If we were to change some part of the way that we did things, we would change some part of who we were. This creates a concern that we will die as a result of this change. This concern, that, by changing our manner of doing things, we might die, and the anxiety that this concern produces in us, creates the major obstacle to change in all of us.

Since I am into alleviating undo concern wherever possible, let me do all I can to eliminate the concern that, by changing your manner of direction of yourself in activities, you might die. Let me eliminate this concern by telling you that if you do change the manner of your direction of your use and the way in which you perform activities, you will die.

You must.

Oh, I know that someday your body will expire and your friends will mourn and your remains will be disposed of in the manner of your choice. I don't mean anything so trivial as that.

Of course, we will all die. That's not important.

What is important is that we generalize the fear of this final bodily death we will all experience, and impose it on our experiences, real and anticipated, of the little "deaths" required when we change.

It is the power of this imposed fear which often daunts us when we dare to change.

The way in which we do things is a product of the way in which we direct ourselves. The way in which we direct ourselves is a product of who we are and what we have experienced and what we believe to be true. In a sense, this composite of experience and belief is the "you" that we all are.

There is no way to change what we have experienced. All that we have experienced is in the past and it will always remain in the past. But, there are many ways to change our beliefs.

It has been demonstrated in many places, at many times, and in many ways with very many people, that all that is required to change a person is to change their values and beliefs. All that is required to change a person is to change the ideas that form their thinking and guide their manner of directing themselves. Change the values and beliefs that people hold, get them to live their lives "AS IF" these new values were true, and, in time, even the circumstances surrounding their existence will begin to conform to these new ideas.

Every success story which you will ever read, see, or hear about begins with a dream or a desire, a commitment to the belief that this dream is already real, and a dedicated life which carries out the actions consistent with the belief that the dream is already real. This belief, in turn, makes the dream happen.

This is a formula for success which is unchanging and without flaw. Everyone who follows it will realize their dreams without fail. But, if the realization of our dreams makes a new person of us all, what has happened to the people we all used to be before the success of our realized dreams?

All of those people are "dead."

If part of what makes us "us" is what we believe and how we do things, then we must change at least some of these beliefs or manners of performance if we are to change at all. By changing these beliefs and manners of performance, we cease to be as we were before. In a sense, even by changing something as simple as the way we do things, the "we" we were before is "dead."

But, in its place is someone new, someone that we will assess and change once more if this new someone isn't to our liking.

And every time we change, the "we" we were will "die" once more.

If we insist on retaining everything about ourselves as we were before, we will never change. If we insist on not allowing any part of our old selves to "die," we will never change. But, if we are ever to improve, if we are ever to reach our dreams, we must change. And, if we change even one aspect of who we were, then who we were before the change, the sum total of ourselves as presently expressed, will always cease to exist.

In other words, to change, "we" all must "die."[1]

Alexander killed off a piece of himself.

By changing from a reliance on feelings as a guide or a judge to a reliance on the procedures he had reasoned out as best for his purpose, he put an end to the person he used to be.

To succeed, he had to carry on with his reasoned procedures even though the procedures felt wrong. To succeed, he had to carry on with his reasoned procedures even though the wrong feeling that these new procedures produced would make him believe he WAS WRONG. To succeed, he had to carry on with his reasoned procedure even when changing his procedures made him feel, quite correctly, that the person he had been would die.

His reliance had shifted from his feelings and his sense of being right to a reliance on the use of his conscious mind to see and project what each activity required. His reliance had shifted from his feelings and his sense of being right to a reliance on the use of his conscious mind to plan an appropriate strategy for the successful realization of his desires. His reliance had shifted from his feelings and his sense of being right to a reliance on the use of his conscious mind to send out the commands necessary for the implementation of his new strategies.

To realize this reliance upon his reasoning took more than the desire to carry out his new directions. To realize this reliance upon the procedures he had reasoned out as best for his purpose required a commitment. It required a trust.

In other words, my trust in my reasoning processes to bring me safely to my "end" must be a genuine trust, not a half-trust needing the assurance of feeling right as well.[2]

This genuine trust in his reasoning processes to bring him safely to his end is the final piece in the puzzle of constructive change. Without this trust and the complete abandonment of feeling for either judgment or guidance that this trust implies, no one can truly raise his mastery of Alexander's work onto the level of conscious guidance and control.

---

1. To many, the prospect of the "little deaths" of our present selves seems too scary to contemplate. The fact remains, however, that for those of us who wish to change, there is at least some aspect of our present "selves" we wished did not exist. As we begin to change and we begin to reap the benefits of our new "lives", we begin to see in a practical way the difference between change within ourselves and the cessation of all life.

2. p. 158 (p. 32-33)

Without the domination of reasoning and the abandonment of feeling as a guide, one would be doomed to a spiraling maze in which one enjoyed increasingly sophisticated forms of better posture, better movement, better performance, greater lightness, more trustworthy sensory appreciation, deeper resonance, clearer thought, more successful teaching and teacher training, etc. without having to change.

Genuine trust is the final key to learning the Alexander Technique, but, it is a key without which the baubles collected along the way cannot be transmuted into the treasures that they truly are.

Students are always trying to catch me in a fault.

Time does not permit a listing of all of the different ways in which they have tried. The fact that they rarely succeed[1] does not disturb them as much as my reaction when they do.

While I might have a number of different reactions - surprise, disbelief, laughter, etc. - my dominant reaction is one of delight. I have worked so hard and so long on this material that any further clue or insight into its meaning is welcome.

"But, doesn't it bother you that you were wrong?" my students persist.

Not really. I've been wrong before. I will be wrong again.

Oh, sure, sometimes I'm embarrassed to find out that I could still act as though I were that stupid, but I'm not surprised anymore.

Years ago, I was at an audition for the Ringling Brother's Clown College. We were all seated around the center ring and, as part of the procedure, a group of clowns were doing some skits. It was a pleasure to be this close to the clowns as they worked because for the first time I realized that the scripts they used had dialogue and that the dialogue was, in many ways, funnier than the actions.

At one point, one of the clowns gave a cue for the next part of the script. The other clown apparently confused the cue in this script for a similar cue in a second script. The first clown gave the cue from script A and the second clown responded with the answer from script B, an answer which made it impossible for script A to continue. The first clown then repeated the cue from script A and the second clown repeated the answer from script B. Then the first clown forcefully repeated the cue from script A once more only to be answered with an equally adamant reply from script B.

This exchange continued for several repetitions and with several variations until finally it dawned upon the second clown that she was in the wrong script. In response to the first clown's next cue from script A, she said, "Faux pas," then gave the correct verbal response and script A continued onward as if there had been no interruption.

---

1. Their low rate of success is not because I am always right. I am not always right. The usual reason why I am able to answer their objections is because I have already answered many of the same objections before.

I have always admired the second clown's response. She was wrong. She realized it. She acknowledged it and went on.

She didn't make a big deal out of it. She didn't apologize profusely. She didn't tear her clothes and beg forgiveness. She didn't feel she was less of a person. She just acknowledged her fault and went on.

The fact that she had made a mistake wasn't important.

The fact that she went on was.

There is nothing wrong with being wrong.

We are all wrong sometimes, just as we are all right at other times.

We all make mistakes. We all make good decisions. We all do well. We all do poorly.

Most of the time our errors have little consequence and, even when there are consequences, it is only rarely that they are unresolvable. But, too often, too many of us treat every little mistake as a catastrophe.

I know this feeling of disaster comes about because making a mistake places us in conflict with our past experiences and beliefs. I also believe that it challenges us with regard to the manner of our performance and puts at risk our perceived need for being right. But, even if we are challenged to the core, there is no way that imperfect creatures such as we are can avoid being wrong at times.

But, that's okay.

There is nothing wrong with being wrong, just as there is nothing wrong with failing.

While it is true that the only way you can fail is if you try; if you do not try, you cannot succeed. The importance in life does not lie in failure or success. All of us will enjoy both throughout our lives. The importance in life lies in having an idea of what we want to do and be, and performing the processes necessary to make these dreams come true.

If we are satisfied with ourselves and our lives, then there really is no need for us to change. The vast majority of people I encounter fit into this category. Yes, if you question them, they will tell you that they might want a bigger TV or a longer vacation or their backs to hurt a little less after gardening. But, if you show them what they would need to do to reach these goals, and ask them if they are ready to get started, much more often than not they will tell you that they would just as soon let it go.

For the rest of us, we believe that as good as our lives have become, there may be something more. As much as we have achieved, there may be more for us to do. As much as we have matured and grown as individuals, there may be a better person yet to come. For us, the acquisition of new knowledge and new ways to improve becomes a joy that surpasses the cost of the acquisition. For us, the potential of learning how to change in constructive and valuable ways is worth the price in time, money, and discipline required. For us, the value of picking up new tools and ideas which will help us reach our goals is worth the heartache and momentary insecurity of putting down what we have believed and held dear.

But, it is not easy. It will take time. It will take effort. It will take discipline. It will take trust.

It will take the kind of genuine trust about which Alexander speaks. The kind of genuine trust to put aside your "stuff" - the things which you believe or feel are true - long enough to put into action the procedures you have reasoned out as best for your purpose.

"But, how will I know I am doing it right?" my students plead.

By measuring your performance against the concepts of your intent long after the action has been performed.

You will make judgments about your degree of success. You will make judgments about how well you carried out your plan. You will make judgments about how appropriate your plan was to your goals.

But, judgments do not have to be judgmental.

Neither do they have to occur NOW.

"But, how will I know I am doing it right?"

You won't. You can't.

I'm not sure there even is a right way to do this work.

I do know that there are a number of discoveries that Alexander made, and a number of procedures that he devised, and a number of skills that he acquired through the implementation of those procedures. I also know that if I will simply do the same things that Alexander did, follow the same procedures, acquire the same skills, "do what he did," I cannot help but acquire at least the same degree of conscious guidance and control which he enjoyed.

"But, how will I know I am doing it right?"

It's not as important to be right as it is to be consistent and persevere.

In beginning classes, we talk about how "thinking" leads to movement and movement leads to change.[1] We talk about how people are always in a hurry to take some new impression or feeling or understanding back into the commands that they are using to direct themselves rather than staying with the ordered directions they have reasoned out as best for their purpose.

There are certain things you will train yourself to "think" as you go into an activity. If the activity is successful, you will "think" these same things again as you go into another attempt.[2] If the activity you have performed is unsuccessful, YOU MUST "think" THESE SAME THINGS AGAIN.

Over the years, student's names have been attached to the various titles assigned to the principles we talk about in class as a reward for meritorious valor, insight, or service. Since I assign the titles, my name is attached to one of the most important of the laws, one which is tricky to understand but well worth the effort.

---

1. See the Box Chart for Beginners in Appendix B.
2. If you go into a different activity, there are certain parts of these commands, the Intrinsic Directions, which you will leave unchanged making only as few changes in the Extrinsic Directions as is necessary or desired.

Dr. Don's Law says that results are no criteria for success.

The easiest level of this law to understand, and the most appropriate aspect of it as it relates to our present discussion, is summed up in the sports cliche: "It's not whether you win or lose, but how you play the game." Someone whose attitude towards success reflects that of Vince Lombardi[1] will not be comfortable with this concept

Neither will they learn Alexander's work. They will be so busy trying to win that they will be unable to see the causal relationship of their manner of performance to their probability of success.

Yes, the Green Bay Packers were the dominant football team for an era. Yes, their passion for success did reflect their coach's, but the way in which they achieved success had more to do with the strategies and procedures written about by one of the team's players named Jerry Kramer.

Jerry Kramer was acknowledged at the time as the best offensive lineman to play the game of football. For years his form and techniques of blocking were taught as the standard. Towards the end of his career he wrote a series of articles which described his procedures. The article which caught my attention was the first one in which he described how to take the proper stance before a play begins.

Kramer said that after all those years of success as a high school player, and after all those years of success as a college player, and after all of those years of success as a professional player, the hardest thing he had to do every fall was to relearn how to get into his three-point stance, the starting position he assumed at the beginning of every offensive play. For the first three or four weeks of preseason practice, he would spend hours each day turning around, trotting seven yards, and getting down into his three-point stance. Once he felt comfortable in his stance, he would stand up, turn around, trot seven yards, and get down into his stance again.

The three-point stance, so named for putting one hand on the ground while bending over, was the basic position from which all of his other techniques followed. Until he had reacquired the skill of getting down into this stance quickly, easily, consistently, and with comfort, he had no foundation upon which to rebuild the rest of his techniques. Once he could relearn how to get back into this stance, he would add in each next part of the process, one step at a time, until he had reacquired a comfortable proficiency in all of his superlative skills.[2]

There are certain things you will train yourself to "think" as you go into activity. If the activity is successful, you will "think" these same

---

1.   Lombardi was the head football coach of the Green Bay Packers, one of the most successful franchises in the history of professional sports. Lombardi was once quoted as saying, "Winning isn't everything - it's the only thing!"
In his defense, Lombardi also said, "We never lost a game. We just ran out of time."

2.   When I tell this story to students they seem surprised that a Hall of Fame player would have to take this long and work this hard each year just to learn how to stand. I point out to them that it was partly because he took this long as he followed these constructive procedures that he became a Hall of Famer. I tell them to remember that amateurs use practice sessions to focus in on those things they already do well. Champions always spend the time practicing the things they do the worst, particularly those techniques which are fundamental to the building of other skills.

things again as you go into another attempt If the activity you have performed is unsuccessful, YOU MUST "think" THESE SAME THINGS
AGAIN.

The reason why your immediate judgment of your success is relatively
unimportant is that your degree of immediate success is irrelevant to the
process of discipline you will continue to perform. No matter what your
degree of success, there are certain things you will train yourself to
"think" as you go into activity. If the activity is successful, you will "think"
these same things again as you go into another attempt. If the activity you
perform is unsuccessful, YOU MUST "think" THESE SAME THINGS
AGAIN because it is the only constructive process to follow in the training of your manner of thinking in this work.

Yes, I know that there is a process of judgment which can be applied
to the assessment of the procedures you are to follow. There are times
when you may want to experiment with the way you are doing these procedures or even the procedures themselves. Whenever you find yourself
wanting to set aside the procedures we have talked about in favor of some
"new and improved" way of doing this work, however, I ask that you keep
three things in mind before you make any change.

First of all, Alexander was a brilliant and insightful genius.

He had to perform experiments which lasted for days and weeks and
sometimes even months without changing his procedures. Perhaps trying
something for a few times in class without success is not a sufficient
amount of practice or time spent for us non-geniuses to acquire these
same skills. Therefore, immediate lack of success is an insufficient reason
to change your procedures or give up.

Second, Alexander applied the Principle of Unavoidability to all of the
changes in procedure that he made. He only changed his processes when
the results of exhaustive, long-term experimentation and the reasoning
applied to the findings of those experiments made change unavoidable.[1]

Most importantly, we don't have to worry, guess, or wonder if the
processes Alexander outlined work or not.

They do.

We don't have to re-invent or improve the work. These procedures
will work just fine without our help.

When my colleagues ask me what I think about their new discoveries
or the way somebody or other is teaching the work now, I tell them that
as soon as I have mastered everything that Alexander showed us, I will
look into the improvements. When they ask me about the best ways to
project the directions or the best design to use for the creation of the
most efficient condition of mechanical advantage possible, I tell them
that as soon as I have learned to eliminate all of the interferences I am
creating in myself in my manner of thinking and movement, I will worry
about how to create something more efficient.

All we have to do to gain the advantages Mr. Alexander enjoyed is
acquire the same skills that he had in the way that he acquired them, and
apply these same processes in all of our activities in the way that he

applied them. If we do all of this, we will not be able to avoid acquiring a level of conscious guidance and control at least as good as Alexander's.

There are certain things you will train yourself to "think" as you go into activity. If the activity is successful, you will "think" these same things again as you go into another attempt. If the activity you have performed is unsuccessful, YOU MUST "think" THESE SAME THINGS AGAIN.

Just as it is a poor trust which requires the assurance of feeling right, it is an even poorer trust which requires immediate gratification or success.

In all the travels, work, and study that I have done, I have never found a tool or an idea as valuable as Mr. Alexander's work. In all of the disciplines I've explored and all of these years that I've searched, I have never found a better way for people to make constructive changes in themselves. Most importantly, in all of these years of experiments and investigation, I have never seen a counter-example to any of the claims of this work nor have I ever seen it fail to provide help or relief to anyone who has tried it on its own terms.

This is something which you may have to take in genuine trust from me, but I would rather that you try it for yourselves.

Just as I have made the invitation to you to join me in my search, there is an invitation for you to show me where I am wrong. I am delighted to find where I am wrong because it is through finding out about our mistakes that we will all learn.

I can't be hurt by having made mistakes. I have made them before. I will make them again. The worst I, or any of us, can be, at any given time, is wrong.[1]

The best I can be involves genuine trust.

First, I must have a genuine trust in what Alexander wrote and what my teachers have demonstrated throughout the years.

Second, I must have a genuine trust in myself that I will follow these procedures and do the work required to gain the skills I need to reach my dreams.

Third, I must have a genuine trust that the manner in which I perform my activities and the way in which I behave is at least as important as what I do.

But, most importantly, I must trust in subjecting the processes directing my use to the experience of being dominated by reasoning instead of by feeling. I must trust in any procedure which I have reasoned out as best for my purpose even when the procedure might feel wrong or make me feel that I am wrong when I use that procedure. I must trust in my reasoning processes to bring me safely to my dreams, no matter how trivial or grandiose they may be.

And this trust must be a genuine trust, not a half trust relying upon the assurance of feeling right or anything else.

---

1. If I have succeeded in my argument, this statement will take on more of the nature of a consolation than a threat.

CHAPTER 17

THE RULES OF THE GAME

Years ago, in Cincinnati's version of Coney Island, my quest for the rules of success by which we can all become the best of our dreams was begun. Because of a general phobia about the feelings associated with rapid acceleration, I was never a great fan of the rides at any amusement park. I liked being there, though, because I always enjoyed being around so many people who were having so much fun.

And there were the games.

I loved playing the games. I loved watching the games. I loved the challenge of tying to win even though the set up of the games made playing them a sucker's bet. I loved the challenge when I played. I loved the excitement when I won.

There was one game in particular which was my favorite.

It was called "Pokerino" and it consisted of a downward-sloping inclined ramp, five hollow, rubber balls, and a flat area at the end of the ramp in which twenty-five holes were drilled. Inside each hole was an electronic trigger which, when depressed by a ball passing through, would light up a specific light on the backboard corresponding to a particular card from a poker deck, e.g. Ace of Hearts, King of Clubs, etc.

The object of the game was to roll the five balls down the ramp and light up the cards on the backboard. After the balls had been rolled and the "cards" determined, you would make the best poker hand possible out of the result. Because dropping a ball through the same hole could only light up a card once, it was possible to have less than five cards in your "hand" even after you had rolled five balls. I remember being consistent enough to have only one card in my hand on many occasions.

Various numbers of coupons were awarded depending on the value of the poker hand made up of your lighted cards. Two Pairs was the lowest "hand" which won and yielded the smallest number of coupons and a Royal Flush (ten through ace in a single suit) was the highest winner with a payoff that seemed phenomenal. The coupons, in turn, could be redeemed for prizes like Teddy Bears and such.

I really didn't care about the prizes, but, because I knew about Poker and because I knew about rolling balls down a ramp, Pokerino was a game which I thought I could learn to play well.

At first when I played, it seemed like I didn't win enough.

Oh, sometimes something would go wrong and I'd win. Usually just enough to keep me playing until my money ran out. But, as time went on, I became aware that I hardly won at all.

Just about the time this knowledge was beginning to seep in, I started to pay more attention to the barker, the man who would call out to people as they went by, trying to entice them to play.

Here I was guarding my chances, hoarding my quarters, putting every bit of concentration I could muster into how I would play each ball in each game, and I hardly ever won. There he was calling out to passers-by, engaging their curiosity in conversation, rolling the balls casually down the ramp, almost not paying attention, and he always won.

I don't mean he often won. I don't mean he usually won. I mean he always won.

Because I went to the park so seldom in any summer, it took many years to establish any kind of a relationship with this man. After about five years, he started to remember me and we became friends of a sort.

And all this time, through all of the demonstrations and all of his barking, he always won.

During this same time, I got a little better. I was able to win a little more, but he always won.

I never saw him lose.

Finally my curiosity overcame my shyness and I asked him how he could do it. I asked him how he won every time. I asked him how I could learn to never lose.

After I had asked him, he smiled a little and told me that it was partly because he played every day and I could only play now and again. I thanked him for his kindness and said that I was sure that practice helped, but he had said that that was only part of the answer and that I wanted to learn it all. When he saw that I was serious, and after he had looked around to make sure that one of his assistants had taken over, he proceeded to give me a lesson I have never forgotten.

For the next couple of hours he described to me the set up of the ramp, the way the ball speeds into the landing area, and the subtle bumps that had been placed in the "flat" landing area. He taught me how to use backspin while banking the ball off the sideboards of the ramp so that I could control the speed of the ball and increase the probability of the ball entering the landing area where I wanted it to. He showed me how the card groupings in the landing area could be bunched together, in your mind, in various ways, to form larger target regions so that, each time you threw the ball, you could aim for a target area which would yield a good result from more than just one hole. He taught me all of the tricks and all of the skills required to play the game at a level of physical command.

Then he looked me in the eye and asked me if I understood all of that. When I said, "Yes," he gave me the five balls and told me to show him.

As I played with his help and his correction, my level of play elevated again and again. He would ask me to make different shots - from the routine to the difficult. I began to win with an increasing regularity. After a while I became confident that I could make any shot that he asked for.

At that point he looked me in the eye again and asked me if I understood what he had told me and if I could do what I wanted to with the ball. When I assured him that I could, he said, "Fine, it's important to have that knowledge and those skills, but it will be next to meaningless if you can't learn what I'm about to tell you now.

"You asked me to tell you the secret of how I won all the time.

"Until you had become a good player, it would have done as much good to tell you as to refuse. Now that you can play well, I will tell you the secret, and maybe now, you'll be able to listen.

"When I get ready to play a game, I decide what the best score is that I could possibly get.

"In this game, it's a Royal Flush.

"I look at the board. I see where the ball has to go to give me the best chance of getting what I want. I decide how I have to shoot the ball to make it go there. I make my shot as best as I can, I keep my goal in my mind, and I accept what happens.

"Then, I look at where the ball goes, and what that means to my goal.

"If the chances for my goal are still there, I continue. If I have to change my goal, I change it and select a new region in the landing area to aim for. I decide how I have to shoot the ball to make it go where I will have the best chance to reach my goal. I make my shot as best as I can, I keep my goal in my mind, and I accept what happens.

"Then, I look at where the ball goes, and what that means to my goal.

"If the chances for my goal are still there, I continue. If I don't get what I want, I decide what the best possible goal is now. I decide where I want the ball to go to make the best goal happen, and how I have to shoot the ball to make it go there. I make the best shot I can, I keep my goal in mind, and I accept what happens.

'Then, I look to see where the ball has gone.

"I see what it has done to my plans. If I can still get what I want, I go on with my original plan. If I can't get it anymore, I figure out the best results I can get with the shots that I have left. I decide where I want the ball to go to give me my best chance to get my best result. I decide how I have to shoot the ball to make it go there. I make the best shot I can, I keep my goal in mind, and I accept what happens.

"Then, I only have one ball left.

"But that makes things easy, because now the best goal I can reach should be pretty clear as well. I decide where the ball has to go to reach my goal. I decide how I have to shoot it to get it there. I make my best shot, I keep my goal in mind, and I accept what happens.

"And that's the secret to this game, son, and any other game you may play.

"Know what you want. Decide how to get it. Learn how to do the things you have to do to get your goal. Do those things as well as you can. Take your best shot, keep your goal in mind, and accept what happens. If you have to change, change; but, take your best shot, keep your goal in mind, and accept what happens.

"Something good will always come to you if you follow these rules."
With that he smiled and walked away.

There was nothing more to say.

I couldn't have said anything anyway, even if there had been something more to say. For, while he made this explanation and carried out his plan, I sat in silence and watched him roll, on demand, a perfect Royal Flush, the most difficult score to obtain.

Alexander gave us rules no less certain and no less precise. He showed us how to direct ourselves in a new and exciting way. He left a record for all to follow of the procedures he went through and of the skills we have to gain.

Then, he urged us on to join him.

He taught us how to think and he shared with us the pitfalls we will all face as we elevate our own general standard levels of use. Alexander believed that the next "great phase in man's advancement [will be] that in which he passes from subconscious to conscious control of his own mind and body."[1] He believed that by achieving conscious guidance and control we can learn to reach beyond our present state, and begin to make real the dreams we hold within.

He warned us that there will be trials and setbacks and frustrations and confusions along the way, but he assured us that we can do at least as well as he, if we will only do what he did.

We can't do just part of it, though. We must do and learn and grow through it all.

We must understand the rules. We must see what needs to be done. We must learn the skills required to accomplish these goals, and then put them into practice. We must learn to watch and assess our results and our procedures, not as a form of guidance, but merely as a part of the conditions present. We must learn to carry on as we have reasoned out is best for our purpose until the need for change becomes unavoidably obvious.

And always, we must learn to implement these skills with a genuine trust that our reasoning processes will bring us all safely to all of our chosen "ends."

We must learn to take our "best shots" and accept what happens.

---

1 Jones, Frank Pierce, Body Awareness in Action, Schocken Books, New York, 1976, p. 24

APPENDIX A

FOR A DARN GOOD REASON

Over the years, much has been said about the innovations which Marjorie Barstow has brought to her teaching of the movement discoveries of F. M. Alexander. People have both praised and vilified these procedures depending upon the fixed ideas which they brought to their process of appraisal

More recently, the advent of the NASTAT organization has fostered a political uproar throughout the profession in this country. This has led to a characterization of various teaching methods as being either "traditional" or "non-traditional." While such labels may be good public relations on the part of the so-called "traditionalists," the labels themselves can be misleading if not intentionally deceptive. "Traditional" in what sense? According to what standards? From which of the many possible starting points does the "tradition" begin?

More importantly, the use of these terms to shape our perceptions about the work, and the methods by which they are communicated to others, prevents us from seeing the true nature of the transactions involved in the work and in teaching it. By taking a closer look at the history of teaching and teacher training, and at the nature of the transactions involved in learning this work, this paper will seek to place Ms. Barstow's innovations in a more appropriate context than is implied by the label "non-traditional," and to reveal the common task which we as teachers all face, a task which provides a more appropriate target for our energies than squabbling with one another.

The use of the term "traditional," in these arguments, creates a myth and a blindspot.

The term "traditional" is being used now to indicate the relative adherence to a certain pattern of teaching and training which has been used in England and the United States for much of the last thirty years or more. In this view, there is a model for teaching the work which underlies these patterns as well as certain procedures for teaching and training which fit the model.

The impression made by the use of the term "traditional" is that this particular manner of teaching stretches back to Mr. Alexander. The word "traditional" implies that Alexander's procedures have been brought forward, through time, intact. As a result, the argument goes, work done in this way is somehow pure and untainted by experiment. There is an implication that only "traditional" work is of benefit, and that most or all "non-traditional" work is so different and inferior that it should even be called by a different name.

As we shall see, this implication is insupportable by the facts that we have. To continue to hold this view requires either a selective memory about the history of the work, or the improbable assumption that a work which deals with change would itself remain unchanged. Most importantly, it misapprehends the basic nature of the work as well as Mr. Alexanders part in it. It establishes concepts about the work which are contrary to fact and counter-productive as a basis for teaching or learning the work.

To avoid the errors inherent in these presumed and fictitious virtues of "traditional" training and teaching, it will be necessary to take a fresh look at our origins in the work once again.

First of all, one does not need a teacher to learn the Alexander Technique[1]. It seems obvious, but I am always surprised by how many people fail to realize or consider that Alexander taught himself. If the acquisition of this knowledge and the capacity to use it was based upon receiving "correct sensory experience from a properly trained teacher," then the whole process would never have been started. The very fact of Alexander's personal success eliminates from consideration the contention that a "properly trained teacher" is required to learn this work.

Alexander learned this work, and Alexander had only himself.

Actually, he had two other things as well.

In the beginning, Alexander started with a problem and an idea.

The problem is well known: his faulty breathing and his throat trouble. So is his idea: that his difficulties were due to something which he did to himself in his manner of performance.

This idea was based on the observation that he lost his voice in performance, but not in ordinary speaking. From this observation, he postulated that there was some procedure, or set of procedures, which he did differently while reciting, which he did not do in ordinary speaking, and which caused his problem. Having come to this conclusion, he then devised an experiment to test his idea.

---

1. The term "Alexander Technique" is used here to mean the broad spectrum of activities and behaviors suggested, altered, or implied by the movement discoveries of F. M. Alexander.

In his lifetime, Alexander never gave a name to the set of principles which he articulated, or to the processes used to communicate these ideas. In fact, many authors inform us that he took great pains to avoid doing so. "How can you name anything which is so comprehensive," he once wrote in a letter. It seems his preference was to refer to the whole of what he thought or did as "the work." The name "Alexander Technique" came to be applied only after his death.

I have heard it argued that the "Alexander Technique" should be defined more narrowly. The argument states that the term should be used only to describe the teaching of Mr. Alexander's principles in a certain way, i.e., in the "way that Mr. Alexander taught them." As we shall see in this paper, that concept is problematic because it is highly improbable that anyone teaches "that way" anymore, nor did Alexander, if the course of his whole career as a teacher is compared to itself.

The major issue involved between opting for the restricted use of the term as opposed to the broader sense is that we must decide whether we are trying to trademark a particular set of protocols for teaching or employing Mr. Alexander's "work," or whether we are trying to identify a group of principles, discoveries, and ideas whose applications are as flexible as the ideas themselves. For the reasons given in this article, the broader sense of the term will be used and meant throughout.

As he carried out his experiments, he gathered information about the procedures which he did use in speaking and reciting. After a long period of experimentation, he evaluated his results. On the basis of the results of his experiments, he was forced to revise his ideas about the source of his difficulties.

His original idea was wrong in one way. There was not some actual procedure that he did differently while reciting. He had the same three tendencies of disruptive movement in both speaking and reciting.

Yet, in another way, his original idea, that there was something different about his manner of speaking and reciting, was right

While the actual procedures were the same in both speaking and reciting, he observed that there was a marked difference in the degree of effort with which these procedures were performed in the two activites. Even when his ideas were wrong, because he followed the five part process of observation, postulation, experimentation, evaluation, and adaptation, he was still able to derive benefit.

He then took his new observation about this difference of degree, formulated another idea about its importance ("that these three tendencies constitute[d] a misuse of the parts concerned"), performed further experimentation, and, after evaluating the results, adapted his ideas once more.

He followed this procedure of observation, experimentation, and refinement again and again and again and again, even after he had already achieved a high degree of success in solving his original problem.[1] He followed this procedure until, to his satisfaction, he had gotten to the root of the solution for improving the use of himself.

Alexander taught himself. He taught himself by using the same process of investigation he used to make his discoveries. It is clear that this process of investigation is a necessary part of the foundation of his lifework. When Alexander tells us that we can do what he does if we will do what he did, he means this process of investigation just as surely as he means "let the neck be free in order to let the head go forward and up in order to let the back broaden and lengthen."

Alexander taught himself through this specific process. With it, he discovered increasingly clearer understandings of how to improve his own self-use. In so doing, he represents the first generation of both Alexander teachers and students.

The next generation of students is represented by Alexander's first students in Australia.

Other people had noticed the benefits which Alexander had gained for himself from his work. They asked him to teach them what he had learned. Here, Alexander's task appeared to be different. Rather than

---

1. "With the prevention of the misuse of these parts I tended to become less hoarse while reciting, and that as I gradually gained experience in this prevention, my liability to hoarseness tended to decrease," lines 148-152 on page 143 from "The Australian Story" in Edward Maisel's collection, The Resurrection of the Body. The entire narrative, as printed in this edition, is 778 lines in length.

teaching himself by following his own procedures to make new discoveries, his new problem seemed to be how could he communicate what he had learned to others. As before, he began with what he knew.

With respect to the work, Alexander had ideas. He had information of value which would benefit his students if only he could communicate his experiences and understandings to them.

But, just as he had no one to teach him the work, he had no one to train him as a teacher of others. So, while we have no certain knowledge of the procedures he used, the most consistent and probable course of action for him to follow was to solve his new problem in the very same way that he had set out to make his initial discoveries.[1]

He started with his ideas. He decided what each idea meant and how it could best be communicated. He made up protocols to implement his ideas to see how well they worked. He evaluated his results. When his procedures worked, he kept them. When his ideas and procedures were proven to be of less value through his experimentation, he changed them.

In other words, when Alexander made a decision about how to teach, he acted upon his best knowledge and understanding, as his experience informed him, at every given moment. When he had an idea, he tested it. If his idea proved unsound (and he had many which did), he set the idea aside or tested it further. If it proved of value, he brought the idea and the procedures derived from the idea into his work, and tested it further.

He always proceeded from an idea. He always tested further. As a result, his process of learning how to teach was not only just as evolutionary as his original process of discovery, but it followed the same process of investigation.

It is important that we see Alexander's work as changeable and changing.

If we lock ourselves into some fantasy that the work is a monolithic, complete, and finished whole, then we will have denied ourselves its essence. One of the hidden pitfalls in our tendencies to preserve any particular protocol is that it gives the impression that we have reached some endpoint in the evolution of teaching methods. In the teaching of a process of improvement, this seems unlikely.

In making his early discoveries, Alexander's ideas were tested. In making his last discoveries, Alexander's ideas were tested. When these tests demonstrated the need, his ideas about the work, and about how to teach it, changed.

By looking at some of the early major changes in Alexander's teaching methods, we can see this principle of constant investigation, constant evaluation, and constant change at work.

For instance, take the issue of the use of hands in teaching. Maisel tells us in his introduction to *The Resurrection of the Body* about Alexander's early work in London. Maisel claims that both Alexander brothers taught

---

1. As we shall see, later examples about how to teach, for which we have some documentation, follow this outline, and therefore support this hypothesis.

by verbal instruction alone.[1] Maisel characterizes the two brothers as being at opposite ends of the studio "shouting their disparate and desperate instructions at [their] victims."[2]

In addition, Maisel gives us the impression that this process was unsatisfactory: "Initially Alexander had attempted - in words, futile words - to teach the new feeling by telling his pupils how to attain it."[3] The problem with this characterization is that, had teaching with minimal manipulation been that useless, one would be hard pressed to account for Alexander's being in London. He was there because of the success of his teaching method in Australia. How can one account for the success of Alexander in Australia if teaching in this way was as futile as Maisel would have us believe?

If we accept Maisel's account (if only to some degree), it is clear that teaching with minimal use of one's hands was possible because the Alexander brothers had success with it. As a result, we have proof, once more, that one does not need proper kinesthetic experience to be imparted by a properly trained teacher in order to learn this work. [4]

Frank Jones' book contains a second provocative reflection on Alexander and his methods with respect to the use of his hands:

> F. M. told me that in 1914 he was just beginning to find a new way of using his hands in teaching. By applying the inhibitory control (which had proved so effective in breathing and speaking) to the use of his hands, he was learning to make changes in a pupil that were different from ordinary manipulation or postural adjustment.[5]

Some take this to be a confirmation of the "hand-less" teaching that had gone before, and suggest that this means that, before 1914, Alexander did not use his hands. It seems more likely to me that he was using his hands to make adjustments in lessons before this time, but, in 1914, he

---

1. Walter Carrington disputes the possibility of teaching without the use of hands in his printed discussions with Scan Carey on page 10.

Perhaps the telling point in this issue is not whether there was teaching without hands, but rather the degree or amount of manipulation used. The more important point may be that, at this time, there was only a minimum amount of manipulation.

Whatever the case, this account will proceed on the assumption that there was sufficient evidence to support a high degree of accuracy in Maisel's reportage. As we shall see, a strict accuracy is not necessary to the main argument presented.

2 Maisel, Edward, ed., The Resurrection of the Body, Shambala Publications, Inc., Boston, MA, p. xxvii.

3 ibid., p. xxvii.

4 It has been suggested by some that this is merely evidence of this contention rather than proof. The point of decision depends on whether or not one is compelled by this information to the acceptance of a truth or a fact.

According to this, there was successful teaching with minimal or no manipulation. Because proper kinesthetic experience can only be an after-effect of manipulation, if there was successful teaching without manipulation, then there was successful teaching without proper kinesthetic experience being imparted. If there was successful teaching without proper kinesthetic experience being imparted, then it can be done, and, therefore, proper kinesthetic experience imparted by a properly trained teacher is not necessary to learn the work. To me, that is proof.

5. Jones, Frank Pierce, Body Awareness in Action, Schocken Books, New York, p. 31.

began to apply his own principles to the manner in which he used his hands.

Regardless of which characterization is true, this is very exciting information on two counts.

First of all, Alexander is reported as saying that he was beginning to use his hands in this way. Alexander did not characterize this change as that he "began," or that he had changed strategies with a bolt of insight and certainty, but that he was "beginning to find a new way of using his hands," as one would begin any experimental practice. In 1914, this application of the inhibitory control to the use of his hands in teaching represented the latest change in Alexander's continuing effort to find the optimum way to communicate the work.

The second point of excitement is that, with this information, we are faced with the certainty that there was successful teaching without the employment of any inhibitory control in the use of the teacher's hands.

By 1914, Alexander had been in London for ten years. He had not only had a successful teaching practice, but, by this time, he had published his first two books.[1] During these ten years, Alexander was enjoying great success without inhibition as a controlling factor in the use of his hands. But, in spite of his success, in 1914, he began using his hands in a new and different way. Why? Because he thought of it; it was consistent with his principles and ideas; and upon experimentation, he found that it worked better than the procedures he was using before.

There can be no clearer proof of Alexander's constant efforts at improvement and change in his manner of teaching.

The need to keep applying these principles of improvement and change to his own manner of teaching and exploration of the work itself was so great that, in spite of his success as a teacher, Alexander continued to submit his work to the very process he used to make his initial discoveries. In spite of his success, he was unwilling to assume that he had reached an endpoint in exploring or teaching his work.[2] As we see this constant change, it is important to remember that the process which he used to discover and refine these teaching procedures was the same process of investigation which he used initially to make his discoveries.

Each time Alexander made a major change in what he was doing he initiated a change in the "generation" of student involved.

His trip to London was, in large part, a change in generation brought about by bringing the work to a larger and more sophisticated audience. Therefore, his interaction with his early students in London can be seen as a "third generation" of Alexander students. It is the nature of the next two generations of students, however, which is the most interesting.

1. The 140-page version of Man's Supreme Inheritance published in 1910 and Conscious Control published in 1912. The two books were combined for the 1918 version published by Dutton with further additions. This version has come to be the standard version.

2. It is interesting to note that Carrington does not dispute this process of constant change (Walter Carrington on the Alexander Technique, Sheildrake Press, London, 1986, p. 18), although he chooses to characterize the nature of the changes as being subtle. One wonders if that over time the accretion of many subtle changes did not amount to at least a few substantial ones.

Students who were given instructions which included more liberal usage of the teacher's hands, instead of primarily verbal instruction, were different from the students who had come before. The use of hands as a primary tool in teaching represents the institution of a new idea and strategy for teaching. It represents an attempt to bring the student more directly into the process of learning by engaging him fully from the outset. The use of hands in teaching was kept, in addition to verbal instruction, because, on testing, it proved valuable.

Those students who began their study (or continued their study with an open and flexible mind) after the change in 1914 were fundamentally different from even students who had been taught with hands before. People who have experienced what it is like to be taught by someone who is not using inhibitory controls in their hands can easily appreciate this distinction. Without the use of inhibitory controls, the teacher's hands feel different. Without these controls, the quality and clarity of the information conveyed is dramatically reduced. The introduction of these inhibitory controls by the teacher in the use of his hands in teaching is a major change which created yet another generation of students of the work.

Those of us who have had the privilege of studying with Marjorie Barstow for a long time have seen this process of creating generations of students at work. With each new major innovation, with each new insight, with each improvement in the process of communicating the work effectively, a new generation of students is created in Nebraska among the students who are beginning their study.

Students who started in Nebraska after the 1985 summer workshop find it hard to believe that we used to stay in one large group in one hot room for four consecutive hours. Students who started in the late '70's find it hard to believe that Marjorie once used "heavy hands" more than "light hands." People who started in the mid'70's find it hard to believe that "doing activities" was not always a priority. Almost everyone who works with Marjorie now finds it hard to believe that we used to get in and out of chairs regularly, that Marjorie would never teach wearing anything but a dress or skirt, or that she would almost never joke or kid around while teaching.

Each change in her work began as an idea. Each change became an experiment. When experimentation proved the change valuable, it was kept.

But, each new student believes that the procedures, methods, and terminology employed when he began his study was the best way to teach and THE WAY that teaching was always done before his arrival.

Each succeeding generation of students in Nebraska believes that the procedures present when they began their study represented a long-standing tradition of teaching which had always happened in just that way. With some of these students it is difficult to persuade them to continue to adapt to Marjorie's new discoveries and methods. In fact, some hold on to their initial understandings and impressions so tightly that accurate predictions about when they began to study with Marjorie can be made by identifying the era during which their fixed ideas about the work were first being articulated.

The present procedures being used by Marjorie at any given time do not represent some unyielding "tradition," but rather the best application of her current thinking about the work and how to teach it. This has always been true of Marjorie's teaching.[1] As we have seen, it was also true of Mr. Alexander and his work.

There never was A WAY to teach the work. There was only a teacher faced with the task of how to communicate the work most effectively and the five-part process of investigation which Alexander continually used - observation, postulation, experimentation, evaluation, and adaptation - applied to the process of learning to teach the work.

The same kinds of changes and the same process of investigation can be seen when one looks at the history of teacher training.

As we noted above, Alexander was required to train himself to teach.

As with learning the work, Alexander's personal success in training himself to teach is testimony that instruction in how to teach from a properly trained teacher is not required to become a successful teacher. This is not to say that the efforts to establish genuine standards and practices to improve all training programs is not important. I merely wish to point out that blanket statements about the necessity of any particular kind of training program to become a teacher of this work are simply not true, and that there is no greater counter-example than Mr. Alexander himself.[2]

Alexander's process of discovering how to communicate his work to others most effectively was never-ending. Neither were his efforts to learn how to train teachers.

When demand for the work grew, Alexander recruited his brother, A. R. (Albert Redden), to join him.

---

1. Although I have only worked with Marjorie since 1971, Frank Jones affirmed this perception from his work with her in the '40's when she worked as A. R.'s assistant in Boston. Others, whom I have met in Lincoln and elsewhere, have affirmed this about her since her return from the training course.

2. Some may argue that it requires a special and nearly unique individual like Alexander to become a teacher without "proper" training, but this is not true. If there is any good news in this work, it is that anyone who will follow the principles which Alexander discovered and use the process of investigation he developed can learn the work. Anyone who then applies this knowledge and process of investigation to the problem of communicating the work to others can learn to teach it.

The undeniable advantage of a training program is a compression of the time required to achieve a significant level of proficiency through the guidance of instructors as well as the wealth of knowledge gained by interaction with a like-minded community. Still, a training program is not required for someone to become a teacher. All that is required to become a teacher is an understanding of the work and of how to communicate it effectively to others. Both of these understandings must be based on an appropriate process of investigation.

Only a training program that accomplishes these things would be of value. But, by the same token, all training prgrammes that accomplish these things would be of value, regardless of their structure.

Certainly A. R. was not the beneficiary of an extended training program. He was trained in Australia during the time that little, if any, work was done by hand. He received primarily verbal instructions in the principles and concepts. His training could best be described as a brief apprenticeship, as he claimed to have needed only six lessons to learn the work[1], and he later boasted that he never required the use of hands to learn the work. Yet, A. R. seems to have been the teacher in whom F. M. showed the greatest confidence.

As such, A. R. represents the second generation of teachers and the first teacher trained by apprenticeship.

We do not know, specifically, how Ethel Webb, Margaret Goldie, and Irene Tasker were trained. Information about this process is sparse.[2] We do know that, by the time the first teacher training course was held, these three women were already trained and working as assistants to the Alexander brothers in both secretarial and teaching capacities.

What is most probably true is that they, too, experienced an apprenticeship with the two brothers in which their own manner of use was improved through lessons and personal application while the mechanics of teaching and the process of investigation was communicated to each commensurate with her capacity and as circumstances required.

I have never heard a disparaging remark about the quality of these women as teachers. In her article about the first training course in "The Alexander Review," Erika Whittaker's comments about Ethel Webb and Irene Tasker, with respect to their training and quality, is typical: 'Neither of them had 'trained,' but what wonderful teachers they were!"

About the worst that I have ever heard said about them were comments about the greater expertise of the Alexander brothers.

This should not be a surprise to anyone, nor should it really be construed as a criticism of their work. Only rarely does the work of apprentices or journeymen exceed that of their masters. And, even then, it is far rarer for this ascendency to occur while the newer adept remains closely associated with the master, particularly when the master continues in a process of improvement and discovery as Alexander did.

Still, we are faced with the fact that before the first teacher training course began, Alexander had already trained two separate generations of teachers, in addition to himself, by apprenticeship.

Even if we consider the backgrounds of the founders of the training program in New York, we find that "neither Judith [Liebowitz] nor Debbie [Caplan] had been formally trained, as it were, but both had learned a great deal over the years"[3] before they founded their training program.

---

1. In conversation, Marjorie Barstow has said it may have taken even fewer lessons than that.

2. Walter Carrington tells us that, when Ethel Webb asked Mr. Alexander for advice on how to teach, he told her, "Just don't do anything you have ever seen me do." Ms. Webb was often fond of saying that this advice "was my training."

3. Carrington, Walter, with Sean Carey, *Walter Carrington on the Alexander Technique*, Sheildrake Press, London, 1986, p. 25. Carrington goes on to point out that not only could people who were not "formally trained" be good teachers, but they could also be effective

Clearly, the oldest and longest-standing tradition in training teachers in this work is brief and extended apprenticeships.

Once we get to the first training course, we come face to face with the original model on which so-called "traditional" teaching and training is allegedly based.

Once again we are faced with the problem of controversy because there is no formal, reliable, contemporary history of the man and his time. Increasingly, recollections are being shared with us by the principals who survived Alexander, but there is so much disagreement that the reliability of these recollections must be questioned.[1]

For instance, Maisel places Alexander's last encounter with the doctor in the year 1888.[2] Lulie Westfeldt says that Alexander had been a successful reciter for years when he began to have trouble in 1892.[3] Frank Jones does not give a specific date for any specific occurence but places the events in the early 1890's.[4]

Similarly, at the First International Congress, Marjory Barlow and Marjorie Barstow were in direct disagreement about the presence and use of a table for lying-down work done by Alexander at the time of the first training program. (Erika Whitaker seems to agree with Mrs. Barlow about the presence of the furniture, at least, by remembering a kind of trestle table in the small back room.) If we cannot reach agreement about such seemingly simple, once verifiable phenomena, small wonder that our attempts to reach agreement about the subtle, substantive nuances of complex ideas and meanings in the work have proved futile!

When looking at the recollections of the first training course, we are presented with varying views of the experience. These views range from satisfaction to strong criticism.

Erika Whittaker's article, although brief, provides a look at the time which is nostalgic and caring. It contains many interesting remembrances about the course and the people in it. It communicates a spirit of adventure and self-reliance which must have been a common characteristic among these pioneering students. While she points out some of the shortcomings of the course's planning and the personalities involved, she, herself, seemed quite capable of changing to meet these challenges and of obtaining value from the experience.

---

trainers of teachers. Liebowitz and Caplan, he tells us, "set up a two-year training course and, although it suffered from a number of inadequacies and shortcomings, some of the people who went through the training have gone on to become established and competent teachers - Frank Ottiwell who lives in San Francisco is a good example."

It is clear from this that it is not necessary to be "formally trained" in any particular way to be either a teacher or a trainer of teachers.

1. In her article in "The Alexander Review," Erika Whittaker says, "If all seven of us first ones in that course were to recount our individual memories there would be quite a diversity of stories - and it must be admitted that we tend to only remember what we want to remember!" (p. 22)

2. Maisel, Edward, The Resurrection of the Body, Shambala Press, Boston & London, 1969, p. xii.

3. Westfeldt, Lulie, F. Matthias Alexander the Man and His Work, Centerline Press, Los Angeles, 1965, p.125.

4. Jones, Op. cit., p. 16.

Mrs. Whittaker's response to the informality of the program approaches delight. "I think the very fact that there were no rules and regulations encouraged us to make use of the time together [on their own and away from direct instruction with Alexander] in a much less restricted way."[1]

She talks of how the students worked together to learn new things even if it meant doing crazy things. "We considered observation, inhibition, direction - we devised various ways of observing each other in a variety of activities .... With non-endgaining and working out means whereby, we had a most interesting time exploring new ways of doing familiar things"[2]

In other words, the manner of her procedure - starting with principle and observation, devising experiments to explore the meanings of these principles, and evaluating the results obtained - fits the model of Alexander's process of investigation, and led her to a very satisfying result.

The most vocal critic of the first teacher training course is Lulie Westfeldt in her book, F. Matthias Alexander: the Man and his Work.

In particular, her assessment of the course and of the progress of the students in the third year was very critical. "We began to suspect that we were on our own.[3] We would have to hold ourselves responsible for learning his work as best we could. Alexander was there, and we might in some way learn how to get what we needed from him, or we might not. We could not count on him for anything.[4]

Although her tone of disappointment is quite clear, her acknowledgement of the student's responsibility for learning the work seems to be consistent with Alexander's views on the subject. In spite of this acknowledgement, and because of the failings she saw in the training course and in their instructor, she later claims that the course was so bad that "if we had left at the end of our third year, we could not possibly have survived as teachers."[5]

Miss Westfeldt then tells us that, in her opinion, two unexpected happenings saved the first training course.

First, a fourth year was added. This presumably gave the remaining students time to overcome the deficits of their first three years of training.

The second unexpected event was when an unnamed colleague[6] pointed out that they had all missed the boat. He had a low opinion of what they all knew and what they could do as teachers. Because of per-

1. Whittaker, Erika, "England - the First Training Course," "The Alexander Review," Vol. 2, No. 3, Centerline Press, Los Angeles, 1987, p. 23.

2. ibid., p. 23.

3. A point which Alexander continually made to all students about learning the work.

4. Westfeldt, op. cit pp. 62-63.

5. ibid., P. 85. It is also interesting to note that Miss Westfeldt also claims that all of the training course members stayed. This is simply not the case. Marjorie Barstow left after the initial three year period. It is not surprising that Ms. Barstow is one of the people who has expressed great satisfaction about the first training course in its original form.

6. Almost all of the principals in Miss Westfeldt's book are unnamed. This is a great disappointment and a constant source of frustration in trying to find through-lines in the

ceived deficiencies in the training course, he said they would have to "somehow or other pull [themselves] up by their own bootstraps."[1]

The importance Miss Westfeldt placed on this colleague's contribution is evident. "Without his (her colleague's) clear sensing of the problem and his creative thought in helping us solve it, we would have failed as teachers, fourth year or no."[2]

Miss Westfeldt's point is clear.

In her opinion, the most important factor in her becoming trained successfully as a teacher was not how long she had studied, or even that she had studied in Alexander's training program. The most important factor, according to her, was what her group did in response to making the observation that there was a problem to be solved. Her group solved this problem by taking independent action.

And what was the independent action that her group - apart from the training course and on their own - took in response to this observation which Miss Westfeldt claimed to make the difference in the success of their training?

"We worked as in a laboratory, using each other as guinea pigs, the group mind gradually bringing to light the problems involved."[3]

They carried out experiments! They evaluated their results! When the results warranted, they changed their ideas! As they carried out this procedure, "simultaneously our minds and our hands advanced in knowledge."[4]

In other words, by Miss Westfeldt's own account, as soon as the disgruntled members of her group in the training programme applied themselves to the learning of the work in the same way that Alexander discovered it, "as in a laboratory," their knowledge advanced. As soon as they relied upon active experimentation with Alexander's principles and ideas, away from their teacher and on their own, rather than relying on being "taught" somehow by someone, they began to experience the same kind of growth in themselves and in their understanding of the work which Alexander had experienced himself.

It was the introduction of self-reliance within a more appropriate process of investigation which saved the course for even one of Alexander's harshest critics as a trainer of teachers. As Miss Westfeldt said, "the factors making our success [as teachers] possible were the realistic appraisal of F. M., belief in and enthusiasm for his work, creative

thoughts of individuals in the work. Reading Carrington's discussions with Sean Carey, on page 11, one is given the impression that this unnamed colleague may have been Patrick MacDonald, but there is no clear proof of which I am aware. (This contention was later confirmed at tea during the Brighton Congress by Erika Whitaker, Marjorie Barstow, and Sir George Trevelyan.)

1. ibid., p. 86. It is interesting to see that although the emotional flavor of the colleague's opinion and Miss Westfeldt's differ from Mrs. Whittaker's, the placement of responsibility on the student for learning the work and the strategy they all employ to bring about constructive change is the same.

2. ibid., p. 86.

3. ibid., pp. 86-87.

4. ibid., p. 87.

resourcefulness,[1] *ability to stand prolonged discipline,*[2] and ability to work together as a group with trust and cooperation." [3] The need for these same factors remains true today.

When we look at the work done by the Master Teachers who founded training programs, we see that all of them have changed the work in some way.

Marjorie Barstow's many changes are the source of much discussion. Walter Carrington tells us of some of the changes which he made in the training course immediately after Alexander's death: the daily lecture, the regular private lessons, the institution of the afternoon "games" in which a specific procedure is worked on in groups of threes, and the early use of hands on the back of chairs as a non-endgaining activity. Similarly, Patrick MacDonald has introduced his series of gymnastics into his work, e.g., the Lunge, the Yo-Yo and Elevator.

Why did these teachers break with the traditions and the manner in which they had been taught to introduce these new procedures into their teaching and training practices? Because these new procedures matched their models and ideas of what they thought the work was, and upon experimentation, these changes proved to be of value to their students.

As their ideas about, and understanding of, the work grew, their willingness to experiment and improve themselves and their work grew with it. As their ideas about, and understanding of, the work grows in the future, I am sure this new growth will be reflected in changes in their procedure.

In this way, it is important for all of us to see that the oldest tradition in this work is not any particular method of teaching or learning, but rather the active investigation of how to improve one's own self-use and how to improve one's own manner of teaching through observation, experimentation, and change.

Even as stalwart a preservationist as Marjory Barlow is not immune to the pressures of improved understanding.

At the First International Congress, Mrs. Barlow, with some delight, showed our group some new discoveries which she had made in the functioning of the foot in standing. She was quite proud and pleased to share it with us, though it was different from how she was taught and not part of "traditional" teaching. She explained her deviation from standard cant and procedure by saying, "I teach everything exactly the way that [F. M.] did, except when I have a darn good reason to change."[4]

As we have seen, her standard for making a change - having a darn good reason based on observation and experimentation - is consistent with the very nature of the work.

---

1. The italics are mine.
2. See Chapters 12 - 14
3. ibid., p. 88.
4. Personal notebooks kept during lectures.

This work represents an on-going process of increasingly fine appreciation of Alexander's ideas which can be taken into activity.

I am constantly amused when I hear myself, or others, say, "Oh! I know what that is!" in a lesson. Each "new answer" which I discover seems, at that moment, like such a final solution. My experience has shown me, though, that my present "new answer" will sooner or later be replaced by another "new answer" which may sound, or even feel, remarkably like the old one.

The most common form this has taken in classes in Nebraska is for the student to say, "Oh! You mean that I should move my head and let my body follow! Why didn't you say that before!?!"

I do not object to this kind of complaint from one of my students. It demonstrates to me that some fundamental understanding in this work has reached some further degree of clarity in thought and action.

What I object to is when my students (or anyone else) take their new understanding and represent it as anything more than just a new understanding. We must eliminate this tendency to accept and propose that any present understanding which we may have is "IT." We must all learn to admit freely that while we may have learned a lot, experimented a lot, grown a lot, and changed a lot, we have not yet reached an endpoint for learning and changing and growth with respect to this work.

In fact, if Mr. Alexander was right in what he said and believed about this work, we cannot reach such an endpoint.

The only way in which it makes any sense to preserve and adhere to any particular form of teaching, without testing it constantly, is to propose that the teachers performing this particular form of teaching have reached some endpoint in the work.

Alexander wrote in the "Introductory" to *The Universal Constant in Living* that "after a lifetime in this new field I am conscious that the knowledge gained is but a beginning."[1] If, after fifty years of investigation, Alexander had just reached the beginnings of the work, it seems highly presumptuous for any of us to believe that in the last fifty years we have found the end.

In fact, there is a way in which picking the final endpoint of the Alexander Technique is like designating the exact moment, "now," by shouting out the word when it occurs. No matter how often you shout, there is always a "now" to come. No matter how often one decides that one finally understands the work, there is another refinement to come.

In the seventeen years I have known Marjorie Barstow, I have never failed to be struck by the amount of substantive change and improvement she has made in her thinking, movement, and teaching during the time we have been apart.

Marjorie's manner of teaching did not spring forth full bloom in its present form as an expression of personality or style. It is very much the product of a reasoned and conscious evolution.

---

1. Alexander, F. M *The Universal Constant in Living*, Centerline Press, Los Angeles, p. xiii.

While it is true that much of what she does appears to be casual, everything which she does (or doesn't do) while teaching has been reasoned out and tested. It has been tried against the standards of Alexander's ideas. Ideas and procedures which have been kept are in use because they have accomplished something new, something better, or they accomplish the same thing more easily. Those ideas and procedures which are discarded are eliminated because they no longer seem of value.

Every new procedure underwent preliminary evaluation and thought. The procedure was then tested. Each experiment was founded upon the ideas which underlay the new procedure. These ideas, and the results which their related procedures produced, were then tested again against Mr. Alexander's ideas and procedures.

This constant process of observation, postulation, experimentation, evaluation, and adaptation continues in every class and every lesson I have ever seen Marjorie Barstow teach. No innovation is adopted without this stringent testing. No change is ever made without a darn good reason.

This universally constant effort on Marjorie's part to improve her general standard level of use and teaching by the application of Alexander's principles and his process of investigation is not only consistent with Alexander's work, but it lies at the very heart of it. Any teacher who is truly following this process of investigation, and who is truly employing these principles cannot help but change and improve in both personal self-use and teaching methods. Any teacher whose manner or methods are constant and unchanging is, at best, suspect and, at worst, the teacher's method may be antithetical to the work.

On the other hand, merely to change one's teaching method for the sake of change is not an answer. Without using Alexander's process of investigation as a basis, this kind of change would also be contrary to the work.

No, the answer lies in the solution suggested by Marjory Barlow. One should stay with what one knows as one continues to experiment and consider. Finally, when one has developed a darn good reason to change, one should change.

We need to see that there is no difference between applying Alexander's process of investigation to the problem of improving our use and applying his process to the problem of learning how to teach others. Our use improves because we learn to prevent interferences of thought and movement behavior which compromise the integrity and coordination of our system. Using Alexander's process of investigation, we learn how to discipline our thinking to employ his principles as the basis for our patterns of directive guidance in the activities of daily living.

All of Marjorie Barstow's teaching, all of her innovations, and all of the ways in which she investigates herself, her movement, and Mr. Alexanders ideas lie exactly at the center of the nature of the work.

They always have.

They always will.

For these reasons, it is clear that all of Marjorie's work is absolutely "traditional."

It is only those who have chosen to isolate, preserve, or fossilize certain elements in this work; only those who presume they have reached an endpoint in this work; only those who believe they know what is correct and incorrect in human movement and performance; only those who make changes in the structure or manner of their teaching, willy-nilly for the sake of variety, fashion, or profit, without genuine concern for the integrity of the work itself - it is only such people and such programs as these that have earned the title "non-traditional" because they have lost their sense of the true nature of Alexander and his work.

The essence of this work is improvement, not arrival.

All that Alexander promised us was that if we do what he did, we will experience a "universal[ly] constant improvement in our general standard level of performance." Regardless of our level of accomplishment, if we follow Alexander's process of investigation and his procedures, we will always improve in our standard level of performance.

We will still have good days and experiences. We will still have bad ones. But, the average quality of our performance will constantly improve.

Always.

There is no destination on this journey we have all undertaken. There is no condition to attain. No final or superior knowledge to be gained. There is merely a process of investigation and change we may choose to employ.

We all have an understanding about this work based on our study and experience. It is not surprising that we all see just a part of a still-developing picture.

I believe that it is important that we stay with methods and concepts which have been proven. But, I also think it is important that we experiment. I think it is essential that we work hard to expand our knowledge of who we are and how we work.

I do not believe that we are anywhere near the endpoint of the new field of enquiry which Mr. Alexander introduced. I do not believe we have even approached such a condition.

I believe we are, at best, deep within the glimmering beginnings of the work which Alexander foretold. Therefore it is our duty, our task, to seek further to clarify the ideas and simplify the procedures involved in the work.

We must seek to understand and build upon what has gone before, but we must never hesitate to carry on. We must see our teachers not as individuals who have held or withheld a completed secret, but as individuals who have dared to challenge what they thought and believed and saw, and who carried out experiments in life and process with a willingness to change.

We, too, must be willing to change.

We, too, must be willing to grow as our experience informs us.

We must respect the past. We must learn from it. But, we must also be willing to go on beyond the ideas and procedures of the past: as long as we have new ideas which are consistent with Alexander's principles, as long as we have new procedures which have been tested and proven, and as long as we have a darn good reason to change.

APPENDIX B

THE INTRODUCTORY CLASS CHARTS

ONE THOUGHT

the poise of a person's head

in its dynamic relationship with his or her body

in movement

is the key to freedom

and ease of motion.

ALEXANDER'S TWO DISCOVERIES

I.

In every movement you make, there is a change in the relationship of your head with your body that precedes and accompanies the movement and which either helps you or gets in your way.

In other words, in every movement there are two movements:

i) a relationing movement performed primarily by the axial structures which either creates a flexible lengthening that improves the coordination of the movement or which creates a general collapse that lowers the coordination of the movement, and

ii) a gestural movement which is made up of changes in angles of the joints of any part of the body and which defines the actual movement itself.

2.

The conscious mind has the capacity to override every system, including the natural ones.

WHAT YOU THINK IS WHAT YOU GET.

THE MONKEY TRAP

Illustration by Sophie Howard

The Problem.

1. There is a nut in a bottle.
2. A monkey sees the nut.
3. The monkey grabs the nut
4. With the nut in his hand, the monkey can't get his hand out.

Other Solutions.

1. Shake the nut out of the bottle.
2. Break the bottle.
3. Get the nut out with chewing gum on the end of a stick.
4. Break the nut in the bottle, take out the little pieces.
5. Get another nut

When the monkey sees the nut in the bottle, he reaches in to get it as he has gotten every other nut in the past. He is acting out a typical stimulus-response pattern for monkeys. Because the opening of the bottle is small, the monkey can just barely squeeze his hand in. Because his fist is larger and less flexible with the nut in it, he can't get his hand out and, hence, he is trapped. In the Alexander Technique, we would say the monkey was End-gaining.

End-gaining is the name we give to the process of carrying out an activity with your attention focused on the end you wish to gain, rather than on the manner in which you will gain it

When we are thinking up other solutions to the problem of getting a nut, our focus is on the means the monkey will use to get a nut. In the Alexander Technique, we would say that our attention is on our Means-Whereby.

Frank Jones has written that most people are caught in monkey traps of unconscious habit.

A SOLUTION TO THE "BOX" PROBLEM

Shown below is a solution to the problem posed in the chapter on "The Monkey Trap". There is no way to solve this problem without going "outside the lines" made by the "box". The point to the whole puzzle is to demonstrate that there really are no "lines" to go outside of. The nine dots are only perceived as making up a "box" because that is an easy convention to use in organizing the nine points in our minds. The problem with this perception is when we let the easy convention of thinking of these nine dots as a "box" prevent us from solving the puzzle by creating a self-imposed limitation that really isn't there.

When I first encountered this problem, I couldn't solve it. I conceived of the dots as making a "box". I not only couldn't conceive of moving outside the "lines" of the "box", but I was sure my classmates had cheated when they went outside the "box" to solve the problem. Since that time, I have become quite adept at looking for solutions outside the "lines".

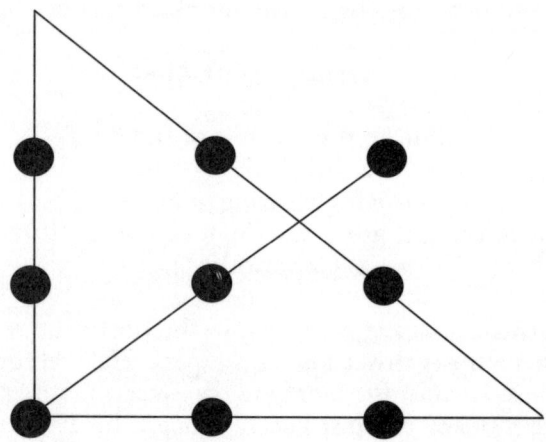

THE BOX CHART FOR BEGINNERS

Part 1:

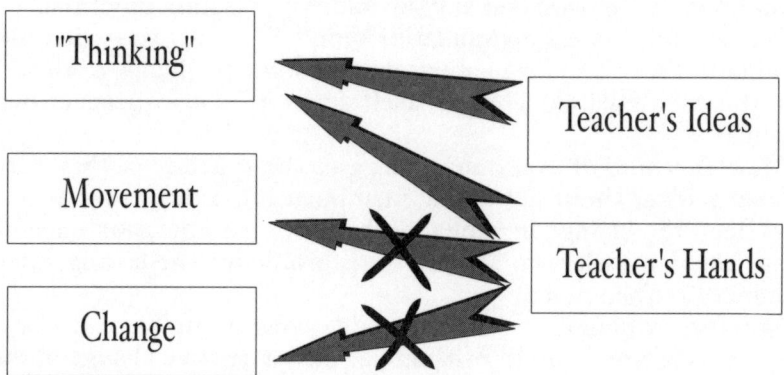

In everyone, thinking leads to movement and movement leads to change. If there has been a volitional movement, there has been a thought which precedes, plans, and directs that movement

Change occurs as a result of movement. Many students in this work try to change before they move, in order to move more easily, but this cannot happen. You must move to change. Hence, movement leads to change.

Everyone understands that the teacher's ideas would be used to make changes in a student's thinking processes. Consequently, everyone understands that the arrow drawn from the teacher's ideas to the student's thinking indicates this kind of transaction.

In a similar way, students want to draw a second arrow (shown on the diagram as the upper broken line with an X drawn through it) from the teacher's hands to the student's movements. While I think it is possible to teach this way, I do not believe that it is a good way to teach, or even a way that we should teach. That's the reason I draw the X through the broken arrow.

In addition, some people think of teaching as though there was an arrow going from the teacher's hands directly to change. They work as though, "somehow", the intervention of their hands is the instrument of "change", rather than having the change occur as a result of movements which the student makes or stops making. Because there is no need for this kind of "magical" teaching in this work, this concept is also represented by the lower broken arrow with an X drawn through it.

I believe that the only transaction we should be performing with our hands in the teaching of this work would be best represented by the unbroken arrow which connects the teacher's hands with the student's "thinking." I believe that the teachers hands should only be used to augment or oppose the student's "thinking." I believe the only effective point of attack in this form of neuromuscular re-education is the "thinking"[1] which directs a student's movement and not the movement itself.

My practice as a clinician has sufficiently demonstrated to me that, while there can be short term changes in movement as a result of manipulation, there is almost never any substantive or lasting functional change as the result of physical manipulation alone. The only time that physical manipulation seems to bring about any substantive change of this kind is when the manipulative change itself leads to subsequent changes in thought.

While this kind of experience may give the appearance that a student has "changed" as the result of the manipulation, in my experience it has always been the change in thought which the manipulation engendered, and not the manipulation, which is responsible for the lasting and ongoing changes in the student.

Therefore, whenever I use my hands with a student, all that I am doing is everything I can to bring about a constructive change in the student's "thinking". This is accomplished either by augmenting the student's ability to do this kind of "thinking", or opposing the student's harmful, incorrect conceptions. In this regard, the physical changes are merely the by-products of the redirection of the student's "thinking", and, hence, are incidental to it. Therefore the transactional arrow on the chart goes from the teacher's hands to the student's "thinking", not to the student's movement.

Part 2:

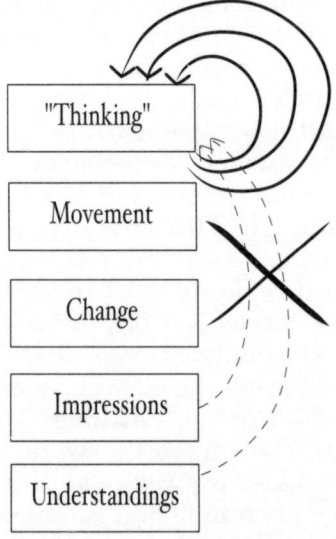

---

1. In this chapter and elsewhere, "thinking" is meant to indicate the kinds of mental processes which Alexander developed to dominate his habitual patterns of directive guidance. These skills are the cornerstones of his techniques and are described in greater detail in chapters 11 through 14.

Because our static position recognition receptors can only fire when there has been sufficient movement for them to reach their firing thresholds, and because movement leads to change, it is the movement changes registered by our receptors which lead to impressions. I choose to use the word "impressions" here rather than "feelings" because it is really our impressions which are important to us.

As I have shown elsewhere (see the chapter on "Feelings and the Time Line"), in the absence of organic or disease deficits, there is more feeling sense data generated every second than we can accommodate. We would probably be correct in saying that, for every movement we make, there is a complete set of data transmitted by which we could appreciate every aspect of the movement. It would also probably drive us crazy to be in touch with all of this information.

What is important to us is the small number of bits of information that get through our filters up to the level of the mechanism where these information bits are turned into impressions. We have complete feedback data available almost all of the time, but only a small part of this information is ever processed as impressions. In fact, it is quite common in a lesson for a student to report that they feel "nothing." One student even told me that once, during her first significant Alexander experience, everything below her jawline disappeared!

The problem with these feeling sense impressions is that we are so accustomed to paying attention to them as a form of guidance that we try to adapt these impressions into the way in which we "do the Alexander Technique."

The most striking example of this occurred once in Nebraska, when a student was asked what she noticed while walking during a lesson. "Oh, I see," she said, "I feel just like a marionette!"

When she first began walking, there was quite a noticeable change in her appearance. Her legs moved more freely and there was an easier motion in all of her joints. It was really quite lovely.

After she had said, "Oh, I see," however, there was more and more of an artificial and mechanical motion imposed on this earlier free movement. There is no question that her initial impression, while first walking, was of moving like a marionette. There was no problem with that. The problem came when she then began moving, not as she had been shown by the teacher, but in accordance with her interpretations of her impressions. There was nothing marionette-like about her movements until she began willfully imposing her imagined marionette-like movements.

What she had done to accomplish these impositions was to take her impressions and to begin broadcasting them as part of her commands for response. She began to move more and more like a marionette because she began to think more and more that she should move like a marionette. On the chart, this is represented by the broken arrow which connects impressions to thinking.

In other words, once she had gotten an impression, she tried to take that impression back up to the top of the chart, and impose that impression on her thinking. This made her begin to move as if she were a marionette, because the commands she was sending out to herself said to move like a marionette. Consequently, what she took away from the lesson was not certain valuable impressions about a new and different way of walking, but a conviction that the right way to walk was like a marionette. Years later, the last time I saw her, these marionette-like movements, which had been unlike any way in which I had ever seen her walk previously before this experience, were still evident in her walking.

In a similar way, some students will be having a lesson and take some idea, or combination of ideas and feeling sense impressions, and have some insight or other. On the chart, this is represented by the box marked "understanding." These kinds of experiences are usually heralded by an exclamation like, "Oh I know what that is!" or "I see what you are trying to say!"

In the same way that our marionette-like friend imposed her feeling sense impressions onto her movement, these students take their "understandings" (the broken line from understanding to thinking) up to the top of the chart, and begin imposing their "understandings" onto their thinking. Because thinking leads to movement, these people will begin moving more and more in accordance with their "understandings," rather than in the way their teacher showed them.

But, this correspondence of subsequent movement and "understandings" is more of a self-fulfilling prophecy than a truth. People move in this new way, not because they are supposed to move in this way, or that this is the way to move, but because they are thinking about moving in this new way, and thinking leads to movement.

WHAT YOU THINK IS WHAT YOU GET!

The X is drawn through these broken arrows to show to the reader that this is not a good procedure to follow.

The procedure to be followed is for the student to do the "thinking" required. This "thinking" will produce a movement, and the movement will produce a change. While the change will produce feeling sense data every time, there may or may not be an "impression" made on the student. While a student may have many "impressions," they may or may not conceive of any "understanding."

Once the "thinking" has been done and the movement initiated, the rest of the possible results will happen, or they won't. Procedurally, it makes no difference. In almost every case, the procedure to be followed is that, after having done the "thinking" required and after having begun to move, the student will go back and do the "thinking" again. This, in turn, will generate a second movement and the student will go back to his "thinking" again and again and again and again.

On the chart, this cyclic return to the process of "thinking" required to make changes in the use of oneself in activity is represented by the unbroken line which circles from a person's "thinking" back to "thinking" again and again.

APPENDIX C

BASIC PRINCIPLES

In 1973, as part of my student teaching experience, I team-taught a class called the Voice/Speech Lab at Washington University in St. Louis, Missouri. The class was divided into two parts. I taught the Alexander Technique to one-half of the students while Sidney Friedman, then chairman of the Performing Arts Area, taught the students the voice work of Arthur Lessac.

This course gave me my first opportunity to work with students in an on-going classroom circumstance. It also gave me an opportunity to explore the practicality of teaching the Alexander Technique in combination with a second discipline. Most importantly, because we had to generate academically acceptable work on the part of the students, it gave me my first opportunity to teach the writings of F. M. Alexander in a classroom setting.

The experience was tremendous! The following year, we repeated the Voice/Speech Lab and I was able to make a lot of refinements in both my approach and teaching methods.

After that, as often as possible, I would introduce Alexander's written work into my Alexander classes. Sometimes the classes would be extended sessions, such as at The Valley Studio in 1975. Sometimes the classes would be weekend workshops at various colleges throughout the country. Then, in the spring of 1980, again under the supervision of Sid Friedman, I was given the opportunity to organize a college course for the study of the Alexander Technique.

I believed then, as I do now, that a person does not truly understand something unless they can talk about it easily and well. The intent of these classes was to introduce Mr. Alexander's work in such a way that anyone could easily comprehend the basic ideas well enough to explain them to others, as well as put them to practical use for themselves.

Over the next five semesters, Drama 318 gradually evolved into an intense, repeatable, 60 hour credit course in which less than half of the class time was devoted to experiential, hands-on teaching. Even then, much of the experiential work done with students in activities was used only to develop or illustrate points which had been made earlier in class.

The tremendous success of these students in learning to do this work easily for themselves at a greatly accelerated pace (when compared with other students I had observed) convinced me that there was great value in this approach to teaching Mr. Alexander's work. The value of this approach was later confirmed when one of my students was included in a discussion of the work at a summer workshop in Lincoln.

This student's command of the information, as well as his ease and confidence in speaking about the work, allowed him to play a significant role in the discussion that took place. When the discussion had ended, the group leader introduced himself as the person who had trained the other teachers in the discussion. He then asked my former student who had trained him to be a teacher. Imagine their surprise when they found out that nearly his entire background consisted of Drama 318 at Washington University.

When The Performance School began in the fall of 1986, this introductory class changed once more into its present form. I call the class Basic Principles because it deals with principles of success and study from many disciplines including the Alexander Technique. Because the class was designed to be a part of a basic curriculum for teacher training at the school, and because there were experiential classes both before and afterwards, I was able to teach this entire first-year course in an interactive tutorial format with very little hands-on work at all.

Through the classes, students acquire a working introduction to some of the written work most basic to the study of the Alexander Technique. They encounter some of the most powerful tools and techniques taught in success education. They have a chance to examine and refine their own ideas about who and what they are and how they work. At the same time, they gradually develop a facility to recall easily the information they have studied, with a confidence that enables them to talk easily about what they know. In combination with experiential lessons in the Alexander Technique, there is no better way to begin learning this work.

What You Think Is What You Get is an attempt to bring the structure, excitement, and ideas of the Basic Principles class into a textbook format. It is designed to introduce the reader to some of the procedures we have used in these classes over the years, and to the concepts which my students have found very helpful in their study of this work.

While I believe that *What You Think Is What You Get* makes an excellent introduction to these ideas, the complete details of the line by line explications performed in class are beyond the scope of any introductory book. These explications are to be written as separate volumes as part of a larger project called The Alexander Commentaries.

In addition to the Commentaries, there is *The Basic Principles Workbook* which has been prepared as a companion piece to the texts used in the Basic Principles course. In the Workbook, there is a section for each of the reading assignments and each section consists of four parts.

The first part of each section is made up of study questions. These are objective questions taken directly from the text which are intended to help students make a close textual analysis of the reading material as they write out the answers to the questions longhand.

The second part in each section is a series of essay and project questions. These questions are designed to illuminate the issues involved in the reading selection and to give the student the opportunity to try and come up with his or her own answer to these problems and issues.

Both of these sections are designed to guide students through their study of these texts by using some of the techniques I have used in my own study of these texts.

The third part of every section is a selection of information bits. These information bits organize what I believe to be the major points contained in the chapters in simple, "bite-size" chunks. This section is intended to make the arguments and ideas in each chapter easier to recognize and understand.

Each of these sections is designed to encourage the use of different study skills and take advantage of different learning tools on each subsequent re-reading of the texts.

The reading selections are grouped together according to author, and at the end of these reading groups, there is a self-administered test. These tests give students a chance to see how well they have mastered the material in any given section.

The intent of the workbook is to provide the same kind of structure in the pursuit of the reading material that would be provided by the instructor in the classroom.

It is hoped that at least some of the difficulties of translating the Basic Principles classes into text will be overcome in these books and that they will prove helpful to students of F. M Alexander and his work. It must be emphasized that while I believe that these books can be an invaluable teaching aid and guide, there is no substitute for lessons in the Alexander Technique. Just as there is no substitute for interactive classroom work with this material. Just as there is no substitute for personal experimentation and study.

Even if it proves possible to translate the Basic Principles course into audio and video tape formats, the advantage of having skilled and immediate assessment of your condition, and a conscious direction of your study by a trained teacher cannot be duplicated or equalled in any way other than through classes and lessons.

On the other hand, no amount of classes or lessons will do anyone any lasting good unless they put in the work and self-study required to make this work their own. In the end, the only genuine importance of the Alexander Technique is how you can learn to use it for yourself to reach your goals and make your dreams come true.

This book and the others which follow it are intended to give you the best possible tools for this purpose.

Donald L. Weed runs classes on the Alexander Technique in England and Europe.

Workshops are held all year round and include a two-week Summer School in August in Birmingham, England. Everyone is welcome and no previous experience is required. If you would like to receive further information please write to:

The Course Coordinator
ITMA
PO Box 181
BRISTOL
BS99 7BH

Donald L. Weed has also written the following books:

The Basic Principles Workbook
Escape from the Monkey Hatch
Four Days in Bristol
Complex Simplicity (about to be published)

These books are available from:
Gil Books, 10 Charlotte Street, Bristol, BS1 5PX, UK.
Tel. +44 (0)117 925 3413
Fax: +44 (0)870 054 8481

Donald L. Weed, D.C., studied the Alexander Technique with Marjorie Barstow* from 1971 to 1993. He has also studied with other teachers trained by F M Alexander, most notably Margaret Goldie and Frank Pierce Jones.

Don Weed has an extensive background as an actor, singer, director and performance coach. He has undergraduate degrees in Human Biology, Music and Drama, as well as a Doctor of Chiropractic degree. However, his deepest and most enduring passion has found expression in teaching others the Alexander Technique.

Don Weed began his professional career as a teacher of the Alexander Technique in 1975, and since then he has taught Alexander's work to many thousands of students around the world. He is the originator of the Interactive Teaching Method (ITM), and is currently training Alexander teachers in Switzerland, Germany and the UK.

* Marjorie Barstow of Lincoln, Nebraska, was the first person to graduate from F M Alexander's first ever training course for teachers in London in 1934. She later taught as A R Alexander's assistant for many years in Boston. In her later years, Ms. Barstow pioneered a ground-breaking approach to teaching the Alexander Technique to groups.